Holosophy
Restoring the Soul's Code

By
Robert Thomas

The Holosophy Foundation Press

The Kosmic Domain Matrix

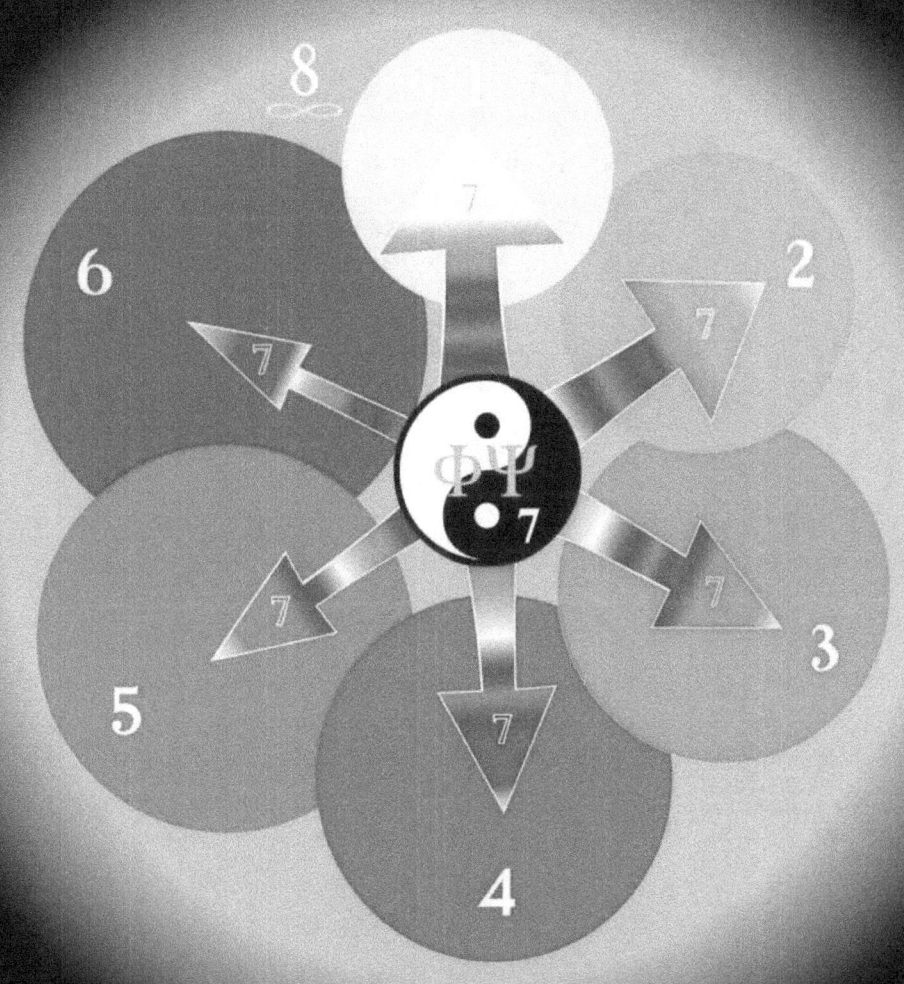

See Appendix 1, page 246 for complete description

Dedication:

To all who helped…
but mostly:
JSJ, LL, KF, DE, JT, PGT, ET, BT, NHT, MG, KM, CM, ACW, PR, A&EM, JM, JLM, AC, RS, JJ, K&JS,
JDS, FF, LW, JC, SR, PL, R&PN, LS

…and of course to
my parents and theirs
who provided my
most recent vessel and
port of entry

Editor: Jennifer St. John

Copyright© 2017 by Robert Thomas
All rights reserved.
No part of this publication may be reproduced, stored in a retrieval system, or transmitted in any form by any means, electronic, photocopying or otherwise without the prior written permission of the publisher:
The Holosophy Foundation Press

Library of Congress Cataloging-in-Publication Data
Thomas, Robert

ISBN-13: 978-0-9984445-9-8
ISBN-10: 0-9984445-9-6

1. Philosophy 2. Metaphysics 3. Epistemology 4. Ethics

B1-5802 2017

The Holosophy Foundation
Holosophyfoundation.com

Holosophy and the Holosophy colophon are registered trademarks
Graphic design by RT, executed by Tom White

> "Ride si sapis (Laugh if you are wise)."
> -- Martial (Marcus Valerius Martialis), Spanish epigrammatic poet

Nota Bene:

The contents of this volume have been compiled from the author's collected lectures, articles, recorded dialogues and seminar materials spanning many years. They have been extensively revised, updated and expanded to achieve some degree of developmental coherence and continuity. An attempt has also been made to use paragraphing, ellipsis, footnotes, and punctuation, to emulate the original spoken words, style, and emphasis, and to accurately characterize the meaning and deepest intent of the source materials; so that any multiple meanings, use of "scare quotes" or instructive ambiguities, can be intentionally stimulating.

This volume is *designed* to accommodate a broad range of study, consulting *and* dialogue applications: First, as a seminar program manual; next, as a guiding philosophical text, coordinated with training drills and transformative exercises, to assist *personal* optimization, study, and Kosmic expansion. The many quotations, which were selected from eclectic wisdom-sources, are intended to encourage thought and dialogue, perchance even elicit a chuckle or two.

And finally, to serve as a general link to the Holosophy Foundation and its broader educational mission, activities, and materials, always with the hope that the concepts and data presented will ultimately invite deeper review and introspection, and emerge "whole" and intact despite *any* deficiencies of literary style, immediate clarity, or challenging access to the presentation, which are, of course, the sole responsibility of the author.

Contents

	Page
Preface	
Introduction	1

Chapter I

Consciousness Revisioned: as an instrument of Kosmic Optimization	14
A Post Traumatic Paradigm: Modality and Mechanism	19
Dialogue as Cognitive Optimization	25
The Mind: Perfect Bio-Computer; Hidden Flaw	29
The *Sub*-Rational Mind: Storehouse of Pain	31
Hypnosis: Taking a "Cue"	32
Sub-rational Survival: The Terra Incognita of Consciousness	38
Cognitive Optimization: Transforming Emotion, Attitude and Behavior	42
Ultimate Responsibility: Primary Kosmic Truth	46
The Cognitive Exemplar:	
How *Optimization* Differs from other Methodologies:	47
Philosophical and Pragmatic Elements of the Program:	47
Assessment Surveys:	48
Standardized and Specified Attainment Levels:	49
Duration of The Program:	50
Personal *Pre*requisite For Counseling:	50

Chapter II

Lila, The *Kosmic* Life-Game Paradigm	54
Some Selected Holosophy Tenets	61
Self-Determinism: Window For *Created* Causation	68
The Kosmic Theatre: Dramatis Personae, and Props	74
Not The Body	74
Not The Brain	76
Not The Mind	78
Not The Mental History or Personality	81
The Holon: Spirit as a Creative Individuality	82
The Holon: A Slice of Infinity	87
Goals of the Game: Incremental Ascension	93
Game Conditions as Benevolent Barriers	95
Rankings in Playerhood	97
Freedom-defining Limits	98
Opponencies: Introduction to the Dance	99
Artful Gradualism: Through, *Not* Over, the Rainbow	101

Chapter III

Dialectical Idealism: Extending the *Kosmic* Game-Matrix	104
Postulation: Metaphysical "Movie Making"	108
Perception: The Playing Field as Imaginal Constraint	108
Action Cycles: The Dynamic Tapestry of Play	111
Problematic Cycles of Action: Redundancy in Action	116
Exchange: Coin of the Domains	117
Ethics: Wisdom's Rational Choices	119
Justice: Benign Umpiring	122
Aesthetics: Qualitative Gateway of the Infinite	124
The Creation of the Game: Maya Modernized	127
Reality: Consciousness *Uses* Process: "Its" from "Bits"	131
Selective Unknowing: Thralldom as Theme	134
Dialectical Idealism: Holon as Observer/Participant/Player	136
Limiting the Infinite: The *Domains* of the Kosmic Life-Game	139

	Page
Errant Domains: Confusions and Blurred Distinctions	148
Universes: Kosmic Windows of Illusion	153

Chapter IV

Life-Gamesmanship: Ability *Dis*ability and Limitations 158
    I. Disabilities Regarding Self 163
    II. Disabilities Regarding Family & Procreation 163
    III. Disabilities Regarding Group & Communities 163
    IV. Disabilities Regarding Humanity 163
    V. Disabilities Regarding Biology 164
    VI. Disabilities Regarding Cosmology 164
    VII. Disabilities Regarding Conceptuality & Spirituality 165
    VIII. Disabilities Regarding Infinity 165

Defining *Dis*ability: Beyond Reductionist Norms 166
Ability: A Kosmic *Re*-Visioning 167

Chapter V

Consciousness, a Triadic Mysterium of: Holon, Mind and Brain 174
Life-Game *Ima*gination: The Purpose of Mind 177
What Does The Brain Actually Do? Correlation vs. Causation 181
Memory: The Mind's Kosmic Library 185
Consciousness Flawed Perfection: A Summing Up 187
The Conscious Mind: Of Wholes and Holons 188
The *Sub*conscious Mind: Mind*less* Precision 191
Robotic *Re*enactment: The hidden menace of "SURVIVE" 194
"Sticks and Stones" and Words Can Hurt 195
"Command-Value": Failure's Warranty 196
Mis-Habituation: A Trauma-labeled "Charge" To *Re*-act 198
Negative Conditioning: A "Revised" Perspective 201

Chapter VI

Success Reluctance: The Kosmic Code sets the stage for Sub-Rationality 206
Error-Limits to a Fault: Redundantly Imprinted Self-Limitations 215
The Retributive Reflex: Kosmic Karma Re-visioned 220
Character vs. Case-Contour: The Primal Error 224
Losing To Win: The Tactics of Sub-Rational "Success" 229
About the Author 238
References 239
Appendices 244
    Appendix I   The Kosmic Domain Matrix 246
    Appendix II   Truth Functions 248
    Appendix III   Kosmic Equation 250
    Appendix IV   Cognitive Optimization: A comparative Analysis 252
    Appendix V   Sub Rational Indicators 256
    Appendix VI   Reality (density) Discrimination Guide 273
    Appendix VII   Is the Brain Really Necessary 275
    Appendix VIII   Excerpt from "Recalling Nana's Face: Does Yor Brain Store Memories?" 278
    Appendix IX   The Paradox: Intimations of Non-duality 280
    Appendix X   The *Powers* of Communication 282
    Appendix XI   The Transformative Dialogue: (Sub-Rational Resistance Markers) 283
    Appendix XII   Kosmic Archetypal Agendas 288
    Appendix XIII   Excerpt from "You Have to be Conscious to Deny Consciousness and Other Conundrums" 289
    Appendix XIV   Consciousness as a Scale of Knowing: An Epistemic Heirarchy 292
    Appendix XV   Seminal Holosophy Canon 293
Envoi 294
Holosophy Publications 302

> "Platonic existence as I see it refers to the existence of an objective external *standard* that is not dependent on our individual opinions nor upon our particular culture."
> -- Sir Roger Penrose, physicist
>
> "Knowing as meaning *creates* being, i.e., is the *source* of experience."
> -- Holosophy Canon

Preface*

In Holosophy the representation of the Kosmos[1], on the previous page, is in the tradition of the Mandala (Sanskrit: circle). In various spiritual applications, mandalas may be used to focus and direct attention to a primal *sacred space*, as an aid to increased contemplative awareness of an ultimate and inherent Source or Ground of existence. In ordinary usage, the mandala has become, generally, a term for any grid, matrix, plan, et al., that represents the totality of existence, *meta*physically and which contains the universal symbolic forms, that, with appropriate contemplation, reveal an *innate* cognitive order, projected, observed, and *utilized,* as the manifest Kosmos.

Orthodox science often offers theoretical appeal to *un*observable entities in nature; multiple universes, extra dimensions, string theory, dark matter, "universal" forces, ionic

---

*Over the last several years of research and writing, it occurred to the author the need for a short introductory overrview of Holosophy more suited to the professional reader or researcher. This preface and matrix description were written in a style hopefully more suited to that purpose. (RT)

[1] Kosmos: an ancient Greek term used by Pythagoras to refer to the *entire* universe in all of its multi-dimensionality, i.e. spiritual, mental, emotional *and physical,* as contrasted with "Cosmos" in its modern usage which refers *only* to the physical realm.

> "In this (subatomic) world of moving things, you can imagine it is something like a great game of chess, played by the Gods, with something occasionally like castling going on."
> -- R. Feynman, physicist

> "Suppose that the parallel universes of the many worlds theory are not material but archetypal in content. Suppose they are universes of the mind. Then instead of saying that each observation splits off of a branch of the material universe, we can say that *each observation makes causal pathway in the fabric of possibilities in the transcendent domain of reality.* Once the choice is made, all except *one* of the pathways are excluded from the world of manifestation."
> -- Amit Goswami, physicist

bonds, abstruse thematical manifolds, and assorted quantum fields, to mention but an unseen few. Why physicists should claim such inferential advantage unavailable to the *spiritually* inclined defies reason. Indeed, with the case of the "multiverse", many scientists would seem to prefer an infinite number of *un*observable universes, than accept a *non*-material causal source of our one *observable* one!

Holosophy however, holds that there is a profound *Kosmic* order in the universe, and that the source of this order stands innate and independent of the manifest existence that is projected from it. This Source of Kosmic order, which Holosophy calls the *actual pattern of existence* has, in various forms, been the subject of mystical and metaphysical contemplation since the most ancient of times. The earliest vedantic mandalas were intended to be a kind of cartography of implicit universal forms, with the potentiality of an *emergent* cosmic pattern (code) of event and circumstance. These ancient "mandalic" beginnings were followed in the west, by Plato's idea that all perceptible *things* derive ultimately from universal *thought-forms*, and that our common experience is an imperfect reflection and extension of those ideal forms; and then Aristotle's entelechy, a *dynamic potential for eventuality,* or "natures that persist", further attempted to describe an order, or reasoned and progressive *pattern* in nature.

Plato's eternal *Ideas* were not just general concepts, but are the innate cognitive prototypes of *all* particular and manifest things. These transcendent formative ideas are not directly perceived by the senses, but are intuited, comprehended, and acted

> "The Transformative Dialogue practice simply removes fixed sub-rational significances from a *past* event, domain, or activity so that it's data can be *conceptually* re-Visioned and used selectively to optimize Kosmic play."
> -- Holosophy Canon

> "Morality is not properly the doctrine of how we make ourselves happy, but how we make ourselves worthy of happiness."
> -- Immanuel Kant, philosopher

upon through concrete experiencing. Plato held that learning is, in effect, remembrance. The *soul (Holon) re-knows*[2], including the emergent and informing *dialectic polarities* and patterns of sense experience, descending from the Ideas. The Holosophy formulation of the actual *Kosmic* pattern (or grid) builds on that tradition, and is intended ultimately to *restore* awareness of the primal Core of Existence, i.e., "nature's DNA", by removing its trauma-associated and *dis*abling mental image encumbrances.

The Buddhist idea of "alaya-vijnana" or "stored *or basic* consciousness", like the more recent example of Jung's "collective unconscious", was based on the consideration that there was a kind of projective formative or archetypal *order* at the source and core of human consciousness that had both purpose, and *reifying*[3] capacity. It is this enabling cognitive source that conceives (Be), actualizes (Do) and perceives (Have) all *innately* generated, and *cosmically* projected (manifest) eventuality.

Consider also the three primal grammatical primitives of *all* language e.g., subject, verb, object; and as cyclical ordering; *be, do, have*; which suggests a common source or "deep structure" of an innate linguistic, and archetypal pattern-logic behind the cognitive orderliness of all grammar, and the event-cycles of common experience. If we add "knowing" as the "fourth" innate

---

[2] In the same sense that Platonic "anamnesis" or guided remembrance, restored the innate but "forgotten" knowledge of the soul, as well as *erasing*, through cognitive dialogue, the *false traumatic copy* and *re-endowment* of the actual pattern of existence.

[3] The word "reify" is used in Holosophy to mean the process of giving innate, non-material concepts, substance and perceptual reality, i.e., "*ideas* made *flesh*" or given "local habitation and a name" as Shakespeare beautifully describes it. It is this "naming" potentially that would seem to refine, combine, and reconcile both the Schrodinger equation (psi) and the "golden mean" (phi). In the first case the potential non-material cognitive context, in the second, it's actual formative and *proportionate* observed manifestation.

> "That there is no such thing as what philosophers call material substance, I am seriously persuaded: but if I were made to see anything absurd or skeptical in this, I should then have the same reason to renounce this, that I imagine I have now to reject the contrary opinion."
> -- George Berkely, philosopher

> "The ancient Greeks had the concept of "arête" as virtue, more broadly goodness, i.e. excellence enacted as a shadow of the ideal"
> -- Holosopy Canon

source from which the more obvious triad of being, doing, and having *emerge,* we can reconcile any apparent conflicting philosophical duality of the triad (3) *vs.* the quaternity (4) as the fundamental existential archetypal order ("three" for the Cosmos; "four" for the *Kosmos)*, i. e., by adding the "infinity" domains (7th & 8th)[4] to form innate algorithmic patterns from which all cognitive and logical order itself seems derived.

Sample Kosmic-Logic Agendas:

Linguistic order:	**Subject**	→**Verb**	→**Object**
Existential order:	**Person**	→**Process**	→**Product**
Metaphysical order:	**Epistemic**	→**Telic**	→**Ontic**
Archetypal order:	**BE**	→**DO**	→**HAVE**

Benefiting from the insights afforded by these enduring wisdom traditions, a *Kosmic* dialectic might then be considered as a *creatively ordered* pattern and (purposeful) progression of opposing *ideas* reified as existence, in a dynamically cascading actualization of historical occurrences. The philosopher Hegel combined these early and seminal ideas of a progressive cosmic "*event*ualization" into a triadic formalism which attempted to logically extend and develop the ancient Heraclitan opposites to achieve a *new* dialectical-historical process[5] or "synthesis", and to integrate what is "true" and valuable in a universal or absolute continuum of projected, historically evolving, and self-reconciling experiential polarities.

Unfortunately, neither the Hegelian dialectic nor its more

---

[4] See chapters 3 and 4, for a more complete description and discussion.

[5] 'Dialectic' refers to the Hegelian process of historic change and descent in which a concept or its realization becomes, is reserved, and Is finally realized, by integration with its opposite.

> "Mind has erected the objective outside world out of its own stuff."
> - Erwin Shrödinger, physicist
>
> "A central failure of "the mind as a computational system" theory is that computations per se, are devoid of *meaning*. They are purely syntactic devoid of semantics. *Meaning* derives from *agency*."
> - Stuart Kaufman, biologist & philosopher

temporal variations (e.g., Marxism) have any place for a creative, event-*causing* and broadly determinant *Holon individuality*. One that could be a central and localized *conscious agency* distinct from the State, and *necessary* to any unfolding dialectic order. Most importantly, there is no insight into the "dialectic" as possibly expressing a soul-encoded, and *consensually templated order* for a universal *game*; or existence itself, *as the Game,* that the "Absolute" could be playing! A purposive, pro-gressive, and *recreational display* of both a kosmically and divinely expressive "Self."

Building on these seminal insights, Holosophy, over many years of research has developed a working modular grid, a kind of logically templated "mandalic matrix" attempting to formulate a primal categorical patterning of Kosmic existence...consistent with, and *extending,* the traditional metaphysical theme of a "Cosmic Golden Ratio" to include an omitted reference to the *selecting* integrity of the rational *persona!* A necessary *personhood* as an instrumental chooser, using a calculus of optimum to less-optimum proportionate selectivity. One that is based on ideally proportional and *simultaneous* consideration of *all* domains of existence, in determining *right action, i.e., an objective "benevolence grid"* or innate Value-Calculus of Optimization, discerning and implementing, *real* and *informed* "increments of betterment," or "greater goods" to actualize the vast Kosmic Game-Display.

Holosophy therefore, interprets any "golden ratio" as more than mere mathematical or numerical abstraction referring only to physical proportion, but more completely to include the non-material *or qualitative* aspects of existence. Personification or a

> "Not all that counts, can be counted."
> - Albert Einstein
>
> "Geometry deals with *ideal* circles and triangles. No real circles are exactly circular, no real triangles are exactly triangular. It follows logically, that in general, all exact reasoning allies to ideas, *not real things*."
> - Lothar Schaefer, physicist

true *agency capacity* for perceiving abstract realms of truth and value, is the basis for the informed calculation of "right-action" (optimization). This *enlarges* the concept of a *selective*; *non-material* scale of values, as an objective, *optimally proportionate*, and domain-inclusive basis for Kosmic choice-making.

The Golden Ratio *concept* is extended in Holosophy, to include various *non*-material value determinants contained in the *full* eight domain-pattern of the universe (Kosmos). This provides informed and proportionate value-ratios to guide rationality in what Holosophy calls Cognitive Optimization; or rational *choices* that recognize, *envalue,* and facilitate, the greater *Kosmic* good by *combining* the cognitive role of consciousness in "collapsing the quantum wave form," with both a *personal and proportional golden mean sensitivity*, when making all reality-projecting and optimizing decisions.

That choiceful capacity and obligation must stem from innate order-based intuition, and that *essence* must also *pragmatically* define, and *usefully* apply[6], the total Kosmic Domain Matrix to calculate optimally, the relative importances and value distinctions both within and *connecting* each domain. This provides a *guiding* "Value-Template" for all Holons to act, with *best efforts,* to produce *ideally incremental* betterment on a rising standard of multi-domain oriented quality and value, but "settling" *actually,* as human beings, for a practical "viability estimate" of actual

---

[6]It is recommended as the reader progresses through the following pages, that it might be a useful if not edifying exercise to periodically review this preface. As an introductory summary it presents a concise, if condensed general review of some main philosophical issues central to fully grasping Holosophy as a subject. Understanding of these issues tends to increase, as counceling and study progress.

> "The Kosmos is not a zero-sum game, since there are *ultimately* no losers."
> - Holosophy Canon
>
> "Why is there something, rather than nothing?"
> - metaphysical query

betterment: one that is based on a real and *personal* capacity for a rational pragmatics, *and* ideally includes no sub-rational memory, and *excludes no domain* from the Optimizing Calculus, which is the goal of the contemplative use of the model Kosmic Matrix-Code and its transformative Life Game applications presented in the following pages.

— The Author

Introduction

Restoring the Soul's Code
Basic Theory and Philosophy of Transformative Dialogue

Fortis Imaginatio Generat Causum'[†] -- Latin Proverb
"The universe is the moving image of Eternity" -- Plato
"People need God … and God needs people" -- The Kaballah
"Almost all the "conventional" interpretation of quantum mechanics ultimately depend on the presence of a perceiving being" -- Sir Roger Penrose, physicist
"Virtue is volitionally superlative functionality." -- Holosophy Canon

Introduction

Holosophy: *(ho-los´-ophy)* n. A body of eclectic philosophical doctrine and precepts based on research into consciousness, life sources and human behavior. It contains transformative principles, methodology and practices, designed to assist in locating, and removing all sub-rational cognitive and memory barriers to the rehabilitation, optimization, and re-ensoulment of the human condition, and in bringing about advanced states of ability and expanded awareness consistent with gradually elevated norms of personhood and value. *[<Gk holos: whole, complete, unitary, self-contained. <Gk, Sophia: wisdom, knowing in the highest sense.]*

What *Is* Holosophy®?

Holosophy, in the simplest sense, is "high-wisdom" *codified,* a body of philosophical principles, tenets, and transformative practices, which holds that, mind, life, and the physical universe *manifests as a spectrum of interacting* and personified, *wholes,* or self-actualizing gestalts[1] and that this primary pattern of existence, although appearing, *materially*, as a dynamically integrated hierarchy of process, form, and substance; *actually emanates from*, the *non*-material, *spiritual* realm of Consciousness[2].

Holosophy further considers this immanent and *Primordial* Consciousness to be, in a Platonic sense, an ultimate Source; a boundless *conceptual* Potentia[3], the orderly projections from which,

---

[1] A sensory pattern of perceived elements which has a *total* unitary aspect greater than the *sum* of its individual perceptic parts. In this sense, perceptions are degrees of *manifest* consciousness.
[2] Holosophy defines Consciousness as the non-material genesis of all conceptual meaning and knowing and therefore, ultimately, of all *manifest* existence, which itself derives *from* that conceptuality combined and projected, as *perceived*, event, form and "substance".
[3] Potentia: An infinite source of *potential* but *unmanifest* actualization and attribution of specified conceptuality, or *meaning;* contrasted with "*actus*": that which *emerges* from the realm of the merely possible to *become* actual as an existence *perceived.*
[†] A strong imagination begets the event itself

Introduction

> "The mind is a conceptual grid that imposes order and form upon perception."
> -- Holosophy Canon
> "The belief that no belief is preferred over another is itself a preferred belief!"
> -- Holosophy Canon
> "Reality is tiered... *being* (as existence) increases as the levels descend."
> -- Huston Smith, philosopher

enable its outer, realized, manifestation first as en*souled* individuality; a *self*-actualized viewpoint of specified identity, as a cognitive continuity or *agency*. Then, through further postulated[4], *shared*, and synchronized acts of creation, the *consensual assemblage* of these viewpoints brings about a *reality;* a synchronized and co-experienced tapestry of individually projected perspectives.

Thus, the *real;* is basically an integrated *conceptual* "binding" of dimension, form, and perception, creatively *combined* as "concept made *flesh*" emerging as the *jointly* attributed, and consensually *observed*, landscape and panorama of existence[5].

Individuality as consciousness, uniquely self-actualized, is considered a *choicefully* enthralled[6] spiritual *agency* or perceiving instrumentality of Consciousness as *Source,* which has selectively *reduced* its native level of awareness, in order to experience the stable and limiting orderliness of a rule-bound, coordinated and persisting cosmic landscape in order to play a larger *Kosmically*[7] *integrated, Life-Game.*

The Holosophy theory of Kosmic origins, following, but building upon, the ancient Vedic *Lila*[7] cosmogony, holds *all*

---

[4] A word used in Holosophy to mean an intentional, unmediated *act of creation* projected by consciousness to *bring* about an *intended viewpioint, condition, effect or cycle of action.*

[5] Consciousness is considered by many quantum physicists to have a central involvement in the "conditions" of *observed* cosmic phenomena, or "reality," a word that in Holosophy implies an active role for conscious observation as projected but "confined imagination," a "bringing about" or "collapse" of infinite possibilities into a *specified* reality.

[6] The word enthrall as in "thralldom" is used in Holosophy to mean a benevolent selective and *willful* self-deception; or "consensus pretense"," in playful coordination with other selves, similarly disposed, to achieve a common unanimity of experience. Much research into the ability of selective groups of individuals to plan, *share*, and report on, mutual vision-states or *dreaming,* is suggestive of this inherent capacity for the creation of such an imaginal "consensus."

[7] See a fuller treatment of the "Lila" concept in Chapter 11.

Introduction

> "Without contraries there is no progression"
> -- William Blake, poet
>
> "Playing a game is like reading a novel…it can give us intense and meaningful enjoyment, even though we "know" it is not literally true and springs from the imagination."
> -- Holosophy Canon
>
> "Science is imagination, in a straightjacket!"
> -- R. Feynman, physicist

existence to be a celestial *Kosmic* Game generated and played by a universal community of individually ensouled entities, or *Holons*[8], on a *playing field* of shared and ascending realms of *consensual* inter-activity, *thralldom, and projected value.*

The common playing field is co-observable, comprised of usefully distinct, and interactive "arenas of play," or Kosmic *domains.*[9] Sub-game sectors that together form a *Holo*archy[10], or graduated "Chain of (qualitative and quantitative) Being"; descend from the highest, most *super*sensible and transcendent realms of awareness and value, downward through the grosser condensations of thought and energy, to an apparently "final" inanimate density of "matter." In all, it is a simultaneous and concertedly *imaginal co-creation* of a totally *ordered* range and scale of significances, fields, particles and energies, which emerges as a vast and nuanced Kosmic stage to *display* it's primal function as *recreational* Holon co-participancy.

It is a basic Holosophy tenet, as well, that *all* actively sentient Holons, existing as *agent*-participants in the Life-Game, have freely *chosen,* and are thus ultimately *responsible* for, being and acting as the primary *self*-determined "units" of awareness necessary to enable, and *volitionally* enter into an original co-existent playerhood with its

---

[8] The word "Holon" was coined by author Arthur Koestler to denote any entity which has the dual nature of being a *whole*, or gestalt *entification* as itself, while also *within* a larger, integrated fabric of co-perceiving, and co-acting Holons: a hierarchical continuum. Holosophy uses, but has expanded, that definition to emphasize the Holon's non-material individuality or *agency* and its ability to cause and create, i.e. to postulate, perceive and act as player within the Kosmos.

[9] A domain is a distinct sector or sphere of the Kosmos as a Life-Game with its own bounded and specified categories, e.g. Person, family, humanity, ecosystem, etc. See Chapter 1.

[10] Holosophy uses the term to mean *a Hierarchy of Holons,* graduated rankings and categorical but interactive orderliness of Holon creativity *constitutes* the manifest nature and form of the *total* Kosmos.

Introduction

> "The art of being wise is the art of knowing what to overlook."
> -- William James, philosopher
>
> "Let us not burden our remembrances with a heaviness that's gone."
> -- William Shakespeare
>
> "Consciousness forgets itself for the sake of *play*. It 'pretends' to forget."
> -- Amit Goswami, physicist

inevitable *descent* into an ever deepening game-enthralled, consensually; i.e. the natural observer-participative and *purpose-driven continuum* of the *Kosmic* Life-Game[11].

However, within the vastness, variety, and grandeur of the Kosmos…we can readily observe the increasing planetary blights of war, insanity, criminality, and all the varieties of *un*reason that seem at times, to menace the very essence and survival of the Holon-players, and even the game itself.

Seeking to build upon and *extend* traditional attempts to understand and *raise* human awareness and ability, Holosophy's purpose is to reveal, access, and *remove* through the full range of its cognitive researches and dialogue techniques, the *actual source* of the varieties of aberrant and destructive behavior that infests the Kosmos. Imposing a *veiled* and "out dated" repository of mentally "pictured" traumatic duress and stress-formed belief systems, it causes a pattern of *sub*-rational *behavior,* a false, and persisting, memory[12] imprint that subverts normative *Kosmic* Life-Game experience.

This hidden, pain-enforced, and *sub*-rationally compelling, encrustation of "recorded" mental-imagery is unconsciously *value*-linked to the *naturally reduced awareness* considered by the players as necessary to both enable, and *preserve,* the continuity of the Game.

---

[11] The self-regulation and managed complexity typical of life systems can be readily modeled as *games*. Many such game analogies have been programmed on computers and designed to display very life-like activities and qualities; one well known example is even called, "The Game of Life;" another recent example "Spore" simulates the creation of life forms and their "seeding" and development in planetary systems, and in a larger "designed" cosmos.

[12] A mentally copied replication of the actual designed thematic pattern of Kosmic existence imprinted deceptively over, and *confused* with, its own natural character, subverting the choiceful commitment to the expressive *use* of that pattern by each Holon as a *selected* basis for game activity.

Introduction

> "Freedom cannot be endowed or imparted. It is self-actualized."
> -- Holosophy Canon
> "Absolute perfection must include the capacity for imperfection."
> -- Holosophy Canon
> "The meaning of the message will not be found in the chemistry of the ink."
> -- S. Kaufman, biologist

This assignment of false "survival" value results in the gradual entrapment of the Holon player-participants within a hidden, *mentally pictured* "veneer" of fixed beliefs and images is formed in response to past traumatic events, and then results when re-activated; as aberrant *behavior in the present.*

Affected adversely by this concealed, and redundant, traumatic-"data-base" of *mental-image feedback*, humankind has gradually reduced the *basic ability to enjoy* and even *play* the game effectively. Life, when detached and insulated from the immediacy of natural expression by the obsessive interposition of mental-imagery of past trauma, and belief, can lose any deeper *Kosmic* "spirit of play" or sense of *fully engaged* role, purpose, or *true self*-actualization.

Imposing past mental-images *retroactively*, also has the effect of blurring real and current distinctions between game-domains, and impeding and distorting the natural value-adding play-activity of *exchanges* between and within them. As stated, Holosophy takes the view that *all* such "neurotic" human life-disability is traceable to this injected overlay of self-generated, but *sub*-rational mental *causation, i.e., the Holon itself, below the level of conscious awareness,* acts irrationally to solve the problems of today with the stress-formed, *fixed and imprinted, beliefs* of the *past*[13].

This forgotten "engramic"[14] store-house of "out-of-date" beliefs, fixed-ideas, and conditioned impulses, deeply rooted in long

---

[13] Insanity has been loosely defined as obsessively making the same mistake over and over, while each time expecting a different result... *fixed* believing.
[14] An early coined word for a mental-image recording of an incident containing pain, unconsciousness, and *fixed* belief systems and out-dated decision making... (See page 15 note 5.)

Introduction

> "The brain is a limiting biological computer that Holons have found useful for temporary occupation."
> -- Holosophy Canon
>
> "The greatest thing a human soul ever does is to *see* something. To see clearly is poetry, prophesy and religion all in one."
> -- John Ruskin, Aesthete
>
> "The Game's afoot." -- Wm. Shakespeare

forgotten Kosmic archetypal themes and patterns, is the remedial target of *Transformative Dialogue,* a Holosophy program of *Cognitive Optimization, for resolving* past traumatic experiences.[15]

Experiencing the integrative *re*-enablement assisted by this dialogue process, provides personal verification that each individual as a spiritual entity or Holon has, innately, a natural and personal game-related impulse for optimal cognitive emergence, which, restored; arrests and *reverses* the decline of awareness and ability associated with the trauma-based, imprinted and *fixed* belief-patterns of the past. The *erasure* or optimizing removal of *all* such cumulative mental-image debris or "feedback" enables a renewed, and naturally incremental ascension-path of playing, and *winning* in the Kosmic game-cycle.

Any receptive individual, properly motivated, with the help of disciplined, challenging, and sometimes rigorous but always compassionate guidance; can enter and utilize the Program which emphases systematic study and assisted self-observation, using proven interdisciplinary practices, drills, and deep-structured dialogue. These are designed to enable, through specifically defined, targeted, and *achieved* realization milestones, a gradual but steady ascent to higher stages of cognitive optimization, with expanding *Kosmic* awareness, *self*-determination, and *applied*-skills enhancement.

---

[15] Just as a computer can be "cleared" of mal-ware, viruses and false data; the Holon has an innate *self*-optimizing cognitive capacity to make sub-rational *mental* constructions *creatively vanish* when completely viewed and *re*-evaluated in a broader, and *fully rational* context.

Introduction

> "We can doubt everything, but *that* we doubt."
> -- St. Augustine, mystic
>
> "The Perennial Philosophy is...The **metaphysics** that recognizes a Divine reality intrinsic to the world of things, lives, and minds...The **psychology** that finds in the soul something similar to or even identical with Divine reality. The **ethics** that places man's final knowledge in the immanent and transcendent ground of all being."
> -- Aldous Huxley, novelist and essayist

In following the ageless and proven consciousness-raising traditions of the "Philosophia Perennis[16]," Holosophy and its dialogue methodology, acts as a non-authoritarian, non-evaluative, and contemplative communication "lens;" which assists each individual to view, mirror-like, and exactly *"as-it-is,"* each self-created envelope or "layer" of parasitic mental-image encapsulation. The truth, revealed in that authentic confrontation, removes or *erases*[17], through a profound and unifying series of realizations, the obsessive but *hidden* mental "creativity" actually underlying *every* life-disability, and irrational goal obstruction, along with resultant "self-sabotaging" *belief* and aberrant *behavior.*

These successive stages of realization, or transformative *insights* are not "arrived at," but are revelatory *re-creations*[18] as the client is systematically but gradually reacquainted, layer by layer, with the traumatically imprinted and encoded "deep structure" of redundant mental "sheathing," that enshrouds and influences, virus-like, the core of his true *Kosmically-integrated* identity.

As this core pattern of *re*-activity (and its cumulative "file" of mentally pictured and emotively charged "trauma-reminders") is gradually contacted, viewed and *erased,* restoring the *self*-determined and *spiritually* directed potential for *rationally* chosen "options of play," the natural, participative, dis*play* inherent in the *Kosmic* Life-

---

[16] This refers to the ongoing mystical wisdom tradition of an attainable higher consciousness, and the philosophical heritage of truths which have validated and expressed it, through the ages. (see Huxley quote at top of page)

[17] Since the Holon is itself *generating,* unconsciously, the unwanted and redundant mental-imagery and belief...it can also upon revelation, *cease* to generate or create the aberrant effects of that *redundant* "mental construction."

[18] In the same sense that Platonic "anamnesis" or guided remembrance, restored, the innate but "forgotten" knowledge of the soul.

Introduction

> "Formation-Transformation; Eternal Minds, Eternal Recreation."
> *Goethe's Faust*
>
> "Essentially, all *apparent* elements of existence are distinct and *conceptual "wholes"* or gestalts; i.e. unitary experiential primitives *derived* from consciousness. Perception is Reified Knowing"
> -- Holosophy Canon
>
> "The quantum mechanical description is in terms of knowledge... and knowledge requires *somebody* who knows."
> -- F. Peirels, physicist

Game, *spontaneously resumes,* and optimally advances; now unimpeded by any hidden, sub-rational restraints or detours.

Thus, in theory, the scope of an individual's consciousness broadens and deepens[19], re-encompassing the ever expanding spheres or *domains* of *inter*active Play, with increasing positive influence and control. What was fragmented, and disjointed, gradually becomes *whole*, unified and focused. Consequently, there emerges a personal and active redefinition *upward,* of the meaning and purpose of what now becomes increasingly *real, i.e., the Holon's* full and *self-causative participation* in all domains of the *Kosmic* Life-Game.

Holosophy seeks to provide:

- A transformative path to increased freedom; for each players *re*-empowerment; a revitalized *Kosmic* agency-participancy and awareness of value, leading to the practice of a truly *rational* ethics[20], i.e. a *value* calculus[21] of balanced, and *optimized conscious* action and decision, that *creates* destinies rather than "suffers" them.

---

[19] It is assumed and demonstrable that the structure and number of traumatically additive elements is *volitionally* finite and when removed, can restore an individual to an original and naturally unencumbered "optimal" state of awareness and ability.

[20] In failing to discover or perceive any innate source of value in our world, we must, then retreat to a shallow, variable, conveniently and situationally "constructed" form of ethical relativism. However, such a denial of *all* or any non-natural or spiritual referents for rational, value-discernment, optimization and choice-making is dramatically refuted and offset by the "dialectical idealism" contained and experiencable in the *innate* value-laden *Kosmic* landscape of play.

[21] A "Calculus of Optimization" would seem to accurately describe the innate capacity for making *rational* and optimizing choices based on the greater good for *all* Kosmic domains. Such a calculus does not *compel* choices, but is simply a reminding "blueprint" for the Holon as free agent, and "architect" of cognitive optimization as reasonably enacted "golden ratio" of *incremental betterment,* extended to include proportionate individuality and a Kosmic calculus of hierarchically scaled value and optimization.

Introduction

> "Look… particles, don't look… waves." -- Quantum theory in a nutshell
> "Individuality is the immediate sense of unique creative continuity that enables Playerhood."
> -- Holosophy Canon
> "The poet…*re*attaches things to the *whole*."
> -- R. W. Emerson, essayist

- A *re*-visioning and re-awakening of each Holon's true origins, and higher purpose; as manifests in the playful Holoarchic[22] actualization of the infinite potentials of *Consciousness, not* as a mere mechanist process of neurologic or synaptic activity, but as the immaterial Source of *all* that "exists," wondrously projected, and unfolding, as an integrated Kosmic Display, enacted and endowed with sublimely proportionate order and *integrity*.

- A guiding value-template for acting with *best efforts* to produce *incremental* betterment on a rising standard of multi-domain oriented quality and value, but "settling" *rationally*, as human beings, for a practical "viability estimate" of betterment. One that is based on real capacity (for a *rational pragmatics*) *and* ideally *excludes no domain* from consideration by the optimizing Calculus.

- A final preliminary reminder: *No* symbology, however pragmatically useful or accurately referential, is *ultimately* Truthful.[23] The Truth lies in the a-priori and *meta-*

---

[22] The use of the word "Holoarchy" has obvious hierarchical ranking implications, of concern to some because of mistaken impression of "order" as an innately rigid or authoritarian structure. But we should not ignore the fact that *every* complex structure or process of a stable and orderly character displays *some* hierarchical organization, seen in atomic and molecular systems; biological forms; and in patterns of behavior in diverse, social, group, or corporate organizations. The hierarchical model is universal in application from the merest and most rudimentary constituent parts or *collections* of physical existence, to the most advanced realms of form and value.

[23] Higher consciousness, as the *ultimate* background of all existence, must contain the transcendent order which makes things manifest. That order must contain within it hierarchic *levels* of truth. These innate epistemic principles form the basis of our enthralled consensual co-experiencing of the Kosmos. *Objective* values including ethics are based on the ultimate primacy of the agreements of all Holons. Earlier agreements have precedence. True and false, bad and good, are rationally and *choicefully* committed to qualitative distinctions, which Holons objectively consult to discern and calculate the true scale of ethical values and actions.

> "There is no morality without freedom."
> -- Carl Jung, psychiatrist
>
> "You must *be* the change you wish to see in the world."
> -- Mahatma Gandhi
>
> "Interpretations *by themselves* do not determine *meaning*."
> -- L. Wittgenstern, philosopher

cognitive *knowingness from which* all mere symbols and their referential knowings are derived. That guiding metaphysical standard, and an expanded and enduring certainty of *personal* access to the cognitive Source behind *all* symbols, is the goal of the contemplative use of the model Kosmic Code and its transformative descriptions and applications.

The foregoing pages were obviously not ones of gradual or easy introductory access. Some of the most fundamental concepts were presented in a somewhat concise and uncompromising fashion. However, we will attempt to further explore, practically explicate, and extend the lineaments of that *super*sensible vision more fully, in the following chapters of commentary.

Chapter I - Consciousness Re-Visioned

Chapter I
Consciousness Re-Visioned as an Instrument of Kosmic Optimization

> "He who knows much about others may be learned, but he who understands himself is more wise. He who controls others may be powerful, but he who has mastered himself is mightier still."
> -- Lao Tzu
>
> "The thought "Who am I," destroying all other thoughts will itself finally be destroyed like the stick that stirs the funeral pyre."
> -- Ramana Maharshi

I - Consciousness Re-Visioned
AS AN INSTRUMENT OF KOSMIC OPTIMIZATION

The vast canopy of stars and galaxies stretching endlessly above us, hints that our own world is but a tiny part of a seemingly limitless cosmos. But how do *we* fit into the awesome enormity of the natural order surrounding us? Humankind has, for measureless eons, yearned to discover in *itself* a cosmic origin nearer to its Gods. Can there be an "imprisoned splendor" within each of us, which transcends, and survives the sufferings and relentless erosion of time and experience?

Too little satisfaction has been found in the countless philosophies, therapies, and the parade of panaceas attempting to arrest or even reverse, the physical and mental decline of a seemingly fragile human mortality; framed by the accident of birth, and the lurking and inevitable annihilation of death. Too often, experiences of pain, loss and failure seem implacably to accumulate, forming a kind of repository of stress-learned resignation; gradually quenching any joy of living and with it, often, the very *meaning* of Life itself.

Yet, consistent with the great idealistic and transformative traditions of East *and* West, long and careful research and observation confirms that there *is,* beneath the facade of each "ordinary" consciousness, beset with the unwanted conditions and

> "Carpenters fashion wood; fletchers fashion arrows. The wise fashion themselves."
> -- The Buddha
>
> "Everything we know about Nature is in accord with the idea that the fundamental process of Nature lies *outside* space-time… but generates events that can be located *in* space-time…"
> -- H.P. Stapp, physicist

Chapter I - Consciousness Re-Visioned

vicissitudes of an often menacing existence, the possibility of a truly *natural* state of a *higher* more *optimized* state of *Kosmic*[1] consciousness.

The vision of such an enhanced level of awareness might seem beyond the norm when compared with what we typically experience in everyday life, but one which practical experience has repeatedly demonstrated, *can* be accessed and realized with diligent and skillfully guided assistance. It is a state of restored *confidence* unburdened from a residual, traumatic past and generally characterized by higher levels of alertness, causation, purposefulness, energy, enthusiasm, and, *above all* a renewed *ability to live more fully* as a *self*-determined *Kosmic player-agent* of influence and action.

This obviously ideal yet fully attainable state of *re*-enabled (and re-en*souled*) consciousness is referred to in Holosophy as *Optimum*. We have used this term, somewhat innovatively in the human cognitive-development field, because it connotes the ideal, natively efficient state of a thing, or the absence of redundant additives (in the language of computers, an *absence* of bugs glitches, or viruses afflicting the data, input, output, or workability of a system). It is a *Consciousness* more *generally able*, in act, intent and judgment.

Those, who have through cognitive means realized a more *optimized* state, exhibit by observation, enhanced levels of ability and awareness e.g., they have a renewed willingness and *ability*

---

[1] Kosmic extends the non-material implications of awareness as contrasted with *cosmic*, which tends to limit it.

> "We do not learn; and what we call learning is only
> a process of recollection."
> -- Plato
>
> "Sense-perception does not provide the data in terms of which
> we *interpret* it"
> -- A. N. Whitehead, philosopher

Chapter I - Consciousness Re-Visioned

to communicate (or *not*) about anything with anyone. They can perceive and take appropriate action to solve any *real externally* situated problem or respond creatively to any challenge: free of stress-formed beliefs of the past.

Their thinking is typically more rational, focused, flexible and imaginative. They can generally recall the past as needed, entertain or disregard with equanimity *any* thought or idea, and freely choose, and *act* to bring about, an optimally conceived future. In short, they are more capable *of being, doing* and *having* a more complete range of options and capacities within the expanded realm of their restored potential as re-*enabled player-agents* in the *Kosmic* Game of Life.

Just as glass can be free of impurities and distortions, just as distilled water is free of dirt, bacteria or chemical additives; individuals restored to an optimal state of consciousness are free of what we term sub-rational (*re*-active[2]) indicators; that is, they are typically *absent* any compulsive cognitive, attitudinal, and/or emotional activity stemming from, or formed *in response to*, past trauma or duress which, when obsessively replayed as if experienced in the present, *characterizes all* aberrant behavior.

Such *reactions* are both *redundant,* i.e. unnecessary because irrelevant to an actual situation and therefore unknowingly counter-productive; *and* sub-rational, or sub-volitionally *unaware*, as is all compulsion to repeat without rational control and analysis, *any*

---

[2] Reactive = automatic; knee-jerk, 'stimulus-response'; or *sub*-rational traumatic re-enactment; occurring without conscious control or full awareness of causation. Post-traumatic or 'stress-cued' and conditioned thought, belief, or behavior, resulting in irrational, *sub-optimum*, awareness and choice.
*to this must be added enhanced, pragmatic, *value* perception and judgment ... hence *cognitive optimization*

> "One does not become enlightened by imagining figures of light…
> but by making the darkness *conscious*."
> -- C. Jung, psychiatrist
>
> "I was angry with my friend, I told my wrath, my wrath did end,
> I was angry with my foe, I told it not, my wrath did grow."
> -- William Blake, poet

Chapter I - Consciousness Re-Visioned

fixed belief, feeling, or *non*-discriminate behavior learned or hard-wired during conscious-diminishing episodic threats to survival. A sample of typical post-traumatic sub-rational attitudinal and behavioral symptoms, indicators, or flags (addressable in transformative-dialogues) is seen below: (a more complete list, with each indicator defined, and the underlying principals, explained more fully, are contained in Appendix V.)

Sub-Rational Indicators*

Addictive Behavior	Dishonesty	Fixation of belief	Regret
Aimlessness	Disinterest	Indecisiveness	Refusal of Help
Alienation	Disorganization	Intemperateness	Resentment
Anger	Distractedness	Isolation	Sadness
Anxiety	Distrust	Jealousy	Self-Consciousness
Apathy	Emotionlessness	Lack of Confidence	Self-Pity
"Betrayed"	Envy	Lack of Interest	Self-Sabotage
Blame	Facetiousness	Lethargy	Sense of Failure
"Can't" Be	Fear	Loss (Persisting)	Shame
"Can't" Do	Generalization	Misery	Tenseness
"Can't" Have	Grief	Misplaced Priorities	Timidity
"Can't" Change	Guilt	"Must" Be	Unhappiness
"Can't" Focus	Hate	"Must" Do	Unforgivingness
Complacency	Helplessness	"Must" Have	Unproductive
Concealed Hostility	Hopelessness	"Must" Change	Vengefulness
Confusion	Humorlessness	Nervousness	Victimization
Criticalness	Illness Prone	"Offended"	Worry
Degradation	Impatience	Obsessive Behavior	
Defensiveness	Inattentiveness	Persisting Upset	
Disapprovingness	Injustice Collection	Procrastination	

Figure 1

* Notice that in Holosophy these are not generally considered normal, "natural," or *inevitable* conditions of ordinary life experience. They are, in fact, trauma-associated, or pain enforced and "imprinted," i.e., *triggered* or cued *re*-enactments from the past, and are quite reasonably *unwanted* as *Conditions*. When fully confronted and understood, in a *Transformative* Dialogue context, they cease gradually to be automatically and habitually experienced. The restored *power of choice* and confidence in the increased

> "Repetition is the only form of permanence that *nature* can achieve"
> -- George Santayana, philosopher
> "Perception is the knowing that enables and locates being"
> -- Holosophy Canon

awareness of volitional causation that comes with targeted dialogue, enables the person to *erase*, i.e. volitionally and with the rational discretion afforded by a newly elevated standard for *optimized*, emotive and behavioral *choice*, to cause to vanish, or *cease to create* any *sub*-rational memory-imaging.

A Post-Traumatic Paradigm: Modality and Mechanism

To further understand and explicate the *sub-rational* theory of the mind, and its components, let's first consider hypothetically, a typical and rudimentary *animal* mentality, largely stimulus-response, with very limited cognitive capacity. It can provide a simple and basic *analogue* for sub-rational imprinting.

Imagine, in a forest setting; an antelope is attacked by a leopard leaping from a large tree, and although injured, narrowly escapes. The terror and pain of the attack causes the meager analytical faculties of the antelope to become attenuated – more and more *un*conscious -- to the point where, instinctively a vestigial *sub*-aware or reactive mentality assumes full command.[3]

The memory of the traumatic experience is recorded and filed away for future "survival" use as automatic or sub-voluntary value-encoded feedback. A kind of mindless (and *timeless*) behavior algorithm[4], designed to compulsively *reenact*[5] *what to a rudimentary and minimally conscious mentality, was a seminal crisis-event,* but *survived!*

---

[3] Interestingly, even a one celled animal, such as an amoeba, can be 'conditioned' to avoid light or other artificially *induced* environmental 'threats'.

[4] A series of steps in a compilation or calculation. In this case a stress imprinted 'menu for survival' behavior.

[5] The capacity for attribution or primary signification is a fundamental capability of consciousness at *all* levels of awareness. In this case, *any* physical continuity has been 're-framed' under *duress,* as a 'now believed to be' valuable '*survival*' event.

> "It is possible to get out of a trap. However, in order to break out of a prison, one must first confess to being *in* a prison."
> -- W. Reich, Founder of Orgonomy
>
> "The highest and most primal capacity of a Holon is to *commit metaphysically* to the intentionality that insures *shared* thralldom, continuity, and existential *playfulness*."
> – Holosophy Canon

Chapter I - Consciousness Re-Visioned

Subsequently, any time the antelope "survivor" approached "that" location in the jungle, the imprinted memory-encoded incident of the survival threat can be *activated* and re-impinged on the animal's mind, commanding AVOID THIS! on *pain of death!* To its traumatically reduced "fail-safe" sub-mind of associative equivalence: TREE = LEOPARD = ATTACK = PAIN = FLEE = SURVIVAL! There is no differentiation of meaning, value or context, just a seamlessly trauma-linked conditioned *re*action! (An algorithm or menu for a mindlessly repetitive, but primal and putative biologically *valuable continuity*.)

Similarly, in a drugged state – under anesthesia during an operation, or unconscious from severe injury or illness – an effected *person* has, *de-minimus*, only a *sub-rational* mind in full operation, but the resulting *post*-traumatic conditioning effects are dramatically and variably complicated by the existence, *at the human level*, of symbolic *language,* and the much more highly endowed *Holon's* cognitive, and *creative* capacity to interpret, and conclude: i.e., *to create stress formed beliefs sub-rationally during the experience!*

Such an individual may not be "aware" of what was taking place, but as will later be discovered heuristically, in dialogue, everything which happened in the original incident (traumatic memory-imprint) was fully and completely recorded as an engram.[6] There is the fully encoded ("survival" re-signified) informational residue of pain, associated with equivalency of

---

[6] A term for a 'memory trace' or imprint coined by Semon in 1920 and used by Penfield, Lashley and others in mnemonic and brain research to refer to mental-imaging of past events. Holosophy uses the term to refer to those incidents containing pain, unconsciousness, and irrational 'survival' decisions or belief-signification of content.

> "*Di*sease is ultimately reactive intention and susceptibility, impinging on biologic structure and function: sub-rational visualization, *materialized*."
> -- Holosophy Canon
>
> "What you resist, persists…"
> -- Carl Jung, psychiatrist

Chapter I - Consciousness Re-Visioned

importance, to all *words, phrases*, and *conclusions* (belief formations) occurring, and *recorded* during the incident.

This information was *un*appraised by the pain-diminished conscious mind and neither evaluated nor reasoned (not *optimized*). Later, perhaps during some other stress, it was *re-activated* i.e. *cued* or *triggered* by, *and equated to, any* generically *similar circumstance* subsequently experienced by the now conscious individual.

When any such subconsciously recorded imprint (*engram*) becomes *re*activated, it can have dramatic *post*-traumatic command influence over the *conscious* awareness of the individual. The *sub*conscious or *sub-rational* mind, auto-cued by some "similar" or *reminder* experience, shuts down the conscious mind to a greater or lesser degree, possibly even to the point of taking over the motor and *psycho*-physical controls of the body.

The stimulus-response re-imposition of the *"forgotten"* experience causes an involuntary behavioral *re*enactment in accordance with the literal *meanings* of the original word and ideo-perceptic content of the trauma: putting this encoded data into an overriding operational control, in an effort to save the organism by mindless and robotic *re*-enactment, *repeating,* with tenacious and "proven" conviction, *what it had already "survived."*

The only sign the individual has that this is happening, is the occasional and fleeting realization of not acting rationally, and

> "Just the act of creating pictures in your 'mind's eye', in a trance state may affect brain function in ways that have direct biological impact."
> -- C. Simonton, MD Cancer Researcher
>
> "The human mind is conscious even during periods of dreamless sleep, and in the mother's womb."
> -- Rene Descartes, philosopher

Chapter I - Consciousness Re-Visioned

later perhaps: "Why did I do (or *think*) that?" Not only is irrational behavior the result of such *re*playing of painful[7] moments, but feelings and sensations (physiological reactions in the *past* incident *sub*volitionally re-experienced) can produce and re-*impose* a full range of inappropriate but seemingly *"present" ideas, attitudes,* and psychosomatic tensions, i.e. "re" active or *sub-rational indicators*[8], on the person's *actual* present-time consciousness and activity.

An example of such an engramic trauma, its imprinted mental-imagery and a later cued and *re*-minded, post-traumatic effect: Mr. A is having an appendectomy under anesthetic.

During the operation, the surgeon, who wears glasses, comments angrily to a clumsy nurse, "You don't know what you are doing." Mr. A recovers. A few months later, Mr. A, a bit tired during a stressful day at the office, has an argument with his boss (wearing glasses), who says, "You don't know what you are doing." Mr. A suddenly feels dizzy, stupid, and gets a pain in his abdomen. At that moment is triggered and installed, an imprinted pattern for future survival-signified behavior and belief; a conditioned "semantic" reflex!

Another example: An automobile accident…

Miss B is knocked unconscious when her car overturns. At the same time, her companion in the car screams, "I'm trapped! I'm trapped! I'll die if I don't get out of here." An ambulance siren sounds in the distance; murmur of crowds, police whistle. A year later, Miss B is driving her car, feeling a bit tired, pulls up to a traffic light at a busy thoroughfare and there occurs by chance, the sound of a siren and the murmur of a crowd. She suddenly feels trapped, accompanied by the irrational urge to get out of her car. Thereafter, with "reminding" cues generalized, she tends to feel very nervous; "believing" that any confined space is "always a threat" to SURVIVAL!

---

[7] 'Painful' can include, for example, the *emotional* pain and stress of loss, menace, confusion, et al.
[8] 'Re' active is used in the sense of a sub (or below) awareness repetitive response level perhaps better described as sub-rational and as unsuitable for rational calculus, as referred to in Appendix II.

> "To look for the ox one must seek out its tracks. To study the Path, seek out mindlessness. Where the mind tracks are, so must the ox be."
> -- Zen proverb
>
> "To secure stability of both our world-concept and *self*-concept, we employ a 'psychic grid' to inhibit certain perceptions which deviate from our 'norms' "
> -- Beatrice Bruteau, philosopher

Chapter I - Consciousness Re-Visioned

The sub-rational indicators, particularly the *sub* rational emotions, called in Holosophy, *mal-emotions*[9], such as anger, anxiety, fear, guilt, jealousy, sadness, and worry, are; of course, very common to human experience. So common, that they often seem to constitute the "norm" and are thus confused with more authentic or effectively *natural* states of mind and emotion. That is why it was suggested at the start that such an enhanced or optimized mind-state might even be regarded as a new and elevated *normative standard* when compared with an ordinary routine or non-optimized mental and emotional experience.

When these sub-optimum affective states are not identified or noticed as indications of sub-rationality, they are automatically taken for "the way things are." or even the way things are *meant* to be. Far from being seen as irrationally imposed *contra*-survival additives (which, in fact, they are), their *mis*-habitual[10] and intrusive *un*naturalness often isn't questioned or even perceived, and is even given a positive belief/rationale, e.g. "Be glad you're neurotic." "It is necessary for an artist to suffer." "We can't help our feelings." "Love is blind." etc.

Upon deeper reflection, such *mal*-emotions *can be* clearly recognized as un-healthy, inappropriate, and *ineffectual*, i.e., redundant and *sub*-rational. Anger, for example, seems more obviously so, because typically, it arises as an impulsive

---

[9] Negative emotions that are inappropriate, ineffective, or irrelevant to the situation and characterized by unpleasant or stressful effect, attitude and sensation, usually cued *contra*-survival reenactments of *previous* painful or unpleasant experience. Generally, free emotional expression which truly facilitates survival is a vital and necessary part of the human condition. However, that expression *can* be selectively optimized, i.e. *framed* by rational choice and diminished reactivity, while *increasing* in naturalness, survival enhancing and *pleasurable* spontaneity.

[10] A Holosophiy neologism for habits or 'automaticities' that are no longer subject to the Holon's conscious control and direction, or normal and graduated erasure or optimized modification.

> "Seek the emptiness prior to the symbol."
> -- Zen proverb
>
> "It is the sequence of cognitive inferences prompted by the dialogue that leads to *erasure,* (or the capacity to *cease to create*) persisting and redundant mental conditions, which is the true essence of dialogue."
> -- Holosophy Canon

Chapter I - Consciousness Re-Visioned

reaction rather than as a reasoned *response* (anger is rarely volitional); it is unnecessarily imposed (even-tempered, undistorted com-munication or action is preferable and *more effective);* and it is destructive since it stress-taxes the body and often violently, and uncontrollably targets others.

Similarly, anxiety can be seen as *sub*-rational because, like anger, it is apparently caused by some unwanted condition or circumstance in the immediate environment; its takeover of the mind seems *sub*-volitional (we do not consciously *choose* to feel angry or anxious); its presence is useless since neither effectively alleviates any unwanted situation. In fact, the experience of it is, like other mal-emotions, destructive in that it stresses the body, suppresses ability and disaffects others.

When the full range of sub-rational indicators cease to be habitually experienced, the *volitional cessation, or* erasure of this traumatically enforced *mis*-habituation is, as has been indicated earlier, definitely realizable.[11] Such an individual obviously feels better, thinks better, and operates better, because he or she becomes an increasingly confident *self-managing cause over* intrusive sub-rational beliefs.

Optimum, defined as a state of being confidently *free* of[12] cumulative sub-rational and obsessive impulses, then, is evidently the *truly* normative, or natural, rational and *re*-storable

---

[11] A rational power of selection is re-enabled in the Holosophy Dialogue or *Cognitive Optimization*, allowing the higher faculty of *chosen cessation* by the Holon, and the now more fully informed causal *capacity* to evaluate and choose rationally.

[12] *Free of* is an active self-determined *choice* as a result of viewing; enabling and emphasizing the all important freedom *to*...rather than a passive and *un*caused *freedom from.*

> "A certain power to alter things indwells in the human soul."
> -- Albertus Magnus
>
> "Blind metaphysical necessity which is certainly the same always and everywhere; could produce no variety of things."
> -- Isaac Newton, physicist

potential of every human being. It is each individual Holon's native-state of causative consciousness or *self-determination,* evidenced by the systematic and successful elimination of *sub-rational* indicators. It also seems ultimately possible, given restored and sustained *willingness to confront;* i.e to erase *all* residual sub-rational impairment.[13]

Dialogue as Guided Cognitive Optimization

Beyond simply using the Holosophy data and precepts on an as needed self-help basis, there are essentially two levels of more systematic address in ridding an individual of sub-rational mental activity. The first way is a method, which we have referred to as the Transformative Dialogue, or direct *assisted reviewing,* "true witnessing." In capsule, with the help of a qualified facilitator, who acts as a non-evaluating "assistant" to the client's naturally inquiring, *rational* mind;[14] there begins a gradual *noticing* that one is "experiencing" a persisting pattern of counter-productive sub-rational mental activity, and/or some *un*wanted problematic condition resulting from that activity.

After the Dialogue process has *fully* revealed the true sub-rational nature and source of the unwanted condition, the client, as Holon, being *innately committed to* responsible rationality, *makes the conscious choice to cease to mentally create (i.e.*

---

[13] The confidence in the capacity to *erase* is regained in incremental levels of *magnitude.* One need not confront *every* past traumatic event to gain mastery over comparable types and *degrees* of traumatic impact, force, or effect. Additionally the ability to perceive and consult the domains, in order to optimize and select relative value (e.g., good, truth, beauty) in making ordinary life choices is restored or enhanced.

[14] The analytical or fully awake, aware, and causative mental vehicle, of the Holon, plus the helping knowledge and skill of the facilitator has proved to be greater than the compulsive irrational force of the sub-rational or reactive mind.

> "An archetype is the a priori guiding potential for representation."
> -- C. Jung
>
> "Negative capability is when a man is capable of being in uncertainties, mysteries, doubts, without any irritable reaching out after fact and reason."
> -- John Keats, Poet

Chapter I - Consciousness Re-Visioned

erases[15]) the targeted activity and its resultant undesired condition, and spontaneously redirects and optimizes one's cognitive capacity. Now free of irrational constraint, the client operates within. the *actual* domains of Kosmic existence instead of the parasitic and traumatic, memorial *overlay* of a falsely valued past!

A simple example: an individual suddenly *notices*, while absorbed in an activity, that his mind has wandered, and upon realizing this, consciously and spontaneously *chooses* after the new *differentiative discernment,* to redirect his attention back to the actual situation in the *present* moment, in effect *"erasing"* (ceasing to create) the minor sub-rational distraction.

In other words, with guided systematic "true witnessing" or *noticing* of a complex reaction-pattern, assisted by the dialogue process, the behavior's *past* episodic origin, redundancy, and *uselessness,* is traced and *seen* with certainty. As one recognizes *fully* that a particular *part* of the false *re-enactment* isn't necessary, isn't really helpful, and certainly isn't desirably present one can gradually, increment by increment, take greater *"re*sponse-ability" and *ownership* for the whole false pattern of belief and *cease to unknowingly re-create it,* i.e., can willfully "deconstruct." discard, or *erase* it, and choose instead to use the mind more optimally, solving *real* problems.

---

[15] To *erase* is defined as: To *cease* to *create* a redundant or unnecessarily additive mental act or image thereby causing its *vanishment;* cognitive closure or *un*creation, *not* a mere sub-volitional 'relocation' to a 'new' mental storage area. Thereby restoring a natural state of uninterrupted continuity of awareness *without* redundant and duplicative superimposition of traumatic mentally *pictured* feedback. Contrasted with a certain 'de-construction' which *reduces* meaning to its falsely assumed non-cognitive constituents i.e. race, class, gender etc., which being perpetual, avoids the actuality of *self-created* meaningfulness and the volitional cessation of that creation.

> "Spirit is essentially the result of its own activity."
> -- G. F. Hegel, Philosopher
>
> "*No* mal-emotion or mental picture, however 'cherished' is ever a rational substitute for smelling the coffee."
> -- Holosophy Canon

Chapter I - Consciousness Re-Visioned

Secondly, systematically expanded transformative dialogue can be used to remove not just one, or a few, more evident "surface" sub-rational indicators (like distractions, disinterest, or a recurring bad mood), but can be directed toward the more deeply rooted and underlying *chronic* trauma-driven belief and behavior-*patterns often* containing a more basic and complex configuration of *many* cumulative sub-rational indicators and behaviors.

Not only can one see that the unwanted conditions stemming from these disabling post-traumatic behavior patterns are not necessary; one can actually trace, through earlier and *linked* "chains" of similar traumatic incidents, back to their fundamental and enabling reactionary core. Just as one can observe and discard obvious sub-rational indicators in the moment, one can, through these deeper, focused, more advanced levels of dialogue, systematically locate, examine and *erase* the deepest, most occluded, and *traumatically installed and resignified Kosmic Game Templates*[16]; thereby re-enabling the holon's fully realized state of *self*-determination, ability, and advanced *self*-actualization which, stated earlier, without obsessive re-activity, can measurably transcend presumptive human norms and limitations.

In summary, just as a misbehaving computer can be *cleared* of its bad data, "viruses" or defective programming, so apparently, can a human being be relieved of his or her sub-rational programs in *toto*, i.e., of the *general* traumatically

---

[16] Trauma-based mental-image surrogates for actual dialectic and archetypical patterns of *Kosmic* existence...

> "Things are not what they seem to be…nor are they otherwise."
> -- Lankavatara Sutra
>
> "*No* mal-emotion or mental picture, however 'cherished' is ever a rational substitute for smelling the coffee."
> -- Holosophy Canon

Chapter I - Consciousness Re-Visioned

imprinted pattern of cumulative and aggregate sub-optimum behaviors, beliefs, attitudes, and emotions which make up the more deeply structured "case-contour,"[17] a *duplicate shadow-image* of one's identity, a *personal* post-traumatic "survival" program, that each Holon as "trauma-programmer" sub-rationally injects, *endows*, and then confuses with *its own authentic character* in the course of living.

The complete *dis*habituating cognitive guidance technology designed to restore rational belief-management, and the *ultimate erasure of the total case-contour* through dialogue, we refer to as *Cognitive Optimization,* within a full *Kosmic* context.

Briefly stated, the program is built on three "pillars" of emphasis and focus: First, the target is *personal* development through erasure, of the individual case-contour of sub-rational aberration and disability. This is achieved through the graduated application of the various Transformative Dialogue techniques.

Next is the ancillary study of Holosophy philosophy and technology itself, which has been found to have additional *applied* cognitive benefit, further accelerating the clients general progress in living. Finally, consultative guidance based on the practical applications of Holosophy to specific life and career-management issues of *client concern*. These can be of particular developmental interest to each client as their broader awareness

---

[17] A redundant mimicry of the actual persona or character by the sub-rational mind, formed cumulatively over time, and comprising the totality of stored traumatic responses which constitute the false 'replicant' pattern of identities and false perception, which the Holon mistakenly endows and enacts as one's "self" depending on the triggering event or circumstance. The word "Case" is used in a multiple connotation; historically; as in "Case Study." The aggregate compilation of sub-rational issues and compulsions which comprise the en*cased* and displaced Holon's *surrogate* "self's," false beliefs, and behaviors.

> "It is our conscious self that is unconscious of something most of the time. In contrast to the unconscious that is *always* conscious."
> -- A. Goswami, physicist
>
> "The natural object is always the adequate symbol."
> --Ezra Pound, poet

Chapter I - Consciousness Re-Visioned

of play-options within the *total Kosmos* expands.

To better understand the program's *Transformative Dialogue* focus and technology, however, it may be helpful to review and amplify, here, in succeeding chapters, and from multiple and varying perspectives, the nature and origins of the various sub-rational mental components targeted for *erasure*.

The Mind: Perfect Bio-computer; Hidden Flaw

The *conscious* mental faculty of a human being i.e. the embodied Holon, is a functional storehouse and processor of accurate, finely differentiated data obtained in the course of living. *Objective* problems[18] in the real world relating to survival are perceived, posed and solved optimally when based on the accurate and readily-available data of *conscious* experience.

In Holosophy the fully *aware* part of the total mental function that consciously records, recalls, and evaluates data; we have called the rational, or "analytic" mind. This aspect of mind is analogous to fully data-accessible and operational computer software, providing swift, accurate choice-capability and informed resolutions to the *real* problems posed by life, modified only by the rational data in-put of the operator's actual situation, education, values, and experience.

The randomly and selectably accessible memory-repositories or "banks" of the Holon apparently contain the complete

---

[18] Real World Problems *without* associative sub-rational traumatic linkage, conflicting belief, content, or imposed past mental imagery and framing. A present 'how to' or a 'whether to' solving, is without any fixed sub-rational conditionality.

> "The study of a stroke event showed that although the stroke had left the patient cortically (brain) deaf, intense focusing of his attention could temporarily *restore* hearing, suggesting that in this case, regardless of brain damage, volition alone can be responsible for conscious perception."
> -- Holosophy Research Archive
>
> "He who despises himself, esteems himself as a self-despiser."
> -F. Nietzche

Chapter I - Consciousness Re-Visioned

moment-to-moment mental record of *all* perceptions of its existence. These recorded moments are evidently "stored" with *full* perception as potentially recoverable mental-images made during times when the individual is functionally *aware* (fully conscious and perceptive), and are normally available as data (or useful knowings) to the perfectly[19] analytical *rational* mind, and constructively applied to daily living.

Let's by contrast, examine again that other primitive or "fail-safe" mental faculty in human beings; (presumably) in part an apparent developmental carry-over from a lower organism conditioned-response mechanism intended to *guarantee biological survival*.

During traumatic moments when one's survival is severely threatened (those containing pain and *un*consciousness), the trauma-disabled individual continues to *record*, with a kind of minimal and *indiscriminate* awareness, sensations and perceptions in literal detail, but files them in a separate, *survival priority*, "memory bin." we have termed the *"sub-rational"* mind.[20]

This primitive and vestigial *read-only* mind "thinks" fixedly, *only* in identities; using false equalities; one trauma-datum equated with others, to form obsessively linked *psycho-*algorithms i.e., survival-reaction patterns that are later

---

[19] Modified of course by individual differences of endowed intelligence and other variable natural capacities and attributes.
[20] Sub-rational, because there is an insufficient degree of awareness present to permit rational distinction or evaluation i.e. a cognitive *response* in contrast to mere compulsive and unevaluated *reaction* to a stimulus.

> "A Holon is essentially a self-intended and reflexive *knowing*ness creatively projecting as *being* and *doing* in order to *have*."
> -- Holosophy Canon
>
> "*Creativity* enables form. Form doesn't enable itself."
> -- A.N. Whitehead, philosopher

Chapter I - Consciousness Re-Visioned

automatically superimposed over reasoned behavior; thus compelling a *re*-enactment of the past trauma, *cue-activated* by any similar "*present*" experience, on a mindlessly stimulus-response basis.[21]

The *Sub*-rational Mind: Storehouse of Pain.

In obvious contrast to the *rational* or "analytical" mind, the *sub*-rational mind; is a stress-imprinted central-command trauma repository for imposing all sub-volitional, stimulus-response, or *re*-active mental activity; a kind of naturally occurring operant-conditioning or knee-jerk post-traumatic behavior-enforcing mechanism. Upon receiving perceptual or episodic cues in life *similar* to those contained in earlier, painful experiences, this sub-mind prompts one to automatically *re*-create and *re*-experience the *sub*-rational mental-image content (and *conclusions*), a necessary re-imposition of the "*survival-valued*" traumatic incident.

The reminder cues which can later command-prompt the sub-rational mind to *react* may consist of *any* perceptions occurring in the *present* environment which *resemble those recorded during past duress*; i.e., any sights, sounds, tastes, and tactile sensations; *any* words,[22] or behaviors of self or others, or any combination of these elements *similar* to the past traumatic incident! People are generally not consciously aware of such cues or triggers, but when they are unwittingly exposed to them, their behavior is influenced instantly

---

[21] Achieving at best, what to a Holon is effectively the redundant and enforced continuity of the case-contour, a traumatic *mockery* of its primal and natural commitment to the self-imposed and *enduringly valued* limits of awareness that guarantee the enthralled (but not *entranced*) continuity of Kosmic play.

[22] Pain-associated words, and their fixedly attributed *meanings,* can have the compelling power of irrationally rooted belief-systems i.e., *charged and sub-volitional mental algorithms* over 'conscious' behavior.

> "Some intelligence or other *knows* how to get rid of warts. If we had any clear understanding of what actually goes on when a wart is *hypnotized* away, we would be finding out about a kind of *super*-intelligence that exists in each of us."
> -- Lewis Thomas, biologist

> "Art is the heightened metaphoric celebration of, and access to, the sublime."
> -- Holosophy Canon

and automatically, in much the same way as a subject might "obey" a post-*hypnotic* suggestion.

Hypnosis: Taking a "Cue"

Actually, *how* the theoretical Rational/Sub-rational Mind relationship works is well-demonstrated in practice by the induced hypnotic state, in which the hypnotist *imitates* (by imposing a peremptory attitude and *intent*[23]). The overwhelming *generic* power of past trauma, with the subjects passive and "believing" acceptance of its "proven" overpowering effect, is, in fact, mildly *re*activating the generic and "commanding" stress-signified repository of *all* past unconscious engramic traumas, and reactions.

By using as the "trigger." or cueing mechanism, i.e., the so-called power of suggestion, the hypnotist actually exploits the existing channel of past *re*active command-value; and, with the sub-aware *collaboration of the subject*[24], "overrides" conscious volition. Hypnosis uses generalized trauma-*simulation* imposed on the subject, *in the present*, to induce operator-directed trance behavior, but such behavior is exploiting an already existing *sub-rational* "survival-valued" path of suggestibility (believability), without actually re-imposing the earlier, *physical* trauma and pain.

Such a suggestion, can have far reaching effects! When given under hypnosis, it can not only influence behavior, but also

---

[23] A "commanding" attitude and capacity well known, and utilized by dog (and animal) trainers to "condition" obedience, often with surprising effectiveness. (A simple example of belief-redirection.)

[24] As we shall discover, the "subject" is not a mere passive receptacle of the hypnotic commands or a mere unthinking pawn of *any* sub-rational imprinted influence. Hypnotic trance is actually a self-generated mockery of the natural, *self-imposed* thralldom capacity of the Holon.

> "What we call a sensation can never be purely sensory. The most primitive sense data we can reach will not be wholly independent of the primitive forms of thought."
> -- Sir Arthur Eddington, physicist
>
> "Meaning is the *beingness* inherent in knowing."
> -- Holosphy Canon

Chapter I - Consciousness Re-Visioned

interfere with the subject's *voluntary* movements, body functions, and even the autonomic nervous system, which controls, among other functions, breathing, heart beat and even the sensation of pain. Hundreds of documented *major surgeries* have been conducted using hypnosis as the *sole* "anesthetic."

Careful experiments have also shown that hypno-suggestion alone, can cure warts; raise *suggested* "burn" blisters on the skin without applying heat; influence acid secretion in the stomach; cause changes of sugar levels in the blood; alter, or remove *symptoms* of pathology, et al., and can remain in effect, even *after* the subject has emerged from the hypnotic trance.[25]

For example, if an entranced subject was given a *post*-hypnotic suggestion that, after being awakened, when the hypnotist mentioned the *pre*-installed word-cue "parsley," he would feel a sudden sharp pain in one foot, hop around the room on the other, and when asked for it, "forget" his *own* name! The subject would obey the word-cue, always inventing ingenious, "analytical" rationalizations (new *reality*-altering "beliefs") to *explain* his odd behavior, and unusual memory lapse.

The *belief* commanded re-enactment imposed by the *sub-rational mind*, however, is actually much more powerful than the hypnotist's suggestion, as *its* commands are further enforced

---

[25] Another well known and documented phenomenon which illustrates the power of the mind over the body is the "placebo effect." By "shaping the expectations of the patient," an emetic can *relieve* nausea, insect dye can remove warts, and distilled water can "cure" bleeding ulcers. Interestingly, a negative, or "*nocebo*" expectation can *produce* a variety of negative psychosomatic symptoms.

> "Modern information 'theory' actually has to do with electron channel capacity, and makes no mention of *meaning*."
> -- B. Hiley, physicist
>
> "It would take a million monkeys a million years just to type out the *name* William Shakespeare. And of course, human consciousness would have to be there to *know* that it was."
> -- Fred Hoyle, astro-physicist

Chapter I - Consciousness Re-Visioned

by the *painful*[26] memory content of the *total generic* unconsciousness; a traumatic threat to survival, *and* the totality of programmed re-enactment already contained in the *sub-rational* mind. Conclusion: What hypnosis can do, the *sub-rational* mind does to an even greater and more deleterious effect, using the *compulsive power of stress-formed belief*s, to achieve the resulting range of compliant behavioral effects.

Importantly, however, when the awakened subject is informed of the suggestion, its power over the individual vanishes! The analogous restorative implication for the Holosophy dialogue "*erasure* effect" is obvious, i.e. the restored-awareness, and *proper* signifying of the post-hypnotic suggestions *actual* real-time relative importance and source removes, or "de-constructs" its *command* value as "hidden" data; restoring it to the Holon's rational and *self*-managed evaluation and control (initiating *rational choice* over the persisting *sub* rational belief and behavior).

To get a more personal sense of this stimulus-response conditioning mechanism, visualize a plump, yellow lemon; mentally cut it in half; then imagine raising it up and squeezing it into your mouth. Notice how this simple mental image or "cue" prompts you to salivate involuntarily! As a comparative implication, have you ever noticed feeling an immediate sense of dislike or distrust toward a stranger who has done nothing to warrant suspicion? And what about the "credible" but irrational

---

[26] The reaction and command effect can be strengthened by the intentional introduction of actual stress and pain (and/or drugs) into the hypno-conditioning setting; a fact well recognized by intelligence services world-wide. Read Richard Condon's *The Manchurian Candidate* for a "fictional" account of effective "brain-washing").

> "Without Ego there *is* no Karma."
> -- Ramana Maharshi, contemplative
>
> "The *sub*-rational mind *enacts* its own Karma…"
> -- Holosophy Canon

Chapter I - Consciousness Re-Visioned

and disabling fears of audiences, animals, heights, the water, or even of being loved? (the full range of *reactively staged* obsessive, and uncontrollable behavior). To further extend the analogy; what would happen if a previously well programmed and functioning computer (Rational Mind) suddenly operated with a hidden, over-riding *input* of data ("virus") irrelevant and actually counter-productive, to the current problem it is solving, and *unknown to the operator? We encounter such situations on a routine and daily basis when our home or office computers are down or otherwise mysteriously "bugged" by malware.* Such are the analogous effects of an intruding sub-rational belief-system, with the resulting wrong answers, and continuing *behavioral* crashes just as devastating to *human* rationality and well-being.

As with the bio-computer example, the imprinted mental image picture-data of such incidents of pain and unconsciousness are neither analyzed nor integrated with present *conscious* experience. In addition, the total memory imprint, i.e. *all* information contained in the "survived" experience is apparently equated with the pain and threat-to-survival theme in which rigid "solving" thought processes (beliefs) are established! In such a primitive computational *linkage of idea and image, it can be decided (believed)*, for example, "I SURVIVED!" *Therefore,* "I SURVIVED *BECAUSE* OF THESE WORDS/PAIN/FEELINGS!" This conclusion (belief-formation) then, like the hypnotists command, "demands" and enforces the compulsive *repetition* of the past engramic behavior-content, when *later* cued; or activated by a similar *reminding* experience.[27]

---

[27] This seeming 'mindless" and basic impulse to continue, copy, or repeat, actually *overlays* and *uses* the Holon's primal, natural, causal mechanisms for the assured continuity of *any primarily* purposeful event or commitment.

> "Even if (Hume) was right to insist that he could not catch himself without a perception he should also have acknowledged that he could not catch a perception without himself."
> -- John Foster, philosopher
>
> "It is the Holon's *tacit* selectivity and *managing* of the sub-rational consciousness that tends to escape notice."
> -- Holosophy Canon

Chapter I - Consciousness Re-Visioned

To borrow again the computer analogy, when the Rational Mind is involuntarily, "fused out" by the overload of severe force, pain, and stress, the Sub-Rational Mind – functionally like a kind of fail-safe shock absorber, *directs emergency control* of the organism. It also records the total experience as survival-priority feed-back to pre-program future behavior automatically in the same "safe" pattern. (Safe only because the organism in the most basic *biological* sense, believes it survived, *because of its recorded response* to the incident.)

In Holosophy, the traditional concept of the Unconscious Mind is updated and advanced by the somewhat startling observation that the "*sub*conscious" (Sub-Rational) mind is a *residual* aspect of the Holon's *total* projected kosmic awareness, and, through which, it is *always "conscious"*! Thus it is in primal readiness to record, react to, and *creatively re-signify the putative value of* the "survived" *experience, even while functionally un*conscious.[28]

This automatic record-keeping mind-mechanism and data-base has an apparent, but specious, usefulness to an individual in emergency circumstances. By imposing a primitive stimulus-response identification process, it, for example, "alerts" him to *pull his hand off a hot stove immediately*, by automatically and instantaneously reminding him of an earlier similar painful experience. Unfortunately, however, the single-valued logic[29] of

---

[28] Some researchers have concluded that, based on the case evidence for a *full* recovery of memory of *any* event, "unconsciousness" is actually *intentional* forgetting, *after* the fact of an actually uninterrupted consciousness *during* an "unconscious experience," i.e. *selective unawareness* in the service of preserving the *limited* ability to confront extremes of force and incident, necessary to localize the Holon's awareness (and game perspective) perimeter.

[29] Every element of perception in the trauma 'equals' a fixed *mono*-toned survival moment. As contrasted with actual *relative* importances, multi-values, and options framing each unique situation.

> "A man tends to become what he repeatedly *does*."
> -- Aristotle
>
> "How can one create a memory? If it is to stay, it must be burned in. This has its origin in the instinct that realized that pain is the most powerful aid to mnemonics."
> -- F. Nietzsche, philosopher

a *sub*-volitional mind cannot apply the real-time *multi*-valued optimization calculus to the novel and complex *present* circumstances, onto which it then imposes the single-valued and fixed-importance framing of past stress "survived" conclusions and behavior.

The more any condition in the present resembles the content of an engram, (trauma), the more the sub-rational mind has the potential to influence the affected individual into *re*enacting ancient, now useless and out-of-context behaviors. The obsolete patterns and *mis*habituating "lessons" (beliefs) contained in the old *undifferentiated* pain-associated and imprinted trauma-lessons are then superimposed over actual experience, e.g. in the example above as "NEVER TOUCH A HOT (*or a cold!*) STOVE AGAIN! (*Ever!*)"

The conflicts, anxieties of spirit, psychosomatic illness, anti-social, and *self*-sabotaging behavior which can result from this so-called "post-traumatic stress reaction," are actually, as we have seen, derived from a rugged, primal, but *mis-applied* "*survival mechanism.*" But, because of the apparent *non*-survival compulsiveness of aberrant behavior, have usually been mistakenly attributed to a variety of hidden and destructive causes, including a primitive, unconscious, biological "death instinct."[30] The precise nature and real *contra*-survival force of

---

[30] Earlier explanation of the supposed "repetition compulsion" of the mind, gave as its source, a primal death instinct. By contrast Holosophy posits a basic *life* intention to *survive*, which is *deceptively* misdirected in the *response* to trauma, endowing and empowering imprinted life game experience to form the *case-contour*; as a redundant 'fail-safe' substitute-identity, displacing the Holon. However, the *basic* motivation of the Holon, although displaced by traumatic imprinting, is always and fundamentally to survive, or to *be*, i.e. in a higher sense to *participate perpetually* in the Kosmos, which is *the* seminal Good, and the true formative essence of the Holon's character. which, through reactive deception, obliquely emerges as the case-contour, a replicant sub-rational mockery of the actual Kosmic template.

> "Words are a way of structuring, manipulating and controlling; thus, if we cannot name it, we cannot control it. Naming gives us power. Control is power, and power is safety."
> -- Sam Keen, author
>
> "The point is not to merely "*SURVIVE*" each moment, it is to *erase* each moment to achieve unburdened novelty and progress."
> -- Holosophy Canon

this apparent "repetition-compulsion," i.e., to fail or succumb *only* by a mindless reenactment of the past trauma, was not perceived and understood, as actually, a *primal, but irrationally channeled effort* to *SURVIVE, as an ultimately committed Kosmic participant!*

Sub-Rational Survival: The Terra Incognita of Consciousness.

Let us review some basic assumptions: The reason this stimulus-response action-mechanism exists at all has to do with the primal human *response* to pain and duress. When we are in a deeply stressful situation, one containing extreme emotional or physical pain, we experience degrees of diminished consciousness--and along with it, the lessening of ability to reason and confront. And eventually, as the situation passes a personally "intolerable" pain threshold, we switch over to the vestigial "fail-safe" Sub-Rational (*un*-thinking) mind; analogous to the "black-box" recorder of a crashing plane.

The enduring problem with this is that the sub-rational mind is very like a hypnotic command center, as we have suggested earlier. Under extreme duress, it apparently records every *percept* of the traumatic experience and *identifies* each one with all others, in a kind of generic *smear* of pain and menace. However, since even the merest urge for survival is apparently *the* most primitive, bio-kosmic *framing* mechanism for *all* experience, these sub-rational perceptions are fundamentally associated with the *repetitive* "success-value" of survival and are covertly affirmed or *believed* at a *sub*-awareness level!

> "Where there are humans you'll find flies and Buddhas"
> -- Zen saying
>
> "Our perceiving self is nowhere to be found within the world picture because it, itself, *is* the world."
> -- E. Schrödinger, physicist

Chapter I - Consciousness Re-Visioned

Since *rational success as survival* is a primary drive and purpose in life, i.e. something we repeatedly and proactively do; experiences that are sub-volitionally *associated with that elemental survival impulse formed under duress,* borrow its creative force. The contents of these events tends to become, like post-hypnotic suggestions, *recued* automatic directives, or charged belief-systems… for *perpetuating and rationalizing* all subsequent sub-rational and compulsive *re*-enactment.

In extreme forms, the hidden directives become full and obsessive repetitions of the past, precisely because that history *was survived* and therefore it has a primitive, compelling, almost *proto*plasmic, urge toward a raw *un*-evaluated survival-assurance! Stressing a *participative identity continuity*[31] that is seemingly nature's most primordial *display* of "success."

Consider also, an additional and often overlooked *contra*-survival dimension of the equation. What *else* is always associated with survival during these sub-rationally imprinted experiences? *Dis*ability! The Sub-Rational mind only takes over when, to some degree, we *lose* consciousness, and generally consciousness is *forcibly* reduced only when, in a primitive biological sense, it is not sustainable; we have exceeded our *psycho*-biological limits and *failed at something.* We have been ostensibly overwhelmed by a superior force; severe stress; injury

---

[31] A quint-essential feature of the *true* character of the Holon seems its primeval and ineluctable commitment to the broad range of *values* inherent in maintaining the Kosmic *game in progress.* The implanted and deceptive *transfer* of that fundamental endowment of energy and intention to the reductive biophysical "survival" priority of the *case-contour*, seems to explain its power to then compel sub-rational and robotic behavior repetition; to succeed, by compulsively *re*-experiencing failure and failing *again*.

> "The world for those who have gained satori (enlightenment) is no more the old world as it used to be. Logically stated, all its opposites and contradictions are united and harmonized into a consistent organic *whole.*"
> -- D. T. Suzuki, Zen Buddhist
>
> "Reality is tiered... *being* (as existence) increases as the levels descend."
> -- Huston Smith, philosopher

Chapter I - Consciousness Re-Visioned

or illness, e.g. a major surgery, an automobile accident, the loss of a valued person or possession, et al. When *any* dramatic failure, or life threatening event occurs, we *accept succumbing* to what we *assume* is more powerful, forceful, or un*confrontably* painful and challenging eventuality.

Such "failed" exercise or interruption of ability or intent, is paradoxically, *also* recorded by the sub-rational mind, *and associated with survival,* just as faithfully as the temperature of the air, the body sensations, *and all beliefs formed* during such traumatic incidents. This is why, when we react automatically to some trauma-based cue in our immediate environment, we invariably *dramatize* (re-enact) some degree of *limiting* or disabled past behavior that is *now* counter-productive.

We are effectively re-*signifying* old *failed* behavior because it becomes unwittingly associated with the primal motive-force of survival[32]. As such, it has almost quasi-hypnotic command *value* over our present awareness and behavior telling us to do *now* what we did *then,* to "survive" (be *right*) again![33]

At times we may even dimly realize this. Have you ever muttered to yourself, "#@!! *Why do I keep doing that?*" after you've just done something silly, stupid or irrelevant--again? There is a driven, *mis*-habituated compulsive quality to the sub-rational mind. We get stuck in the ancient, habitual belief and action patterns of such "successes," even though they are no

---

[32] It may be interesting, at this point, to observe that, in the deepest sense, the Holon is dedicated to the *persistence* of the Kosmic game, a consensual and rational thralldom that is, through response to historical trauma, converted into a compulsively *pictured* sub-rational trance.

[33] A paradoxically "successful" *failure!*

> "Transformative Dialogue simply *de*-constructs the *sub*-rational mind and its skill sets."
> -- Holosophy Canon
>
> "He who would do good to another must do it in minor particulars."
> --Wm. Blake, poet

Chapter I - Consciousness Re-Visioned

longer useful, simply because they have become repetitively value-fixed, ingrained and reinforced over time.

Any challenge to drop these inflexible patterns and employ new strategies tends to be ignored or automatically rejected, not because the new strategies are faulty. (They are usually far superior!), but because any new pattern of behavior goes against the old, ingrained, "this-always-equals-SUCCESS" (survival) and *mis*-habituating[34] *conclusions* formed while surviving some forgotten traumatic menace.

Such "habits," which have come to feel "natural" and *right*, like the comfort of old shoes, or a flawed but "natural-feeling" golf-grip,[35] resist change and ensure a perpetual, but disabled continuity; a kind of "psycho-sclerosis" inhibiting the Holon's free-flowing native capacity for rationally effective *flexibility*.

The individual, in reverting to the familiar, safe pattern -- i.e., the "old shoe" syndrome, finds himself in a downward spiral of covert self-sabotage in order to survive *now* as he did in some forgotten *then*. In fact, it has been observed that the acute repetitive pattern of any particular traumatic imprint may, through repeated *re*activation in the course of living, become an encrusted layer of the individual's chronic and frozen veneer of false and redundant *virtual* self re-construction, or replicant character armouring (Case-Contour).

This *core* and self-eclipsing program of traumatic mal-ware

---

[34] To emphasize again, sub rationally generated habituation without control, tends to persist with a kind of normalcy bias."

[35] One might hearken again to the oft-quoted Einstein definition of insanity: "repeating the same mistake over and over while expecting (believing in) a *different* result."

> "The eternal objects are the pure potentials of the universe. Actual entities differ; in their *realization* of potentials."
> -- A.N Whitehead, philosopher
>
> "That which you are looking for, is that which is looking."
> -- St. Augustine

Chapter I - Consciousness Re-Visioned

and (to borrow again from our computer analogy) or true identity *hi-jacking*, i.e., *dis*placing with mental-image mimicry, the *authentic character* of the Holon, manifesting instead as a *replicant or* egoic *shadow persona* of tension and emotional charge,[36] composed of a cumulative traumatic configuration of outdated beliefs, purposes and mental images from the past.

The case-contour is in essence a Holon-*surrogate*, a mosaic of traumatic self-replications, fused into a sub-rational pseudo-player in the Life-Game, which the Holon, mistaking for its *own character*, endows obsessively as a virtual self-image, thereby condemning "itself" to an endless episodic re-experiencing of the now *sub*-volitional, destructive, and *grafted on* game-patterns of a residual, but forgotten and falsely *survival-valued* past.

Cognitive Optimization: Transforming Emotion, Attitude, and Behavior.

The Cognitive Optimization Program, as will be fully described throughout this volume, involves using, systematically, a series of *Transformative Dialogues;* designed to locate, re-examine and through heightened *cognitive discernment, erase* the persons hidden, trauma-related *core beliefs*, and the associated fabric of environmental *cues*, which *activate* the totality of *sub*-rational impulse and behavior.

One might casually liken the process to the sport of skeet-

---

[36] Psychophysical distress or traumatic tension stored, but *re*creatable, from cued mental image imprints.

> "The *sub*-rational mind provides an automated servo-mechanism for the *fixed* re-naming, valuation, and *use*, of traumatic experience."
> -- Holosophy Canon
>
> "The real point of the incompleteness theorem is the irreducibility of semantics to syntax."
> -- Kurt Gödel, logician (in conversation)

shooting in which a clay projectile is mechanically launched as a shotgun target in a repetitive but carefully timed and *ordered* sequence…Pull, Shoot, *Hit!,* Repeat…until precision, skill, *(and awareness)* are enhanced, with *increasing levels of confidence.*

Comparatively, the Holosophy Counselor initiates a series of *personalized,* carefully selected topical assessments, dialogue tactics, and exercises to gently and repeatedly target and activate the sub-rational mind (*Pull!*) As a relevant mental-image picture emerges into his field of rational awareness, the individual observes it with precision *(Shoot!).* Then the reactive imagery, and any associated belief-system, when *fully* and honestly observed and *communicated* (*Hit!*), *erases*…because, like the accurately targeted clay, it obviously has no further legitimate use![37]

The mental image pictures which are thus elicited, or "re-cued" by a graduated series of planned and confrontable questions, are, of course, associated with traumatic and emotionally charged events of the past. Initially, these images may consist only of intimations and inferences of actual incidents; i.e., the client may at first view seemingly unrelated or, fragmented memories, impressions; or even experience various seemingly "unrelated" issues, emotions, attitudes, or physical sensations.

As the dialogue progresses, however, the gradually re-accessed

---

[37] A Dialogue action consists of comfortably graduated and *confrontable* communicated 're-activations', which enable the Holon to causatively 're-create' the targeted events, and through newly rational inferences and realization gained in dialogue, *erase, through cognitive closure* (cessation of creation) the re-dundant trauma-related imagery and *belief-content* of the case-contour.

> "If one is master of one thing and understands it well, one has at once the insight into many things."
> -- Vincent Van Gogh, artist
>
> "Consciousness forgets itself for the sake of *play*. It 'pretends' to forget."
> -- Amit Goswami, physicist

impressions, images, and feelings are recognized with increasing implicative clarity as portions of entire incidents directly linked to underlying (earlier and similar) patterns and ideomotor memory sequences, ultimately stemming from an even more basic and formative *core architecture, or a whole patterned and thematic tapestry of traumatic content.* Material is volitionally and *gradually* discarded that was compulsively experienced, *before* disclosure and erasure, as a complex and diffused memorial-construct of irrational beliefs, emotions, and behavior.

What has been basically observed by the author and many colleagues over more than forty years of counseling practice and research is that, as an individual systematically and accurately views and *repetitively* discusses, (strictly within the exacting parameters of the above communication paradigm)[38] the charged[39] incidents of his early past, he gradually, through revelatory and volitional acts of *cognitive closure*, i.e., *erasure;* unburdens himself of their associated aberrant beliefs, disabling psycho-physical effects, and general sub-rational influences.

Simultaneously, the lower extremes of chronic emotional-tone, self-sabotaging attitudes, and succumbing behaviors, gradually shift *upwards* from those of a perpetually victimized "loser" to a self-determined *winner,* from the passive and defeated *emotional* depths of *re*enacted traumatic failure, overwhelm, and dark despair; up through and *out* of, the

---

[38] Consider the ancient Platonic concept of *zetema* or 'quest' for true knowledge, as an inspirational precedent. The dialogue process allows some flexibility of interpretation and application as long as erasure is achieved and the client's serial attainments of cognitive closure are authentic and *self*-confirmed. See Appendix IV.

[39] *Charge* is defined here as stored and unreleased psycho-physical and emotive tension associated with past pain, enforced ideation, conflict, and stress.

> "Optimization is Kosmically coordinated, meta-programmed, transformative *de*construction of *dis*ability."
> -- Holosophy Canon
>
> "Comedy is *acting out* optimism."
> -- Robin Williams, actor, comedian

Chapter I - Consciousness Re-Visioned

numbing and previously disabling bands of chronic "*mal-emotions.*"[40]

As the tactically organized dialogue program unfolds the Holon ascends, through ever more proactive, positive, *success*-directed attitudes and emotions, and finally, up to the cognitive pinnacle of relieved cheerfulness; increasing awareness and confident causativeness; a newly framed and *un*filtered access to each, infinitely contextual, *present* moment.

This on-going remedial dialogue-cycle of incremental betterment has its generic, life-defining, *attitudinal* nuances, as well, which also progress upwards as more *re*active belief-content is consistently unburdened, from the depths of a perhaps chronic apathetic hopelessness, anxiety and fixed introversion, up through increasingly positive emotive and attitudinal transformation, to a *fully* extroverted, confident and stable, peak realization of *actual* self-*re*impowerment as "Holon in-Charge."[41]

Each incremental stage of the program involves discarding, letting go, or *volitional cessation* of the *redundant*, core traumatic imagery and false egoic displacement by the case-contour which, after erasure, is no longer compulsively (and *absurdly*) endowed and sustained as one's *authentic* character.

---

[40] Painful and stressful emotions that are characteristic of trauma and threats to survival. They become the *chronic* emotional tone of the Holon, when it is consistently displaced by the case-contours malemotional content.

[41] It has long been observed that during the dialogue of a specific traumatic event, that, as the incident erases by incremental repetition, there appears *routinely,* a kind of generalized taxonomic scale of emotional states; ranging upward from the apathy of total overwhelm, up through improving "recovery states" of higher more aggressive emotions like anger and antagonisms 'up' through boredom to the final *cheerful* revelation and release, of *erasure*.

> "If I *like* it, I say it's mine. If I don't, I say it's a fake."
> -- Pablo Picasso, artist
>
> "Everything is in physics, *if* we define physics *to* include everything."
> -- E. Squires, physicist

Chapter I - Consciousness Re-Visioned

Ultimate Responsibility: A Primary Cognitive Truth

As the program proceeds, the individual will gradually discover, in a series of cognitive epiphanies resulting from the deep and systematic self-observation, that *all* traumatic *framings* of fixed beliefs, and *mis*habituations previously described are, at their core, also *self-determined!* He or she will realize that the apparently random sub-volitional responses to the cues from the environment have a deeper pattern and background of purposefully *postulated selectivity*[42], and that this selective un-awareness, even when perceived as an "obviously uncaused" traumatic effect or victimization is, at its creative inception and core, *volitional,*[43] *and kosmically meaningful.*

This personal discovery is not a matter of "faith-based" precept or belief, but a matter of a *demonstrable* self-realized capacity. The destructive sub-rational patterns of compulsively repetitive mental-imagery which gradually dissolve with dialogue and counseling, are discovered to do so because of the restored awareness of their hidden, however *mistaken, volitional initiation by the Holon* and the increasingly confident certainty of being able to also *cease obsessive* replay of *all* such trauma-responsive *mental creation.*

---

[42] A creative bringing about of a *conceptual* potentiality into a preferred and purpose-related *actual* existence. The Holon is always exercising that potential, overtly or covertly.

[43] As one increases the ability to *erase*, i.e. to *un*-create mental images, one may eventually realize by implication and through inference the nature and source of their origin, Holosophy *re*-visions the traditional and supposedly inevitable 'Karmic' source of unwanted conditions replacing it with a primal and remedial *self*-determination.

> "*Show* me your mind, that I may pacify it."
> -- The Buddha to a disciple
>
> "Esse Quam Videre: To *be*, rather than to *seem* to be."
> -- latin phrase

Chapter I - Consciousness Re-Visioned

Thus, as the being's personal responsibility and *power of choice* is revived and optimized, he can ethically discard or *cease to create* the buried irrational and contra-survival, *mis*-habituative "creativity" of the past and begin to live more optimally, with full and choiceful awareness of the present, *as it actually is*; a perpetually inviting portal to a Kosmic future.

The Cognitive Exemplar: How *Optimization* Differs from other Methodologies

This process of Cognitive Optimization is distinctly characterized not only by its basic mental image--theoretic perspective (e.g., the rational vs. sub-rational mind duality) and its systematic dialogue approach to cognitive and belief *dis*habituation, but also by its idealistic and non-reductionist philosophical context. Additionally it employs selective use of objective assessment surveys, confirming research technology, and finally *specified* pre-set goals and *standardized* attainment milestones that define each successive level of the transformative staircase of the Program.[44]

Philosophical and Pragmatic Elements of the Program

As an emerging cognitive-development modality, Holosophy counseling can provide a meaningful philosophical context for understanding life from a multi-dimensional perspective, which emphasizes volition, balance, harmony, and integration. Holosophy, while likening life to a game, uses the more expansive Life-Game paradigm to re-vision the higher goals and

---

[44] See the Psych/ology/iatry reference comparison and attainment descriptions in Appendix I and IV as well as the 'Three Pillar' methodology description on pages 22 and 23.

> "Rational choice enacts finite increments of Kosmic betterment."
> -- Holosophy Canon
>
> "The meaning of the message will not be found in the chemistry of the ink."
> -- S. Kaufman, biologist

Chapter I - Consciousness Re-Visioned

values of the *fully realized Kosmic* game as ideally *playable*.

This would include our deeper spiritual nature as players; the fields on which we perform and play; the primal dialectic formation and thematic conditions of the game, and, most importantly; *how* the phenomenon and mechanisms of the sub-rational mind which supplant and suppress our native ability to win or *succeed* in the game, can be identified, and *un*-created[45], or erased.

The *Kosmic* extension and refinement of the ancient Life-Game paradigm (presented more completely in Chapter 2) is extremely important, for it suggests more extended, *workable*, and *ideally proportional standards* of rationality and ethics. These are vitally useful in discerning and gradually eliminating from one's life the *unwanted* conditions and adversities of play that, even though usually accepted as "normal," are *not* broadly *rational,* i.e. not, on balance, contributing to, and *upgrading* the quality, *meaning* or betterment of one's total and personal experience of the game of living.

Following is a review, in brief, of some of the distinguishing features of the program. A full understanding of both its facilitative and *pro*scriptive elements are vital to individual successes in its application.

Assessment Surveys: The Program normally begins with a comprehensive personal interview designed to determine *where*

---

[45] "*Un*-create" is used to mean the volitional cessation of the *sub*-rational trauma-associated *creation* of mental-imagery... resulting in a cognitively optimized spontaneity of experience based on *conceptual* familiarity un-mediated by redundant and sub-volitional mental *picturing* from the past.

> "Consciousness *subtracts* the actually possible from the realm of the Infinitely potential."
> -- Holosophy Canon
>
> 'Truth is the approximation of the thought to reality...it is thought on its way *home*."
> -- Brand Blanshard, philosopher

Chapter I - Consciousness Re-Visioned

exactly, among the many unique experiences, exigencies, relationships, and endeavors of the client's life, the salient issues of *sub-rationality* actually lie. This survey is systematic and precise, provides clearly identified targets of focus for the interactive dialogues to follow, and thereby curtails random and protracted search for *personally* relevant material.

In addition to the preliminary survey, other directive re-assessment methods may, at times, be used further along in the program to locate specific areas of tension or conflict which were previously hidden and unconfrontable, but which surface unburdening has subsequently made accessible; or have been unearthed because of *"charge"*[46] removed, or insight and abilities gained, in the earlier stages of the program.

Standardized and Specified Attainment Levels: While this technology can be utilized in short-term facilitation to help individuals achieve relief from specific and immediate subjective or unwanted problems, issues of concern, or to attain certain limited goals; the basic program, in its entirety, is conducted more broadly through a series of precisely-defined stages, each of which is designed to facilitate realization of the standard pre-set and incremental goals of *reduced* sub-rationality with a precisely *described increase* of ability and confidence characterizing each level.

---

[46] 'Charge' refers to both the psycho-physical tension and encysted emotive energy, contained in the full range and reservoir of traumatic memory, from surface level '*cued* reactions' to their underlying engramic sources, *as well as* the Holon's deeper conflicted *belief resistance* to the re-experiencing or recreation of *all* sub-rational memory content, since erasure is perceived *sub-rationally as loss* of valuable "survival" data.

[46] E.g., by C. Jung as early as 1907, to find word associated stress.

> "Visualizing mental formations either voluntary, or *not*, is a most mysterious process. What becomes of those creations? Do they, like flesh and blood children, escape our control and play parts of their own?"
> -- Kushog Wan Chen, Tibetan Lama
>
> "God is being... itself."
> -- Paul Tillich, theologen

The attainment of these goals, which the client and the facilitator *both* confirm and *attest* to, as they are achieved, provides additional *objective para-normal* milestones that demonstrate in vivid and *personal* terms, that the Program is an effective tool, and that through its use, he or she is achieving *real* and meaningful improvement.

Duration Of The Program: The amount of time required to complete the Transformative Dialogues varies widely from individual to individual, but generally each stage can require about fifteen to twenty hours of personal consultation, the scheduling of which is highly flexible, and requires *consistency* and honest dedication of purpose. Some individuals prefer scheduling weekly sessions of an hour or two each, for example, and might complete the basic program within a year or less.

For those who prefer a more accelerated pace, each stage can be conducted in personal intensives, which are available by special arrangement. This schedule can also be amplified at the discretion of the client to accommodate additional consultation for selected life and work situations, or a special interest in Holosophy Technical Study applications as outlined in the "Three Pillar" program model described earlier.[47]

Personal *Pre*-Requisites For Counseling: With few exceptions, virtually any sane and healthy individual of average intelligence can benefit from Transformative Dialogue, *if* he or she is also sufficiently *motivated* to honestly examine, confront, and volitionally relinquish long-standing, often deeply habituated, but self-defeating beliefs and patterns of behavior.

> "The next best thing to playing and winning; is playing and losing!"
> -- A. Alverez, writer
>
> "Overcome any bitterness felt because you were not up to the magnitude of the pain entrusted to you."
> -- Rumi, ancient poet

Chapter I - Consciousness Re-Visioned

The self-assessment inventories, attestation formats and sub-rational-*indicator* lists, provide examples of many of the specific unwanted conditions, problems and disabilities, which can be successfully addressed, resolved and/or improved through applying the dialogues and other aspects of the multi-faceted program.

The importance of *ethical motivation* cannot be overstated, however, for engaging in any part of the program requires of an individual not only a significant investment of time, and resources, but a deep, *honest* and enduring cooperative commitment to confronting *and* assuming *ultimate* personal responsibility[47] for *whatever* unwanted or sub-optimum condition he or she is experiencing as a *Kosmic* player.

The types of individuals for whom the program *may* be inappropriate or contra-indicated would include persons who are currently or who have recently been addictively dependent upon drugs or alcohol; those with a history of medical or institutional treatment for neurosis or psychosis; those who are currently engaged in, and *committed* to, strictly secular, *victim-oriented* helping practices, and those who rely heavily upon, or are unduly influenced by, the support, actions, or counsel of any individual, agency or group who may be antagonistic toward the spiritual goals of self-actualization, restored personal empowerment, or individual responsibility.

---

[47] In fact this volume is designed to accommodate a broad range of study and/or consulting applications. As a seminar manual; as a guiding vehicle to assist personal study; or as a general link to the Holosophy Foundation and its educational mission and ancillary study materials.

> "All evil is based on creating, asserting and *acting* from, the substitution of pictured traumatic conditioning, identity, and belief for the *actual* character and intent of the Holon."
> -- Holosophy Canon

> "First get the facts, then you can distort them at your leisure."
> -- Mark Twain, novelist

The reasons for these exclusions are quite simple and perhaps obvious. Any ingested substance which artificially alters an individual's body chemistry, mind, mood, or perception, will necessarily obstruct or obscure direct contact with areas of tension or stress. The endorsement or reliance upon radically reductionist philosophical or "helping" paradigms can (and in our experience usually does) prompt conflicting, entrenched, and counter-productive comparisons with the spiritual ideals and practices employed in the course of counseling.

Finally, the necessary willingness to assume greater personal responsibility for one's condition in life is generally found to be incompatible with any *dependent,* intransigent, reliance on an outside source for any support or advice that limits or negates *full* commitment, or reduces a client's *freedom* to make rational self-helping choices consistent with *Kosmic Optimization*.

Chapter II – Lila; The Life Game Paradigm

Chapter II
Lila, The Life-Game Paradigm, a Kosmic Enchantment Displayed

> "The notion of Lila or "divine playing" occurs at least twenty-eight times in the Rig Veda, and is fully represented in the Bhagavad Gita and Upanishads, and we find references to a "Buddha-Lila" in Buddhist texts (Ja·takas)."
> -- Ananda Coomaraswamy, religious historian
>
> "The quantum mechanical description is in terms of knowledge… and knowledge requires *somebody* who knows."
> -- F. Peirels, physicist

II - Lila; The Life Game Paradigm
A *KOSMIC* ENCHANTMENT DISPLAYED

Within the Vedas, the sacred 10,000 year old hymnal scriptures from which (in part) modern Hinduism derives, lies a seminal concept which the ancients believed both summarized and explained existence in a single Sanskrit word: *Lila.* Literally meaning "divine play," Lila suggests that the totality of existence *is* a Game; *not* a narrow entertainment based on chance, or a mere trivial recreation, but a vast *Kosmic*[1] Display of Divine Self-Actualization.

Kosmic Reality as we both *construct and perceive* it, is a universal consensus *creation;* an ultimately sublime interactive *complicity* comprised of volitional rules, proportions, boundaries and limitations[2] that we, as inherently immortal Holons, have initially, and through time, imposed upon ourselves for the purpose of perpetually actualizing the *co*-created and *enthralled sharing necessary for the playing* of *the game.*

It follows that any incidental "suffering" of unwanted conditions we experience is *ultimately* the result of a *selective unawareness* or "needful forgetting" of these natural *self-*imposed limitations. Then, responding to traumatic

---

[1] Kosmos: An ancient Greek term used by Pythagoras to refer to the *entire* universe in all of its multi-dimensionality, i.e. *spiritual*, mental, emotional *and* physical, (as contrasted with "Cosmos" in its modern usage which refers *only to the physical realm).*

[2] Any game requires a limiting, rule-enforcing, or "umpiring" (*not* "regulating" or controlling) authority as a supervising and stabilizing arbiter within any arena or boundary of play. The "hidden" but accessible truth or standards of that authority *guides* the activity of play and needs to be *playfully* and temporarily concealed, as the play activity continues. Just as we are "guided" by the sun's light, only if we do not look at it *directly.*

> "The problems and baffling paradoxes associated with human experience, are seen as contrived deceptions invented by Universal Mind and built into the Kosmic game. The ultimate meaning of human existence is to be an ultimate actor and playmate in that game."
> -- Stanislaus Graf, psychiatrist

> "The wall of paradise within which God dwells, is made up of paradoxes (contraries), and the straightway, in lies *between* them."
> -- Nicholas of Cusa

interventions, which imprint redundant and deceptively "real" surrogate mental-imagery, we falsely attribute our travails to the causation of others, blind chance, various deities, or to the circumstances of a menacing and seemingly unchosen material existence beyond our control.

Whether or not the mythic concept of the Lila cosmogony reflects literal truth, few would deny that *life* and the seeming mathematical order of a universe available (or constructed)[3] for its habitation and development, can be usefully *likened* to a game process, and that, like any sport or board game, it can be viewed as having players, established conditions of play, playing fields, strategies for winning, and degrees of effective performance!

If players, for instance, can be defined ideally, as *individual Holons,* willingly and completely aligned with others for the optimally competitive pursuit of "*win*ables," or survival-valued goals, exchangeables, or qualitative desiderata of some kind, then we as human beings certainly *qualify* as players. The further, rather obvious implication, is that such playerhood requires the larger and necessary defining context of a *constructed Game to play*[4], and at least a minimally propitious Universe *in* which to play it.

We are all in collective pursuit of the most basic and primary *win*able *survival*, if nothing else. But beyond the goal of mere

---

[3] A group of theoretical physicists have recently hypothesized that the cosmos is analogous to a cinematic "matrix-like" *constructed* universe.

[4] An interesting Buddhist variation on the "Lila" concept is the Tibetan "Game of Liberation" played within a "Map of the Universe" containing 104 squares.

Chapter II – Lila; The Life Game Paradigm

> "They are playing a game (but), playing at *not* playing a game. If I show them I *see* they are; I break the rules and they will punish me. I must play their game of *not* seeing the game."
> -- R.D. Laing, psychiatrist

> "Not that this joy first began with the creation, no! The creation is the same sport out of Himself."
> -- Jacob Boehme, contemplative

biological sustenance and continuity, we can and do seek heightened and *qualitative* expansion of the game's many playing fields and activities. Ideally, as a community of rational human beings, we tend to protect, support and *perfect*, to whatever degree, the *playing fields and participants* of the game: our environment, species, race, nationality, family, relationships, extended values, and *ourselves.*

In so doing, we each play or perform certain roles or occupations to achieve valued exchanges, according to our unique abilities, talents *and* interests, routinely giving ourselves titles, licenses, credentials, and even uniforms to make our particular rank, designation, or player *status* more readily apparent within the "Game Holoarchy" i.e. it's interactive, *hierarchic,* orderliness.

As we pursue our personal goals in life; self-actualization, raising a family, developing a career, we seem to inevitably encounter the fundamental conditions or *defining characteristics* common and necessary to *all* games. These include goals and purposes, limiting rules and ratios; freedoms, barriers, opponents, exchanges, ethics, justice and aesthetics, among others.

Within these tacit and necessary *game constraints*, or boundaries, we create, and contend with ever more game sustaining strictures. By introducing specific and living rules of play, such as evolving laws, policies, conventions, procedures, mores, customs, courtesies, etc. we attempt to produce and *maintain* through an enduring

> "Reality is the leading cause of stress amongst those in touch with it."
> -- Jane Wagner, playwright
>
> "Reality is that which when you stop believing in it, doesn't go away."
> -- Phillip K. Dick, novelist

Chapter II – Lila; The Life Game Paradigm

player-hood, (apparently even beyond a single life-span),[5] an *optimized balance* of interest, opportunity and predictability within the games interactive "arenas" of play.

Obviously, there *are* such playing fields in life. On a gross cosmological[6] scale, we *play* as Holons, within the stable physical boundaries of an inevitable and emergent "observer participancy;" a quantum mechanical "averaging of illusion," or a uniformity of *universal* experiencing, literally *brought* into existence by a *jointly* observing and *measuring* aggregation of consciousnesses.[7] e.g. our cosmic universe with its galaxies, solar systems and planets.

On a planetary scale, we play within continents, countries, regions, cities and towns. On a more local scale, we play within our homes, factories, offices, public places, roads, and rooms. Every environment we can name contains and supports *some* boundary or perimeter of defined social order, inter-play, and exchange; be it business, recreation, politics, intimate relations, physical maintenance, or any combination of these.

It seems difficult, in fact, to see *any* way in which life does *not* resemble an elaborate, on-going game. Actually, far from

---

[5] Although generally accepted for thousands of years in Eastern cultures, the "transmigration of the soul" or reincarnation as a belief system in the West, has been beset by competitive orthodoxy. Recognized for centuries by the Jewish Kabbalists, the sect of Essenes, and contained in the philosophies of the earlier Church Fathers, Origen, and Justin Martyr, influenced by Plato, and the early Greeks, historical evidence also suggests that it was part of early Christian and Gnostic doctrine. However, in a series of Nicean Church Councils, the Biblical sources and Foundation teachings were revised and renamed; and reincarnation was declared heresy and anathema in 553AD.

[6] Extended participation beyond the mere physical realm to include the *full* existential spectrum of play, including the epistemic and divine, defines the *Kosmic* Life-Game.

[7] A majority of physicists ascribe to the "standard model" of quantum mechanics which holds that an *act of conscious* measurement or observation "collapses" the background wave function of the *un*-observed quantum physical universe from *possibilities* into perceived *realities*. Just *how* consciousness achieves this transformative "extraction" is left to conjecture (and some dispute).

Chapter II – Lila; The Life Game Paradigm

> "We have lost our awareness of union with spirit; not at the "beginning" of evolution, or during the early years of life – but at the beginning of *involution* – or what happens prior to our birth in time."
> -- Ken Wilber, integral philosopher

> "Thralldom creatively adjusts the primal categorical opposites to accommodate and *enable* the projection of ordinary experience."
> -- Holosophy Canon[9]

considering it merely an analogy, the authors of the Vedas presented the concept of *Lila* or the "divine play" as a literal *fact* of ultimate spiritual truth, and many modern-day proponents still do. In *Meditations and Its Methods According to Swami Vivekenanda*[8], for instance, the renowned Indian scholar and teacher suggested as much when he wrote:

"It is all play. Play! God Almighty plays. That is all. You are the almighty God playing. If you want to play on the side and take the part of a beggar, you are not to blame someone else for making that choice. You enjoy being the beggar. You know your real nature is to be divine. You are the king and play you are a beggar. It is all fun. Know it and play. That is all there is to it. The whole universe is a vast play."

Again, does the ancient *Lila* cosmogony-mythos reflect actual *meta*physical truth? Are we *really* biologically encapsulated divinities intentionally forgetting who and what we are *for* the sake of being convincingly enthralled[9] in a game of our own *Kosmic* devising? Is the possibility *too* difficult to imagine? Consider the unspoiled delight of children entering games of "pretending." They naturally (and arbitrarily) select and enact roles, instantly becoming warriors, doctors, parents, et.al in the realms of their imaginations, and have little, if any, distracting consciousness of themselves as really "just children" until their co-participative gaming spell is broken, by a call to supper, or back to class.

Obviously *some* volitional "suspension of disbelief" is required to

---

[8] Meditation and its Methods According to Swami Vivekenanda, Second Indian Reprint, July 1981, The Indian Press Pvt. Ltd., Calcutta- 700 013, India.

[9] "Thralldom" in Holosophy usage is is used to mean that state of "*creatively tacit* un-*knowing*" or selectively forgetful pretense, during which a creative instantiation, or bringing about, is employed to accommodate and impose the convincing r*ecreational display* of novel*ty*, and the otherness of existence; a paradox central to all creative activity!

> "The universe looks like a 'put up' job."
> -- Fred Hoyle, astrophysicist
>
> "Imagine, that behind the scenes God and the Devil were the closest friends but had taken opposite sides to stage a great cosmic *game*."
> -- Alan Watts, zen author

Chapter II – Lila; The Life Game Paradigm

initiate all truly imaginal (creative) endeavors.[10] Unless we have some *indirect* numinous experience of this seminal dual-identity, i.e. of being, at once *both* human and celestial; "plant and phantom," to borrow Nietzsche's elegant phrase, we can't "not know" with any degree of *certainty* that we *are* actually amnesiac Kosmic game-makers.

We cannot, however, say we did *not* create the rules of life, or even life itself, simply because we do not "recall" having done so, any more than we can say we did not kick our mothers while in the womb because we do not remember having done so, or cease to *exist* as Holons, because of *any* profound state of *temporary* unconsciousness. (Such "un-consciousness" is no excuse.)

Without subjective confirmation by deep and *personal* revelatory intimation or recall, *or* direct "scientific" evidence, the question of ultimate cosmic origins and causation risks becoming a mere polemic, centering on an academically interesting but *personally* irrelevant spiritual enigma; or instead becomes completely a matter of asserted belief; of accepting it one way or the other as an article of faith, or because some authority whom we admire, or respect, (or fear) *says* "It is so!"

But, suppose for a moment, that the "life-as-a-game" theory[11]

---

[10] An actor when totally spontaneously absorbed in a part, is, at once, creatively *non*-conscious of *self;* while *consciously and creatively playing an imaginal characterization;* an act of cognitive *pretense*, and self-enchantment that when authentic, engages and "enthralls" the actor, and audience, as well.

[11] Actually there is growing scientific consensus that the universe was in fact intelligently designed to *accommodate* life and its apparently innate and *purposeful* survival capacities. In this anthropic theory, contrary to the strictly materialist Darwinian hypothesis of life evolving from a series of random, accidental "natural selections" and mutations, there are too many vastly improbable "coincidences" of physical circumstances propitious to the entry and development of life to explain away. In the words of one prominent physicist, "The universe must have *known* we were coming!"

> "We are the toys of God, and should dance accordingly, as if playing at the finest games!"
> -- Plato

> "Sense impressions without the innate categories of understanding are meaningless."
> -- Immanuel Kant, philosopher

Chapter II – Lila; The Life Game Paradigm

is literally valid, and that a *chosen*, committed, enthralled descent, as Holon-players into human form, *however* accomplished, was the original entrance requirement or "ante" into the game; which has *de*volved through time and the experiential (and traumatic) exigencies of play, to what is observably, a present condition of *entranced forgetting*;[12] reduced to mere troubled, aberrant, and protesting, but seemingly *condemned victim*-occupiers. What, however, would such a *restored Lila-Context* imply, if true, about our personal responsibility for both our ultimate, and immediate condition and existence, as *primarily self*-entranced Kosmic players?[13]

The body of theoretic Holosophy principles and practices which constitute the metaphysical Kosmic Life-Game construct, and its explanatory corollaries, validates and incorporates, after many years of consciousness research, the Vedic "divine-play" mythos; and presents a number of key points of a *Kosmic* Paradigm for further *personal* investigation, contemplation and evidentiary confirmation.

Some Selected Holosophy Tenets:[14]

1. We human beings, as Holons, theoretically *were*, and innately still *are*, divinely heritaged Spiritual Beings who could and *potentially can,* know anything, *be* anything, *do* anything, and *have* anything *creatable.*

---

[12] Trance is the sub-rational reduction of thralldom defined in Holosophy as playfully *knowing* pretense; to obsessive and convinced *re*enactment *without* awareness.

[13] Is the adventurer who *knowingly* ventures into a savage jungle responsible for what possible harms and dangers he or she experiences within it? How might this analogy apply further to each individual's simple and very *real* commitment, made daily to *continue living* in this world of uncertain eventuality and vicissitude; when a local *suicidal exiting* is always an open (if extreme) *choice*?

[14] See complete Publications List Appendices for further references.

> "Man is not the creature of circumstance. Circumstances are the creatures of man!"
> -- Benjamin Disraeli, Prime Minister
>
> "If the picture makes no sense, examine the *framing*…"
> -- Holosophy Canon

Chapter II – Lila; The Life Game Paradigm

2. To accommodate creation of the limiting perimeters necessary for the purpose of Kosmic Play, we have selectively (and collectively) chosen to reduce our innately endowed capacities, i.e., to know, be, do (or *not*), and have certain agreed upon things, or "boundary conditions," in order to tacitly establish a co-experienced, convinced, and enduring field of play.

3. For the purpose of the sustained thralldom necessary to keep the game of life *real*, we have elected to forget, with selective but unconscious precision, who and what we really are, and as a result, have immersed ourselves, by volition, into a kind of consensually enacted, or tacitly designed and en*thralled* verisimilitude, a *convincing Kosmic recreational display,* or stage for enactment.

4. *Our* self-imposed participative limitations and choices form the fabric of all conditional apparencies of the *Kosmic* game, and are *not* merely the "given facts" of a material, uncreated "natural" world. In acts of conscious observation, *we* create or "bring about" our reality, by postulate-belief and projection; and within certain tacitly shared game-preserving proscriptions, we can optimally modify or *erase* (*un*-create) all its *rationally* unwanted conditions.[15]

5. Ethically determining and optimizing through *free* and

---

[15] Consider the role in quantum mechanics of physicist and mathematician John Von Neumann's theoretic "abstract ego," the final and necessary observational and *causal* link of *consciousness* to the requisite selective "knowings" that *ultimately* constitute the "reduction" of *implicit* wave-forms of probability to the *explicit* appearances of reality.

> "The substance of God touches the substance of the Soul."
> -- St. John of the Cross
>
> "God made everything out of nothing, but the nothingness shows through…"
> -- Paul Valéry, poet and essayist

rational idealized choices, the local conditions, goals, limitations and quality of our lives *is* fun, i.e. the essence of ethical gaming and display (*lightness* of being, playfulness, unalloying pleasure, qualitative action and *value*-adding creativity).

6. Thinking, believing and *living* as victim-blamers or "as if" other beings, objects, past events or external conditions, ultimately and immutably determine our lives, without *any* degree of personal causation or responsibility, is *not* effective or fun. It engenders instead, darkness, confusion, angst, dread and deadly *seriousness* and interjects redundant and endless *irrational* pain, penalty, and circumstantial adversity into the game.

7. The secret to enjoying life, lies in *increasing* one's conscious *self*-determinism and causativeness, with regard to the purposes, barriers and *full* choiceful participative *framing* of life, a completely life-engaged and *pro*active quality of experience, accompanied by elevated mood and positive and increasingly expansive emotive "tone" levels of *Kosmic* Playerhood.

While these few preliminary tenets may seem jarring to some of us in the West; properly viewed, they are actually not that foreign to our own contemporary thought. There probably isn't a reputable "life-change" consultant in practice today, for instance, who would argue with the value-primacy of *self-determination*. The free exercise and power of choice has obviously proven throughout the ages to be inherently

> "Space is only a word we have believed to be a thing."
> -- Henri Poincare, mathematician
>
> "If a man has nothing to eat, fasting is the most intelligent thing he can do."
> -- Herman Hesse, novelist

preferential, both personally and practically, to tyranny, aberrant mental compulsion, authoritarian domination, repression, or blind obedience of any kind or degree, political, doctrinal, or *internal*.

Who among us would *sanely* and willingly negate their own capacity to make *free* choices? In fact, one's degree of self-determination in any area of life, can be seen to be a direct and even imperative measure of one's health and success in that area... The more conscious *control*, or power of choice, a person can assume over his personal life situation, the happier and healthier he is. Conversely the *less* his presumptive (*believed*) capacity for causation and control, the more emotionally distressed, ill, demoralized or "victimized" he is apt to become.

There is obviously serious debate over the fourth tenet: that we are each *ultimately* responsible for the conditions in which we find ourselves. How many would reasonably contend that suffering victims[16] of violent crime are personally responsible for the emotional scarring they experience after an assault, mugging or rape, for instance; or that property owners are "responsible" for the damage to their homes and disruption of their lives caused by hurricanes?

Yet most of us have observed that, while some people seem permanently scarred, embittered or "destroyed" by painful experiences, others somehow manage to move beyond their

---

[16] Consider the distinction in attitude and behavior between receiving an unwanted or injurious effect as "victim" without any degree of awareness of ultimate personal responsibility or remedy, and the certainty and restorative capacity as an *aware* Holon, to erase any lingering mental effects of such an event.

Chapter II – Lila; The Life Game Paradigm

> "The *Holon* is defined as the non-material *being*, persona, or agency: *Holos* as the action-principal of *doing*; and Holism as the final projected conditionality of *having* and perception…"
> -- Holosophy Canon
>
> "Interpretations *by themselves* do not determine *meaning*."
> -- L. Wittgenstern, philosopher

scars and buffetings and even be somehow strengthened and positively *transformed* by fully confronting and accepting[17] them; which, like the intense but natural pain of a mother's childbirth can quickly fade from her daily memory and concern.

This crucial difference in *response to adversity* is obviously generated only by the individual, *not* merely by the event! Truly *self*-determined and actualized people *cope* with adversity, can quickly heal and move on; while people with *sub-rationally selected victim attitudes,* obviously continue to *blame;* languishing in unduly prolonged negative life-conditions, and are seemingly self-condemned to being perpetually "poised for outrage," since a blaming mind-set *requires* a complete denial of, or *any* degree of *awareness* of a personal and *causative* participation in the basic or *extended Kosmic* dimensions of Play.[18]

What if the original *access to* the *Kosmos* (and, of course, by implication, also to one's *current* lifetime) proves to be, *itself,* ultimately self-determined? If, for example, one is *fully* aware of the dangers of entering a jungle containing dangerous wild animals, and yet decides to enter, is one "responsible" for being savaged by a particular tiger in any ensuing adventurous enterprise? To extend the analogy, would the immediate and obvious fact of the *volitional,* daily exhibited, choice to reject suicide, and to *continue to inhabit* an existing and dangerous

---

[17] In Holosophy, "transformative acceptance" (with *erasure*) is not mere resignation or a passive and regretful sufferance. It is the fully enabled and *volitional* passage of the Holon into the *next* full and free *moment* of choiceful possibility, without residual *sub-volitional* effects from the past: the "creative advance into novelty."
[18] More complete awareness of the 7th and 8th domains of the full *Kosmic* Life-Game seem to accompany and sustain the higher perspectives and abilities required to rise above any enduring victimization by adversity.

> "In Physics, everything that *might* have happened influences what actually *does* happen."
> -- Richard P. Feynman. physicist
>
> "The karma of all sentient beings that inhabit the universe, plays a role in shaping the formation of the universe."
> -- Dalai Lama

Chapter II – Lila; The Life Game Paradigm

world, on what is obviously an assumed-risk basis, have any practical relevance to each Holon's ultimate (and immediate) actions and responsibility as a *player-agent* and *choiceful* game participant?

Obviously, the Kosmic origin or "birth"[19] of the Holon-players suggested by the Lila exemplar and reflected in tenets one, two and three are subject to lively philosophical (and theological) debate. Yet *most* ancient *and* modern religious traditions, assert that man, by nature, has free will, which implies and *requires* an innate capacity *as an agent* for self-determination, and implicit *social* accountability.

Since all such teachings urge human beings toward *some* form of ultimate spiritual reconciliation or union with a Deity, they likewise imply an imminent *potential* for a freely acting, realizable, unity or *interactivity* with an omnipotent Supreme Being; Creator, cum Game-Maker; or whatever designation the inadequacy of mere language affords to reference it.

Our purpose here, however, is only to show that the Vedic concepts which undergird the *Kosmic* Life-Game paradigm are actually quite Universal, and need not conflict with anyone's personal spiritual or religious beliefs to have *some* degree of "user friendliness" in a helping *life* application.

But the issues of any "ideological" polemics or the conflicting exegesis of dueling dogmas is perhaps irrelevant, for the real test of the validity and value of *anything* lies in one's direct

---

[19] If consciousness or *essence* truly *precedes* existence, it could hardly have "evolved" *from* it.

Chapter II – Lila; The Life Game Paradigm

> "Everything we know about Nature is in accord with the idea that the fundamental process of Nature lies *outside* space-time; but generates events that can be located *in* space-time."
> -- H. P. Stapp, physicist
>
> "The sage is never other than the real self of the disciple. When the self is realized, there is neither Guru nor disciple."
> -- Ramana Maharshi, contemplative

experience, and the only truly confirming experience that matters here is the fulfilled testamentary promise of tenet seven: *the restoration, through* cognitive optimization, *of a more complete, enlightened, and able playerhood* with gradually expanded awareness and participation, encompassing *all* domains and dimensions of *Kosmic* existence.

This ideal but actually *winnable* accomplishment seems, from long experience, to rest on the perceived "warranted assertability," risked embrace, and committed *use* of, the basic Holosophy tenets. This provides a *pragmatic*, if initially assumptive, framework for directing the spiritual will, and the disciplined endeavor, necessary for graduated reduction and erasure of *all* sub-rational influence.

Suppose that you *could* actually achieve that promise. That you could, in fact, increase your self-determination, your ability to be, do, or have, in the service of any rational aspiration; or to *not* be, *not* do, or *not* have any reasonably *unwanted* condition, and therefore enjoy, as a player, the *total* process of living as much as you do participating in *any* transient sport, hobby or game? Put aside for a moment any ideas about *why* this may *not* be possible, or the many "convincing" negative examples of others who are obviously *un*self-determined, and consider:

If you *could* change all *fixed* beliefs, and better call the shots in your own life, if you could up the performance percentage[20] of *winning* desirable goals; achieved in a way that was fair,

---
[20] In baseball, for example, the difference between a "300 hitter" and one who bats .275 is perhaps 1 hit in 15 times at bat. And of course, a few million dollars in annual compensation!

> "If you are distressed by *anything* external, the pain is not due to the thing itself, but to your estimate of it and *this* you have the power to revoke at any moment."
> -- Marcus Aurelius, Emperor of Rome
>
> "The sun, the stars, and the seasons as they pass; Some can gaze upon these with no strain or fear."
> -- Horace, poet

beneficial, pleasurable and without actual harmful consequence for all concerned; wouldn't life be a little less weighty and "serious" and a lot more *fun* for you, and those around you? Wouldn't day-to-day living seem more and more like an absorbing and fulfilling *game* in every novel and expanded sense of the word?

Self-Determinism: Window For *Created* Causation

The essence of the Holosophic Program is, in fact, the *graduated increase* of *confident* self-determinism; i.e. that state or degree of personal creative causation and self-actualization wherein the individual can control or *agree* to be controlled *by*, any game environment according to his own *free choice*.

Theoretically, *real* sanity could be considered self-determinism, or freedom to act without sub-rational compulsion, rated in degrees on a taxonomic scale of awareness-levels extending all the way from "zero" (death and *below*) up through increments of increasing consciousness, and ability to consider and *cause* effects, to some ultimate *degree of* co-existence as *a* projective *Infinitude*[21], i.e., an *acting* and self-realizing immortality. This is Holosophy's highest estimated level of the Holon's potential *extendable* individuality, ability, and causation.

In a previous chapter we have reviewed the mechanisms and

---

[21] It might be constructively imagined that Life-Games are vast Kosmic cycles endlessly renewable and recurrent; knowingly created from a "remotely involved" and infinitely potential *source* of order *senior* to any conditions of existence that it projects; and in which, the apparent separation of *creation* and *discovery* are unified as a Thralldom.

> "If I were in this business, for *business*, I wouldn't be *in* this business!"
> -- Sol Hurok, impresario
>
> "When one tries to change institutions without having changed the nature of men, that unchanged nature will soon resurrect those institutions."
> -- Will Durant, philosopher

sources of sub-rational behavior, now to be underscored again by the additional, profound insight, that decades of cognitive research extending into the earliest of Kosmic histories and origins,[22] have revealed and confirmed. An individual reduces his self-determinism and ability *only by his own hidden and sustained decision, conclusion, or belief;* made during the self-generated solving-*reaction* to some injury or apparent loss he has either received, or more importantly, *earlier caused another.*[23]

If he first *decides,* and also *believes,* that something has overwhelmed him; he then tends to sub-rationally accept the *pattern of influence* of that "defeat" *and also all* sub-rationally "related" things, *in slavish perpetuity*, as absolutely *vital* to his survival. And so, by *his own* hidden choice, becomes increasingly diminished, *other*-determined (unfree), *dis*abled and *un*well.

His activities become thereafter, incrementally *un*causative and irrational and he seems to go wherever the environmental (*other*-determinism) influences push him. The Holon, *displaced* by the *pictured* "self" of the case-contour, has to that degree become merely a *reduced* adjunct and pawn of the physical universe.[24] As can be observed, a man is as spiritually *un*able as

---

[22] The basic or "core" dialectic pattern or thematic "code" of Kosmic existence has evidentially been deceptively replicated, traumatically pictured, and *volitionally* endowed by the Holon as reality and false "fact," thereby becoming the residual "case-contour" with its *sub*-volitional command value over rational consciousness and action.

[23] The Holon's sub-rational attempt to "balance the scales" through a *compensatory iteration* and receipt of the "same" harmful effects that were visited upon others - a kind of "retributive reflex."

[24] It has been said that the creative projection of each single "right *action*" within the *daily* self-enchantment of the Holon's participation in the Kosmos, is itself a "miracle" in disguise, since *every* creative act, even if constrained by limit is intrinsically *Super* Natural.

Chapter II – Lila: The Life Game Paradigm

> "To suppose that the eye with all its inimitable contrivances for adjusting the focus to different distances, for admitting different amounts of light, and for the correction of spherical and chromatic aberration could have been formed by *natural selection* seems, I fully confess, absurd in the highest degree."
> -- Charles Darwin, evolutionist

he has made fixed but *forgotten* "ability-reducing" decisions in his past. And, as we have emphasized repeatedly, he is as *able* and aware as he is *relieved* of this persisting, but hidden, lost-learning fixation and restored to authentic *Self*hood as Holon.

When, however, we talk about dramatically extending or increasing *self*-determination, we are *not* talking about returning without *Kosmic* sanction, to some omnipotent state, or obtaining similarly, lost and miraculous powers. Perhaps such powers are occasionally accessible to some very rare individuals. Pantanjali's *Yoga Sutras* are descriptive of such abilities called "Siddhis." Vivekenanda also made cautionary comment on them in his book, *Raja Yoga*.

In the book *Autobiography of a Yogi,* as well, Paramahansa Yogananda attested to witnessing such manifestations as he recalled anecdotal encounters with those who could levitate, read minds, produce scents and objects from thin air, and dematerialize, etc. The annals of para-psychological research also abound with both anecdotal, and more carefully researched, references to many such anomalous extensions of human ability.[25]

But, as the ancient's cautioned, self-determination even at this advanced level, unless guided by *ethics and enlightenment*, would inevitably result in a deterioration, scarcity, and finally even an *absence* of game; evidenced by a *non-level* playing field

---

[25] Robert G. Jahn at a Princeton research lab studied the ability of consciousness to influence matter (telekinesis), this research over a 25 year period has demonstrated that awareness and intention can cause measurable and repeatable effects on physical objects, including computers.

Chapter II – Lila; The Life Game Paradigm

> "I believe that the modern physics has definitely decided in favor of Plato. In fact, the smallest units of matter are not physical objects, in the ordinary sense. They are *forms,* ideas which can be expressed unambiguously only in mathematical language."
> -- W. Heisenberg, physicist
>
> "Sometimes I've believed in as many as six *impossible* things before breakfast."
> -- Lewis Carrol, author

and the potential subjugation of other players. Such an advanced restoration of power would require commensurately greater *ethics* and *high*-wisdom, since as the early sages of Vedanta aptly put it, "A man who is stupid on the earth is also stupid on the moon."[26]

Apparently and as the positive results of Holosophy applications suggest; in fact, the ancient traumatic-imprints of harmful *misuse* of siddhic powers and abilities (or *any* power or ability that far exceeds or violates the established norms of an existing game) can be a precursor to the present-time self-sabotaging restraints and sub-rational "karmic" limitations of *success-reluctance;*[27] a later topic.

For our more mundane, (and *sub*-lunar) purposes, effectively increasing one's self-determination in the *Kosmic* Life-Game simply means restoring, through increased awareness, the degrees of ability confidence, freedom, energy and joy that make day-to-day, rational self-management and control of one's mental *and* physical life a more fulfilling *adventure.* Stop for a moment to consider what "Winning at Life" really means. It is a phrase so commonly used in self-help fads, and "pop"-psychology that we can too easily dismiss it as a cliché; and miss its actual significance.

Ideally, Winning at Life means being able to *choose* whatever

---

[26] His life orientation has remained merely *Cosmic* as opposed to *advancing to Kosmic*!
[27] A sub-rational restraint to restoring any creativity or capacity that would s*eemingly* violate what the Holon considers to be his agreement to be "ethically" limited; and therefore might "spoil" the Game which requires such limitation.

> "Imagination is the living Power and prime Agent of all human perceptions."
> -- Samuel T. Coleridge, poet/essayist
>
> "Don't think, look!"
> -- Ludwig Wittgenstein, philosopher

goals we wish, and then being able to enjoy the *journey* of accomplishment, not only the destination. Full engagement in the dynamic process of effectively applying our creativity, intelligence and available resources to all related and goal-directed problem-*solving* is required in order to implement a linked and prioritized series of "winnable" steps to achieve an idealized vision or higher aspiration.

We seek to expand the wondrous and interwoven goal-tapestry of all such freely projected *Kosmic ideal*-scenes, *whatever* they might be: a fulfilling relationship, a rewarding career, financial security, physical fitness, philanthropic assistance, refined aesthetic pleasure, or spiritual enlightenment. But, concurrent, and consistent with this increase in self-actuated ability must be the emerging higher-*wisdom* to perceive and *choose* the appropriate *ethical* goals and actions that consider and *optimize* ever more broadly, *all* of the interactive *Kosmic* domains of participation and play.

Therefore, when we talk about increasing self-determination and restoring our ability to play and *win* at life, we are talking about truly "filling the moments" of our lives, living causatively, rationally and responsibly, not as mere victims of circumstance. We are always *potentially* in control[28], and at cause, if not completely, in some immediate traumatic and "overwhelming" situation, then potentially of our *current or future response* to it.

We are *always* inherently able to impose *some* degree of

---

[28] We can always assume retrospective control of any event past or present by simply erasing its persisting mental image, along with any deleterious effect it imposes in the present.

> "The Kosmos is the Game of Games."
> -- Holosophy Canon
>
> "It is difficult to find happiness in one's self, but *impossible* to find it anywhere else."
> -- A. Schopenhauer, philosopher

Chapter II – Lila; The Life Game Paradigm

causation, some *finite increment of betterment*, if only by rationally exercising the power to *"move on,"* i.e. to "unfix" our attention and freely choose our *next response* to any actual event;[29] or to *erase* a painful and irrelevant past, when it is seen clearly, as an illegitimate "hack" of our present awareness.

It is only when we can knowingly and responsibly cause ever-more-optimal *shared* effects including *all* players and at the same time, consider and *optimize* the broader effect on *all* domains, that we can *fully* participate in, and win,[30] *any* game in *Kosmic* life.

As was suggested in the Introduction, this is the essential function of *Kosmic* optimization; consistent with the theoretical premise that the origin and meaning of life is illuminated by the *Ideal* that living may indeed be the display-sport of an assemblage of enthralled and self-concealing "divinities"; and that it is conducted as, and within, a Kosmic game whose hidden truths can be revealed, mastered, and ethically expressed, in the fullest measure, as *right* (optimal) action.

Holosophy seeks, therefore as a philosophy, and also as a spiritually-oriented educative and cognitive *practice,* not only to attempt a logically coherent *theoretical* understanding of life's ultimate nature and source, but to provide a workable, systematic method or *praxis* by which we can restore our ability

---

[29] For example, we have the power to forgive an "offending" event or person for having *been there* and/or acted, and thereby erasing the harmful "pictured" continuity of *that* past.

[30] Holosophy stresses a "multi-sum" game, i.e. *a win-win* game as opposed to the "zero sum" game wherein someone always *loses completely.*

> "Truth, if ever, is found in the simplicity of things, never in the multiplicity and confusion of things."
> -- Isaac Newton
>
> "If stupidity got us into this mess, why can't it get us out?"
> -- Will Rogers

to play with a fully engaged and integrated spontaneity with a benevolent ferocity[31] of intention which seems to ultimately characterize the truly *realized spirit* of Play.

The Kosmic Theatre: Dramatis Personae and Props

If life is a game, and we human beings *are* players, what is our planetary or even *cosmic* role? What, as yet unvisioned, *galactic* moves are at our disposal? What are we ultimately playing *for*? To *consider* the full range of options of play at the *Kosmic* level of the Life-Game, let alone win at it, we need *initially* to know, more fundamentally, who and what we are, and perhaps just as importantly, by reasoned as well as evidentiary inference, who and *what we are not.*

Not the Body: One of the most common reductionist[32] mis-assumptions we make about ourselves is that we, as beings, are "nothing but" our bodies. The identification with bodies is so strong that we believe that we cannot possibly *exist* without the obsessive concern, caring and feeding of them. But is this really the case? We *use* bodies. We are *recognized* via our physical embodiment, in much the same way that athletes are recognized by the numbers on their jerseys.

We obviously suffer if our bodies are damaged, stressed, or poorly maintained. But just as a programmer is not the computer he operates, nor the driver the car he drives, we are *not just* our

---

[31] Reference the early brushwork depictions of Zen masters with their playful and beaming ferocity and *laughter,* both "empty, and *marvelous.*"

[32] Reductionism is the assumption that consciousness life, indeed *all* existence derives from "nothing but" material elements arranged in various configurations. i.e., one single cosmic domain of exclusively *physical* existence.

Chapter II – Lila; The Life Game Paradigm

> "Reductionism is the philosophic belief that all human activities can be 'reduced' to, i.e. explained by, the behavioral responses of lower animals – Pavlov's dogs, Skinner's rats and pigeons, Lorenz's geese, Morris's "naked apes" and that these responses can in turn be reduced to the physical laws that govern inanimate matter."
> -- A. Koestler, essayist & author

> "*Enough* is a feast."
> -- Zen Saying

bodies. For we apparently can, and often do, have as Holons, a certainty of existence, awareness, and *agency*[33] quite separately from them. Continuity of *being* is not equivalent to embodiment.

Impressive evidence of this fact is actually quite varied and abundant. For example, in his ground-breaking, often referenced book *Life After Life,* physician-author Dr. Raymond Moody presents many anecdotal accounts of out-of-body experiences reported to him by people who had been medically pronounced dead or dying, and then resuscitated after heart attacks, drownings, failed operations, accidents, and many other assorted, but extremely traumatic events.

In most, if not all of these cases, the individuals interviewed claimed they were aware of or "saw" their dead bodies at a distance; observed, and remembered in *detail* (often with later carefully documented confirmation), other people such as paramedics, nurses and physicians conversing and attending them and *watched,* usually from "above," the attempts to bring their bodies back to life. Here is a portion of one such interview, conducted with a woman who "left her body" following an accident:

> *"There was a lot of action going on, and people running around the ambulance. And whenever I would look at a person to wonder what they were thinking, it was like a zoom-up, exactly like through a zoom lens, and I was there. But it seemed that part of me -- I'll call it my mind -- was still where I had been, several yards away from my body. When I wanted to see someone at a distance, it seemed like part of me, kind of*

---

[33] Agency refers to the Holon as a *subject or continuing non-material identity.* A self-actuated, self-generated and accountable source of thought and action, a self-created window of perception and causation, as opposed to a mere material object or "blank, slate" written upon by cosmic circumstance.

Chapter II – Lila: The Life Game Paradigm

> "There is nothing of which every man is so afraid, as getting to know how remarkably much he is capable of doing and becoming."
> -- S. Kierkegaard
>
> "Human beings can alter their minds by altering their attitudes of mind."
> -- William James

like a tracer, would go to that person. And it seemed to me at the time that if something happened anyplace in the world that I could just be there."[34]

Dr. Moody's book is by no means the only credible study of out-of-body (OBE) experiences, as a glance through the "metaphysical" section of most any bookstore or relevant website will confirm, such accounts are many and various. But if out-of-body accounts are difficult to accept as evidence of our ultimately *non*-corporeal nature, consider individuals who have lost major body parts, or been born without them. Are they really less than whole and complete as *personalities*, despite their incompleteness as biological entities? Of course, if the Holon as a *non-material Consciousness, survives* bodily death, the question is moot.

Not **the Brain?** Obviously, and reasonably, one might counter that, while we can still function as our essential selves without bodily extremities, we certainly cannot do so without our brains, long considered by orthodox science[35] the seat (and source) of consciousness. But apparently, even this is not beyond evidentiary dispute. There are numerous citations in the brain research literature of instances in which individuals with massive cerebral injuries and loss of brain tissue, have been restored to normal conscious and functional viability.

Consider the interesting case of Louis Pasteur, the great chemist and bacteriologist, who suffered a severe stroke in mid-

---
[34] Moody Jr. M.D., Raymond A Life After Life, New York, Bantam Books, 1975
[35] The trend of "scientific" materialism is to equate consciousness, mind and brain. Ignoring alternative paradigms like philosopher William James' hypothesis that the brain acts only to modify or limit mind and consciousness like an intermediate prism modifies the perceived light of the sun.

> "The more I study physics, the more I am drawn to metaphysics."
> -- A. Einstein
>
> "Earthly things must be known to be loved. Divine things must be loved to be known."
> -- Blaise Pascal

Chapter II – Lila; The Life Game Paradigm

life. He recovered and spent the last 26 years of his life with full faculties and creativity. After his death, an autopsy examination, showed that *half* his brain was atrophied and functionally useless. Obviously, Pasteur *as Holon*, didn't require it to be *fully* aware and conduct a flourishing intellectual life.

Even more astonishing, individuals born genetically defective and *without actual brain structure,* have not only matured to adulthood, but have exhibited average or even *superior* intelligence and lived quite normal, productive lives. Among such anomalies cited is the following, taken from a description of the extensive researches of British neurologist John Lorber:

> *A colleague (of Lorber's) at Sheffield University came across a student with a slightly larger-than-normal head. The situation was not causing the student any problems, but because of Lorber's interest in such matters, the student was referred to him. Lorber ran a CAT scan on the youth and discovered that although he had an IQ of 126, had gained a first-class honors degree in mathematics, and functioned in all other ways as completely normal, he had "virtually no brain." Lining his skull was only a thin layer of brain cells a millimeter or so thick, and the rest of his cranium was filled with cerebrospinal fluid.* [36]

The implications of Lorber's research into *many* such cases, while controversial, are supported, in principle, by more recent discoveries of other neurophysiologists such as Jeffrey Schwartz, MD[37] who has been studying the electrical and sequential activities of the brain, and finding them *to result from*, rather than cause, volitional impulses of the conscious *person;* Suggesting that indeed, the Holon exerts a certain existential seniority over mere synaptic function and "brain-

---

[36] Talbot, Michael, Beyond the Quantum, New York, Bantam Books, 1986. (See also Appendix V)
[37] Jeffrey Schwartz, M.D. "The Mind & The Brain: Neuroplasticity and the power of mental force" (Harper Collins)

> "Professional Philosophers think up the notion that there are no *thoughts,* come to believe that there are no *beliefs, then* feel strongly that there are no *feelings.*"
> -- Sir John Eccles, neurophysiologist
>
> "Action is eloquence."
> -- William Shakespeare

states" which are often cited as the "source" of consciousness. But, apparently, when people change their minds[38] they also *change their brains.*

Adding further to the growing body of research of brain function which disputes materialist reductionism, Australian neurophysiologist and Nobel Prize winner, Sir John Eccles, concludes from his own extensive studies; *"We have here an irrefutable demonstration that a mental act of intention initiates the burst of discharges of a nerve cell."*[39] In other words, that a *downward non*corporeal cause initiated by the Holon (you!) can somehow produce a resulting, however correlated, (but more importantly, *chosen and causative)* body/brain effect.[40]

Currently then, extensive and responsibly chronicled "out-of-body" (and therefore out-of-*brain*) experiences, *as well as* research on actual brain function, strongly suggest that, although each of us *uses* a body, no human being *is* the body (or brain!), in the essential "supervening" sense. Apparently, the body can change, be missing parts, a complete brain, or even cease to function entirely; while the personality (Holon) that *owns, uses, and occupies* it, can continue in some important sense, to *exist;* emerging intact, and often willfully paying a return incarnate *visitation.*

Not **the Mind:** A second, similarly questionable, presumption

---

[38] Mind is senior to brain. *Holon* is senior to mind. It is quite common for clients to have "out of body *and* mind" experiences during the Transformative Dialogue program.
[39] Eccles, Sir John and Daniel N. Robinson, The Wonder of Being Human (New York: Macmillan, 1984).
[40] Mental activity is obviously correlated with, but not equated with or *caused* by, brain states; any more than a radio broadcast is "caused by" the radio that receives it.

> "The Mind is de-void of mind."
> -- Dalai Lama
> "A thing constructed can only be loved after it is constructed. But a thing created is loved *before* it exists."
> -- G. K. Chesterton, writer

Chapter II – Lila; The Life Game Paradigm

often made about personal identity is that we *are* the "mind." While this may be apparently closer to truth than a body/brain-equated definition of self, it is still short of the mark. Holosophy considers the mind to be an organized and controlled *system* of projected mental-images that are useful *imaginal* notations or representations of *conceptual* activity that both monitor and service personal identity, intention, and action.

Mental "things" that can be seen as analogous to "bytes" of computer code are not to be confused with the innate *meanings* which those encoded images and "applications" represent and are derived *from*. As with bodies, we as Holons (spiritual agents) *use* minds. We *mean* with, and *through* our minds. We are characterized by our minds. *"We"* suffer if *our minds* are malnourished or abused. But we, as Holons, are *not* our minds and *not any* projected *viewable* mental process, perspective or image. The viewer is not the viewed.[41]

The validity of this assertion is first, common-sensibly demonstrated, by the ordinary proprietary references we make *to* our minds. We say, *"I've had you on my mind,"* or *"This isn't what I had in (my) mind,"* or *"I've changed my mind,"* or *"I'm about to lose my mind!"* If we were *only* mind and not its separate and conscious witness, how could we possibly comment on "our" minds, or *see* its images, as distinct from us? A computer for example, evinces no emergent "I" or real *self-*

---

[41] To be "seen" would seem to require the intervening medium of space and therefore, independent existence of both the seer and the *seen* object or perspective. Simple logic would seem to dictate that to "see" requires space and distance *from*, but, from *where* does one *see* "oneself"? Is every "viewpoint" an act of *creative self-location as player-identity*?

> "Each self is a divine creation."
> -- Sir John Eccles. neurophysiologist
>
> "As soon as man apprehends himself as free and wishes to *use* his freedom, his activity is *play.*"
> -- John Paul Sartre, philosopher

Chapter II – Lila: The Life Game Paradigm

referencing capability, unless programmed to *simulate* such personhood by a programmer who *is already* herself, a distinct and separate observing *I, and a volitional agency.*

How then, does even the *idea* of an apparent or supposed separation between mind and Holon emerge in our consciousness? If we as Holons were indeed existentially inseparable from the mind as process; how is it that, while no one *frame* or moment of the stream of mental activity is the same as another, "we" nonetheless distinctively remain, and continue *witnessing* while our perceived *mental* perspectives and activities come and go?

The ability to observe the constantly changing mind from a unique, stable and unchanging, but *distanced* viewpoint speaks well for its innate qualitative separateness. In fact, this restored sense of the Holon as a self-realized agency and personhood is an important cognitive "lever" that enables the Cognitive Optimization Program.[42]

One could, in fact, maintain, that the *existence* of mind as a vehicular *servo*-mechanism, is essential to being, and remaining, a *humanized* Holon. It would seem to be an indispensible *tool we use* to process and *limit* information about our surroundings; to communicate with other beings and to maintain the network of a constant flux of mental images, symbols, energies, and

---

[42] The true witnessing necessary for erasure requires the capacity to "not be" that which is truthfully perceived. A Holon capability for *distancing* from the mind and its imagery or thought process is a core requisite of *any* traditional transformative practice. This is not to overlook or minimize any presumed psychco-physical correlation with a volitional imaging process of mind (or brain) necessary to reduce the quantum potentia of the sixth domain to the actual occasions and observables of the other domains of existence.

> "To someone who could grasp the universe from a unified standpoint, the entire creation would appear as a unique truth and necessity."
> -- Jean d' Alembert, mathematician
>
> "I'm a *deeply* superficial person."
> -- Andy Warhol, artist

Chapter II – Lila; The Life Game Paradigm

masses, which (minus any *sub* rationality) we *use* as momentary *imaginal* aides, to remember, communicate and compute as and within, an established game-parameter of awareness. A secretary however, is *not* her notes, *nor* the painter his brush.

Not **the Mental History or Personality:** If we are *not* our minds, *not* "nothing but" our bodies or brains, we certainly are *not* our memories or educational experience, our profession, our sexual preference or marital status, our mental acuity, our taste in art, our weekend hobbies or any of the temporarily useful decorative or recreational, but insubstantial accouterments of our personalities.

We *can,* and often do, adapt, drop, change, and embellish these mutable conditions and characteristics of personality in the course of a lifetime without ceasing to be essentially, and recognizably the same enduring and sustained *being* who does so. The Holon, cum *persona,* agent, or innate self-actualizing essence, is quite distinct from the perso*nality*, as an avian's essential *bird*ness is distinct from its mere form and plumage.

To get a more direct intimation of this concept of a non-material Self or *I-ness*, try the following exercise: Imagine a three-dimensional mental-image of a *pink* dog. Place the dog about fifteen inches in front of your face. Have it wag its tail, scratch an itch, bark at you. Now make it run in a circle. Now bring it closer to your face. Mentally pet it. Feel the texture of its fur, the motion of its breathing. Then, *you* make *it* disappear!

Now ask: *Who saw* (at a *distance*) that pink dog? Who is it that

Chapter II – Lila: The Life Game Paradigm

> "By space the universe encompasses and swallows me up like an atom. But by thought, *I* comprehend the world."
> -- Blaise Pascal
>
> "How is the water of the brain turned into the rich wine of consciousness?"
> -- Colin McGuinn, philosopher

heard the dog? Who is it that *felt* the dog's presence? It was you. *You,* not your eyes; *you,* not your ears; *you,* not your hands; *you,* not your memories, for that imaginary dog did not exist[43] until you created it; *you,* not your profession, your age, your appearance, your talents or any other characteristic that *you* typically manifest.

What seems truer and more pragmatically warranted? To assign creation of mental-images, or functions, to an *assumed* but imperceptible[44] electro-chemical "process" in the brain? Or to your own direct and distinct knowing and *demonstrable* creative management, perception, and control, of those functions and images in *your* indisputably private, mental space and domain?

It is only when you progressively realize that it is an integral *you* (when rational) who manage these things, rather than *they* which manipulate you, that you become truly free and able to create a *preferred* destiny of purpose-driven and executable *ideal*-scenes with Optimum qualitative benefit and value across the multi-domain spectrum of the *Kosmos*.

The Holon: Spirit as a Creative Individuality

When we realize that body, mind, mental history and personality are merely composite *external* aspects of what we call

---

[43] Imagination is *not* the mere re-combination or permutation of past memories, images which can't themselves, seamlessly recombine into gestalts; which are by definition, *more* than the sum of their parts. The Holon is the basic agency and imaginal *source* of combined *and unitized conceptuality* as distinguished from the *projected* images or *representations* it creates and *projects*. Even a "self-image" must be *meaningfully known* to be such.

[44] It would also seem reasonable to expect that if mental processes and images were "nothing but" microcosmic electro-colloidal events, they would also *appear* to us as such. Another interesting experimental exercise: close your eyes and hold your head in your hands for several seconds, now look forward *mentally* at that solidly, feel "the lump of flesh" between your hands. Are *you* "in" that? Try it a few times; to some it can prove insightful.

Chapter II – Lila; The Life Game Paradigm

> "The mathematician plays a game in which he himself *invents* the rules. While the physicist plays a game in which the rules are provided by nature. But it is evident that the rules the mathematician finds interesting are the *same* as nature has chosen."
> -- Paul Dirac, physicist
>
> "If such (psi) phenomena do indeed occur, no change in the fundamental equations of physics would be needed to describe them."
> -- G. Feinberg, physicist

a human being, rather than that *irreducibly individual Holon essence* that animates or defines it we begin to see, with increasing certitude, that our true metaphysical nature is neither physical, symbolic nor temporal, but Spiritual; an immanent transpersonal witnessing nature which escapes definition as all else.

We are eternal, noncorporeal beings, spiritual agents, or *awareness-of-awareness units*, who *use* personalities, bodies and minds to have experiences on this physical plane as a projected expression of an innate and invisible but participative, spiritual order emanating as the Holoarchic Domains of the Kosmos.

"Spirit" is defined by Webster's Dictionary as *"an animating or vital principle held to give life to physical organisms,"* and also as *"a supernatural being or essence."* As with most dictionary definitions, they are essentially circular; "Spirit = Soul = Innate Principle = Being = Spirit" but what is it that can read or hear these numerous and linked verbal descriptions and yet intuitively understand the underlying context and *meaning*?[45] What *is* "spirit" exactly? How is it characterized? What does it do? How does it relate to what we call the human condition?

From the perspective of Holosophy, we have earlier defined spirit as a non-material agency, or *potential for*, consciousness; and a *particular* spirit as a self-actualized "unit" of *knowing and creative* consciousness; or *Holon*. A human being is in essence, a composite *vehicle* of consciousness, "occupying" and using a

---

[45] Capacity for meaning and the *understanding* of it, does not "bubble up" from some pre-biotic soup, or emerge from some random flux of synapses, it comes from non-material *consciousness with powers of attribution,* which is distinct from and "pre-dates" its creations.

> "Most of our assumptions have outlived their usefulness."
> -- Marshall McLuhan, futurist
>
> "The soul is the source of thought activity."
> -- Catholic Encyclopedia

Chapter II – Lila: The Life Game Paradigm

particular body, mind and personality. It is by acquiring useful knowledge of the nature and potentialities of the spiritual domain--i.e., of *higher* consciousness and its manifest *and* innate faculties; that we increase our real understanding of what an individual Holon-player can accomplish in the *Kosmic* Life-Game.

Such a self-actualized consciousness has as *itself*, no physical mass, energy or form. One cannot "see" it in the way one sees a physical object, nor is it ultimately bound by time, space or location.[46] It is like a non-material mirror, if one can imagine such a thing, as the innate point of *emanation* of the formative conceptualities that it also "reflects," i.e. percepts, thoughts and actions, but is no more *defined* by these things, than is an ordinary mirror defined by the fleeting images on its surface.

Idealistic philosophers of all ages and cultures have variously considered mass, energy, time and space to be the perceptic *products* of consciousness, and *not* its constituent parts; for consciousness *is* awareness *per se*, and as such is the generative, and qualitative *source,* of *postulating and perceiving* things, not of *itself* being those things.

At this point it may be useful to attempt a theoretical ranking distinction between Holons, e.g., between all self-actualized *units* of consciousness, and the concept of a Deity or *Supreme* Being. Consistent with the highest spiritual insights of traditional

---

[46] As to origins: One might ask, "Where does that which *creates* location come *from?*" Or, "What *comes before* that which *creates* time?" Or, "Is that which assigns or attributes truth, existence, or process, *itself* the projected object of its own creating? Does process *create* (and perceive) process?"

> "Those who cannot remember the past are condemned to repeat it."
> -- George Santayana, philosopher
>
> "Esse est percepi (To be, is to be perceived)."
> -- George Berkely, philosopher

mysticism, Holosophy holds that the Supreme Being is *not* a mere *omni*-personality, however vast and omnipotent, but is the transcendent epistemic source of *all* "Being" *or* appearance. It is *infinite* potentiality for reified *thatness;*[47] an undifferentiated and ultimate Knowingness; "neither the one nor the many," but the unlimited, non-dual, Source of *all specifiability* of knowing (i.e., meaning). It follows therefore that *all existence* is an enthralled *selective subtraction*[48] from that infinite Knowing*ness, exemplified* creatively as the Kosmos!

The Holon, as a conceptually *unitized* spiritual being, could be said to "be" a *uniquely conceiving* "window of individualization" of that ultimate Infinite Potential; *one* creative and *witnessing*[49] expression of the potential to display cognitive specificity; to *knowingly* be, do or have, or *not*; as uniquely distinct from all other Kosmic domain expressions of that unlimited Potentia.

Thus by "borrowing" or *subtracting* from infinity the specified conceptuality of an "individuality" as an expressive *vehicle,* the Holon acquires a unique meta-physical integrity as an agent-entity and player *distinct* from, but ultimately compatible with, the ultimate and innate Ground of all other *possible* existences.

The neologism "Holon" was introduced, as explained earlier,

---

[47] "That." "A senior" potentiality which might also enable a Kosmic assemblage of lessor "co-cognizant" deities.
[48] Each existence or manifest conceptionality might be considered a postulated negation of, or subtractive exception to, an *infinite* potential which also contains it as a "specified finitude."
[49] Witnessing in the sense of true contemplation (from the Latin "contemplare"; "to gaze attentively"; observe) is an act of acti*ve, engaged,* and *intentionally focused* attentiveness *or interest.*

> "I simply believe that some part of the human self or soul is not subject to the laws of space and time."
> -- Carl Jung, Psychiatrist
>
> "Time and space are fragments of the infinite for the use of finite creatures."
> -- Henri Amiel, critic/essayist

because the words "spirit" and "soul" are used so often in so many different and confusing contexts. In this text, we will, following other researchers, continue to refer to this indivisible unit of individual agency-consciousness; the fundamental being; the *one* who is *aware of being aware,* as a Holon; *the* first supersensible Domain of the *Kosmos,* the primal, *non-egoic Self.*

As previously cited, extensive researches of "out-of-body" experiences would seem to confirm that Holons *can* and do exist in a *dis*embodied state. Yet, despite having no "materiality," they *are* detectible, at a minimum, through various higher communicative and perceptic modalities, by other Holons who are *perceptually* sensitive to the unique empathic quality of *aliveness* held in common by each such animating spiritual being.[50]

When an *able* Holon is associated with a body, there is a sense of an archly *knowing* "presence," a playful *élan vital,*[51] an aliveness, or vital energy, that can be *sensed* deeply "within" or *behind* the eyes of an embodied, but also actively en*souled,* personage. Which is why philosophers and poets alike, have maintained that the eyes are indeed, the "windows of the soul," and that the "doors of perception" *are* the cognitive portals through which the Holon as authentic *character,* and player both witnesses and enters the game.

---

[50] From the strict "natural scientific" or *materialist* viewpoint, however, nothing non-material can, in *principle*, exist. If it can't be *physically* observed or measured, (like consciousness) it is unreal and not a proper object for study; an extremely self-limiting standard, since it requires *conscious* and selective elimination of "awarenesses" from observation!

[51] A phrase meaning "*vital* force," famously used by philosopher Henri Bergson to refer to the unique non-physical creative energy, existence and motive power of *life itself.*

> "By limiting through subtractive specification, the infinitely *possible*;
> Holons create the finitely *actual*."
> -- Holosophy Canon
>
> "A particle must be thought of as a series of events. "Matter" is not a part of the ultimate material of the world, but merely a convenient way of collecting *events* into bundles."
> -- Bertrand Russell, philosopher

The Holon: A Slice of Infinity

A Holon's *individual* consciousness can be viewed as a potentially *un*limited *agency* of entrance, to the higher Kosmic domains that *requires* it to be also an intentionally un-abled and limited brain-*filtered* instrument of causation: *infinite* consciousness *artfully* and tacitly rendered finite, but consensual.

Consciousness's general *orientation* within the Kosmos is a self-managed and synchronized diminishing of native capacity, necessary to achieve and maintain an enthralled co-participancy in the devolving Game-Cycle. By a *subtraction* of ability and awareness from Infinite Potential, the Holon can, with *selective unawareness* create a finite, optimized, and *occupiable* reality.

Confirming evidence of this role of "*practiced* awareness attenuation," and filtration of Holon ability, to accommodate "everyday" playerhood can be seen in certain individuals effected by psychedelic drugs, brain damage, or esoteric practices; and especially in the astonishing abilities of so-called "idiot savants" where the *filtering* of higher cognitive capacity has apparently been temporarily suspended, resulting in a light-emitting "Crack in the Kosmic Egg" with constrained ability-potential shining through.

Well documented cases of such ability-accessing anomalies are many and varied: An English savant who can multiply numerical products to 8 digits while conversing, or calculate the value of "pi" to 2200 decimal places (a world record) but cannot

> "Mr. Duffy lived a short distance from his body."
> -- James Joyce-*Ulysses*
>
> "*Anything*, past, present or future *can* be changed, one may, however, need to create an alternative universe to *contain* the change."
> -- Holosophy Canon

perform simple tasks like driving a car, or telling left from right.

A *blind* savant-pianist who played a complete Tchaikovsky concerto after hearing it *once*, and without ever having a lesson.

The real-life "Rain Man," who could read two pages at once (one with each eye!), recall verbatim over 7,000 books he has read, and for recreation routinely memorizes telephone books, containing *millions* of entries.

Animal and insect abilities can also dramatically exceed the human norm: powers of smell, vision, navigation, telepathic herd cooperation, etc; each demonstrating the vast range of higher capability potentially, but *selectively* available to *all* life forms.

Such cases which abound in the (less perused) investigative literature, are usually *explained away* "scientifically"[52] as caused by brain damage or some abnormality like "autism" or epilepsy, which *might* explain *dis*ability or *dys*function, but would hardly account for such astonishing *increases* in ability.

We can theorize, consistent with Holosophy's view of the Kosmos, that there is an *ethically* filtered, and *engaged* , quotidian and probabilistic *normalcy-bias* accomplished through the *limiting* mechanisms of the healthy human mind and brain; a self-actualized continuum-perspective *through* which the higher,

---

[52] In 1792, on an occasion of a fall of meteorites, the French Academy of Science adopted a resolution categorically rejecting such "anomalies." Raison D'être? "There are no rocks in the sky," so, obviously, none could be falling! Modern science has routinely excluded from existence a much broader range of "anomalies," oddities; and all the unexplained and "unproven" i.e., *dis*proven phenomena of *extra*ordinary experience!

Chapter II – Lila; The Life Game Paradigm

> "Originally, there is not a single *thing*."
> -- Bodhidharma
>
> "Similarity has limited explanatory power. Under analysis it tends either to vanish entirely or to require for *its* explanation just *what* it purports to explain."
> -- N. Goodman, philosopher

metaphysically thematic domain-realms of the Kosmos are accessed and made manifest.

The natural cycle of birth and death is also a fundamental and *limiting* game characteristic of the Kosmos. When a Holon disassociates from its body at corporeal "death," massive and well researched evidence suggests that it *re*incarnates in a new body to continue its self-elected and archetypically "referenced" *full domain* participation in the *Kosmos*.[53]

Child prodigies are certainly suggestive of this apparent continuity, as is anyone who enters the world with unusually distinctive aspirations, characteristics or temperaments, or who feels an intense and enduring, but inexplicable déjà vu affinity or repulsion toward certain people, places, things or activities.

Perhaps one of the most credible bodies of evidence (apart from one's direct *personal* realization) is to be found in Dr. Ian Stevenson's decades-long research project at Duke University. A meticulous scholar, Dr. Stevenson, a psychiatrist, not only investigated the testimony of *thousands* of children who, unprompted, claimed to remember former lives, but also researched a significant number of those who actually sought out, found and demonstrated their familiarity with surviving relatives.

Some even had birthmarks on their bodies where they had

---

[53] Reincarnation, if factual, would seem to constitute proof that the *only* thing that "returns" is *not* the *Holon*, as a non-material and *timeless potential to reincarnate* or continue as *agency* or Kosmic player, with multiple identities and garbs. In that sense, as a timeless potentiality; *it* never leaves.

> "Reincarnation is a fact, but not a Truth."
> -- J. Krishnamurti, contemplative
>
> "Paradoxically, an *immortal* Holon seems committed to, and unduly concerned with, the survival of *personal* identity."
> -- Holosophy Canon

experienced severe, even *lethal,* traumas during the past lives being investigated. Others had special knowledge, skills, or traits seemingly transferred to the new identity from the previous incarnation. Stevenson also collected the abundant testimony of townspeople, neighbors and family who corroborated the children's claims and experiences, often in great detail.

Stevenson's careful investigations of apparent reincarnation cases number over 3000, and is now carried on by other researchers at Duke[54]. The following case, summarized in the book *Intangible Evidence,* is a typical example:

> *"Victor Vincent was a Tlingit Indian living on one of the small islands off Alaska's southern coast. In 1946, when he knew he was dying, he told his beloved niece Mrs. Corliss Chotkin that he would be reborn as her next son and that she would know this by two scars the child would receive from him. Vincent had a livid, one-inch surgical scar on his back and a less distinct scar at the base of his nose. A year and a half later, Mrs. Chotkin gave birth to Corliss, Jr., who has two birthmarks that exactly match the scars on Vincent's body. Dr. Stevenson examined the one on Corliss' back and noted, "Along its margin one could still easily discern several small round marks outside the main scar. Four of these on one side lined up like stitch wounds of surgical operations."* [55]

As the junior "Corliss" grew a few years older, more evidence of a pre-existence emerged. He spontaneously recognized people on the street whom he had previously known as *Victor*, he could recount incidents from Victor's life about which he had never been told, he stuttered like Victor, and he demonstrated a precocious affinity for repairing engines, a task at which Victor had been

---

[54] See "Life before Life" by John B. Tucker, MD (a child psychiatrist who continues to direct further research at the University of Virginia).
[55] Gittelson, Bernard, "Intangible Evidence," New York: Fireside, Simon and Schuster, 1987 (an independent survey of reincarnation researchers).

> "I want to be with those who know *secret* things, or else, alone!"
> -- R. M. Rilke, poet
>
> "Sometimes it proves to be the highest understanding *not* to understand."
> -- B. Gracian, philosopher

Chapter II – Lila; The Life Game Paradigm

notably skilled.

Stevenson's inquiry also includes the examination of birthmarks and deformities that may be suggestive of inter-birth transmission:

> *"For there is a common suggestion that a violent death, for instance by a bullet wound, may result in a birthmark in the next incarnation at the site of the wound inflicted in the previous life! One of his subjects, a Turk, claimed to have been, in his previous life, a gangster in Istanbul who was killed in a struggle with police. He pointed to a spot on his head where, he claimed, the bullet had entered. Stevenson, after having made a notation of the facts as claimed, reflected that if the bullet had entered the Turk's head at that spot and in the direction that had been indicated in the claim, then it must have exited at another spot, the location of which could be approximately determined. He then went back to re-examine the Turk's head. The hair was bushy at the hypothetical spot, so that no birthmark could be easily detected. After Stevenson had parted the Turk's hair, however, he found exactly the sort of second birthmark he had hypothesized, though the Turk claimed at that time never to have known anything about such a mark."* [56]

It is interesting to observe in passing, that to completely, and "scientifically" discredit any reincarnation hypothesis, one must believe that literally *hundreds of thousands* of recorded observations world-wide, by *scores* of highly qualified investigators, both anecdotal, and carefully researched and documented, are each and *all* either fraudulent or heuristically flawed, or both! Many who, even so, question or reject the concept of reincarnation often ask why, if it does in fact occur, so few of us actually recall our former lives.[57]

---

[56] MacGregor, Geddes, "Reincarnation in Christianity": A New Vision of Rebirth in Christian Thought; Quest Books, Wheaton, IL.

[57] Another objection is that as the population expands, where do all the new souls come from? If the Kosmos is a vast evolving playground, it would seem reasonable that there could be an abundance of Holons "waiting" to be restored to human player status through a local planetary embodiment.

Chapter II – Lila: The Life Game Paradigm

> "One must go from type to *prototype. T*he true artists are the ones who strive to approach the secret depths where the *prime* law fosters development and metamorphosis."
> -- Paul Klee, artist
>
> "Language is fossil poetry."
> -- R. W. Emerson, essayist

Apart from the obvious difficulties in recalling *any* "early" traumatic experience, another interesting explanation already touched upon, is that a *total* recall of one's past lives might seem to vitiate the normalcy-biased *filtering* of perception and ability that accommodates the *convincing authenticity* of every day human experience.[58]

It would challenge as well, one's narrower sub-rational and "unknowing" participative status in the *Kosmic* Life-Game, and prevent employing the *sub rational* "must *be* and *stay* human" dictates of the case-contour to guard against "unleashing" any *prior* "evil" higher awareness "ability" or a knowing and *re-enabled* volitional emergence from any between lives "amnesia."

Perhaps the ordinary exigencies and *drama* of life and death might indeed seem less "convincing" *if* we realized *fully* that we *are* actually self-concealed immortals. Yet such an enlarged perspective, which obviously includes the total certainty of survival of bodily death, can and does in fact, greatly expand and extend the quality of the Holon's personal, social and *Kosmic* playerhood paradigms and perspectives.

It is this heightened awareness and changing perspective that we wish to *gradually* achieve through Cognitive Optimization procedures and dialogue. For this reason, the recalling and re-visioning of the sub-rational influences anchored in both recent traumas *and* their underlying, primordial formative *dialectic*

---

[58] Consider the Platonic myth of the "Waters of Lethe," consumed "between lives" to produce a "merciful" forgetfulness to soften (and obscure) the "shock" of rebirth.

> "Most of our assumptions have outlived their *uselessness*."
> -- Marshall McLuhan, futurist
>
> "The soul is the source of thought activity."
> -- Catholic Encyclopedia

patterns of sub-rationality can, as erased, reveal ever deepening levels of spiritually "transformative" purpose and meaning.

One of the first notable gradients of increased understanding clients achieve, is that, as Holons, we are senior to, and responsible for the unwanted conditions of body and mind. The progressive increments of awareness provide a growing confidence that our creative *essence* as Holons *precedes all perceived existence,*[59] since consciousness is not merely a passive receptacle *of* perception, but is itself, a *timeless generative and projective* prerequisite *for all* realms of its experiencing.

Goals of the Game: Incremental Ascension

The primary goal of Holons within[60] the *Kosmic* Life-Game seems to be, to *play* it, in real time, and *authentically*.

To create and realize aspirations (a house by the sea, a career in science, attaining a higher state of consciousness, even travel to distant planets and beyond) *all* happily, adventurously and gradually attained, while gradiently neutralizing whatever obstacles we may pose or perceive that counter their realization.

There is apparently no *ad-hoc* externally imposed, "meaning of life." We *give* meaning to Life, *within* a framing *Kosmic* context, and the higher the informed spiritual perspective, the more profound the potential for the optimized cognitive

---
[59] Au contraire, in reference to John Paul Sartre's, "Existence precedes essence."
[60] There is much truth in the cautionary admonition to the risk-averse: "You've got to be *in* it, to *win* it!"

Chapter II – Lila: The Life Game Paradigm

> "The ultimate work for civilization is the unfolding of ever deeper spiritual understanding."
> -- Arnold Toynbee, historian
>
> "The true poet, dreams while awake. He is not possessed by his subject, but has dominion over it."
> -- Charles Lamb, essayist

valuation and *rational consistency* of *all* actionable meanings projected, and the resultant enhanced quality of life-experience.

What makes the Game *truly* satisfying, is not just "solving problems" chosen arbitrarily, or even solving *en passant*, the daily tasks of ordinary survival that we routinely select to perceive and address. What constitutes the *highest* reward seems to be *solving* problems as concealed *ends within means*; in order to reveal, ascend to, and joyfully experience, a gradually *wider* and higher, quality and *meaning* of the total Kosmic *Game-Cycle* itself!

Each gradient and productive value-step of this improvement we term in Holosophy an *"increment of betterment;"* i.e., something *real* volitionally made better; or a step-by-step enhancement of the general quality of life; directed toward bringing about a greater good or *ideal scene* through rational application of an informed *"Calculus of Optimization*[61]*,"* an inherent cognitive mechanism for *rational choice* in selecting a course of action with balanced, and proportionate valuation of *all* domains.

Anchored in an innate Kosmic paradigm for optimizing (a benevolent adding of value), it guides the bringing about, in each single act or decision, an increased qualitative good for the *maximum* number of dimensional aspects, or *domains* of the

---

[61] It seems a useful and reasonable *standard* for making ethical choices, however, as human beings with necessarily limited faculties for information gathering, our calculations must be spontaneously but *limitedly* comprehensive, *and* pragmatic, i.e., our choice must rationally settle for maximizing benefit impacts within our *highest* and best analytical scope of awareness; *omitting* no domains. It is the understanding, refinement, and use, of this innate "Calculus of Optimization" for making rational selection of action and exchange within and between the play-domains, that is the essence of Holosophy Ethical Theory.

Chapter II – Lila; The Life Game Paradigm

> "The will is infinite and the execution confined, the desire is boundless and the act, a slave to limit."
> -- William Shakespeare, *Troilus and Cressida*
>
> "First realization of a Warrior is *not* knowing."
> -- Bushido Code

Game. It is this *rational free choosing* in *acting* to overcome real obstacles to any rational aspiration that Holosophy holds to be the ethos and essence of a true *spirit of play*. This in itself, seems an *objective*, i.e. reasonably consensual, *and* workable, standard for happiness. Achieved *incremental* betterment!

Game Conditions as Benevolent Barriers

Since the *Kosmic* Life-Game is an on-going creative activity, the apparently unyielding conditions or barriers we face daily while playing it, ideally change with game-enhancing progressivity, every time we realize they are *solvable*. For instance, while "no water in the dessert" may cease to be an obstacle to survival when irrigation is introduced, it may then be replaced with "no understanding among the local people of how to manage it" as the *next* barrier requiring a related "increment of betterment." New solutions to continue and *optimize* the Game toward a rational *ideal-scene* which includes an ongoing pragmatic adjustment to new challenges and circumstances.

Similarly, (to use an ordinary business example), when "No clients for a new consulting initiative" ceases to be a barrier to the sale of services, a *new* situational challenge of "no ideas" for creating and launching a broker competitive marketing strategy may be the next requisite for expansion.

It can be observed however, that any *persisting*, unchanging, sub rational mental-image *framed* unwanted *condition* is always a *false* and subjective "problem." An *actual* problem, is a *factual* real-

> "Some corporations are ships that leak from the top."
> -- Apple Board Member
>
> "The Tone at the Top is the key to managerial success."
> -- Anonymous

Chapter II – Lila: The Life Game Paradigm

world circumstantial obstacle requiring the decision "*whether* to," or "*how* to" take any action-steps necessary to effect real progressive or optimized change[62] of the condition, *or* to cease "trying to solve" *false* and subjective (fixed past-focused) *mental* problems that seemingly "demand" solutions. Ultimately, *there* are *no* permanently fixed or *inherently* "insoluble" or unwanted *objective* (i.e. external) conditions in the *Kosmic* Life-Game[63], only *concealed* opportunities for incremental betterment.

For example; a continually *fixed-image* condition of "no money" is *not* the problem: "*How or whether to* obtain money" *is! E*ven a "terminal illness" is *not,* "itself" a fixed, *subjective* problem: "*How or whether to* respond, in the moment, to the illness" as an *objective* biological condition *in flux,* is! All persisting mental or *subjective*, (internal) unwanted "problems" are really *fixed* pictured "conditions" overlaying the actual *changing* objective circumstances. They are *believed ideas and images* in "double-bound" opposition, held in place by a hidden, frozen, and conflicting *balance* of intentions, or "solved confusions" resulting in persisting false dilemmas that are discoverable and *erasable* by cognitive inspection and dialogue.

As each false "problem *as* condition" dilemma is erased, it is replaced with the perception of new and *self*-determined *objective* problem-opportunities at ever expanding levels of play. An array of options with gradually increasing consciousness of the higher

---

[62] Often a review, redefinition, re-framing or *re-visioning* of the apparent insolubility reveals it to be conflicted and "stuck" mental imagery, falsely *imposed* on actual circumstances.

[63] The mere presence or absence of a physical condition is not itself a problem. An effectively managed *countering* response of *some* incremental betterment is always an option. Even a planetary cataclysm does not suspend the inherent power of the Holon's ultimate choiceful response, which reigns in perpetuity.

> "Reality is apparently an agreement projected consensually through a core *lens* of triadic Order."
> -- Holosophy Canon
> "Be *wisely* selfish."
> -- Dalai Lama

contextual *Kosmic* realms of applicable value and aspiration.

In other words, the more successfully we "play" at the game, by removing false trauma-based subjective, or conflicted mental-imaged problems[64], the more sophisticated, challenging and value-enhancing are the *real* objective problems *we* challenge ourselves to *select*, experience and resolve by *taking* action; or *not taking immediate* action. *All* actual Life-Game problems are seemingly *designed* to contain opportunities for producing incremental betterment and realizing personal transformation.

To illustrate; a person may experience a convincing "lack of something desirable," but on closer inspection, may discover his or her *own* hidden trauma-formed belief-*intention* is opposed to having that very thing while *at the same time* consciously demanding it! The erasure of *all* such sub-rationally "balanced," but also conflicting and *fixed*; problematic *mental* intentionality, is a basic transforming and re-enabling objective of counseling in Holosophy (Cognitive Optimization).[65]

Rankings in Playerhood

Since goal-directed *team* play is obviously, a necessary (third domain) characteristic of the *Kosmic* Life-Game fabric, its players will be seen to naturally occupy positions of greater or lesser status relative to others around them; an *earned* ranking position or status

---

[64] Problem-solving could be considered as a temporarily *focused response* to effectively *counter* and *deconstruct* circumstantial or ideological barriers to selective goals and attainments.
[65] The restored certainty that one can erase subjective problems, and *solve* objective problems (and perceive the difference) is a basic goal of all rational intentionality.

> "In holding a cup of tea, sensory experience is like touching the cup with bare hands. While "thought" is like touching it with one hand covered with a cloth; a metaphor for the concepts and language which comes between observer and object when "thought" operates."
> -- Dalai Lama
>
> "History repeats itself. *That's* what's wrong with it!"
> -- Clarence Darrow, attorney

Chapter II – Lila; The Life Game Paradigm

(whether President or Pawn), that is commensurate with their mastery, skill, or worth (value-adding capacity) in a particular Holoarchic context of group or team play.

A corporate CEO, for example, bringing greater experience, expertise and leadership to his company from the perspective of value of command, outranks his staff. A quarterback, bringing greater athletic and *strategic* ability to his team, outranks his tackles. The more an individual is able and willing to act effectively, to enhance conditions for his fellows or the common good, the higher his rank and scope of influence in society or organizations will tend to be.[66] Conversely, the *less* an individual does to manifest his full potential, the lower his (or her) rank will be. Never fixed or assured, rank is a variable game-status and team effort, ideally depending on *real* merit and ability.

Freedom-defining Limits

Since games require rules and limits, one's defining freedoms[67] or *scope of volition* within the *Kosmic* Life-Game shift, increase, or decrease according to one's degree of awareness and willing participation, *and* the agreed-upon rules governing it in a particular place and time.[68] For example, one can now legally drive 65 miles per hour on most open U.S.

---

[66] Example: wealth *creation* as an activity would seem to out rank wealth *consumption* as an optimizing social good.
[67] In Holosophy, freedoms *to*, i.e. unfettered exercise of volition in action is emphasized over freedoms "from," or mere passive removal from unwanted influence or conditionality.
[68] Human societies apparently have law, custom, and mores, as a communal counterpart to the brain as the Holon's limiting "reducing valve." However, societies too, can further "evolve" or *optimize* as planetary populations are freed of *sub-rational* limitations.

Chapter II – Lila; The Life Game Paradigm

> "All aberration is basically composed of unwarranted *solutions*, fixed beliefs, and behavior, from the past, frozen into a fixed and persisting web of 'unwanted' conditions."
> -- Holosophy Canon
>
> "We must, as second best, take the *least* of the evils."
> -- Aristotle

highways; but one can drive *much* faster on the German autobahn. An executive may elect, or be "free to" play golf with a client during the work week, but a common laborer is ordinarily obliged (not forced) to stay on the job site, as is the office worker to "punch the clock."

There are no fixed or *absolute* freedoms. Ideally, they are self-imposed based on *reasonable and known* conventional and situational limits, and are always subject to random and non-coercive revision, extension or elimination, *but* as "trauma-generated" *charged* beliefs, are *sub*-rationally and harmfully *imposed* to dominate and coerce. This is done *not* for the greatest good; since, such activity, being *sub*-rational, is factually "out of phase," i.e. it is based on a hidden *traumatic* memory containing *past*, deleterious and *un*ethical, pictured identities, intentions, and *beliefs*, which are false post-traumatic additives to the actual *gaming* challenges of the Kosmic *present*.

Opponencies: Introduction to the Dance

Games also require opponents (not necessarily enemies or *losers*). An opponency is simply an intention or force in some degree counter[69] to another. All play, even *perception* itself, requires *some* sensed degree of countering opposition: an expression of an innate inter-active *duality* however slightly manifest, in order to contact and experience *any* sense of *otherness* and opposition. If we are playing a game of chess, for

---

[69] In this sense, to counter is to rationally oppose with minimum *effort* and maximum ease of optimizing effect, in contrast to "resistance" which tends to sub-rationally energize the unwanted condition or opponency, since one must continually *put and keep* it there, subjectively, to be able to resist it.

> "No one knows or even feels, that anything is a limit or defect until he is at the same time above and *beyond* it."
> -- G. W. Hegel, philosopher
>
> "One's reach should always exceed one's grasp."
> -- Anonymous

instance, our opponent's desire to checkmate first, is obviously contrary to ours.

If we are pursuing a new business opportunity, our desire to win that business is opposed to that of our competitor's and hopefully to a lesser degree, the sales resistance of the prospective client! If we are attempting to gain the attention or favor of a love interest, our goal may run counter to the prospective beloved's first responses, or to that of another suitor's. If we are attempting to run a faster mile, we "oppose" the laws of gravity and inertia.

Even *dancing* with a skilled partner has a certain beneficial aspect of *opponency*, in that there is a jointly imposed spatio-temporal limit, within which, the mutual, and artfully managed, interaction or *controlled resistance,* of the dance, can manifest as graceful and dramatically expressive coordination and even joyful synchronization of the partners.

No one and no thing is inherently or *fixedly* an opponent. The highest concept of Game is one in which every participant wins *some* perceived benefit at end-game.[70] Opponency is as conditional and subject to change as are obstacles and freedoms. Especially important, is that an opponent is *not an enemy.* Opponents play *with* us. Enemies may intentionally seek to destroy us or *prevent* our playing the very game itself.

---

[70] To rationally *counter* or constrain is in contrast to the sub-rationally normal tendency to *resist* by force any perceived opposition or obstacle. Holosophy posits more optimum *multi-sum* games in which everyone wins *something* as contrasted with "zero-sum" games in which there are *total* winners and losers.

> "God is not a 'what,' He is a 'That' - *there* without qualities."
> -- Scotus Erigena, mystic
>
> "Tao never *does* anything. Yet through *it* all things are done."
> -- Lao Tzu

Chapter II – Lila; The Life Game Paradigm

This is not to say there *are* no enemies! But an actual enemy, viewed in the wider and more lofty context of opponency, i.e., *as a sub rational opponent*, however irrational or "evil," is more easily neutralized and effectively *countered,* because actual harmful intent, however masked; being *sub-rational*, is more identifiable, tactically predictable, and, also being *sub*-rationally "self"-defeating, is therefore more vulnerable to *counter*-measures.

Artful Gradualism: Through, *Not* Over, the Rainbow

Since the "limiting" but transient persistence of *overcomable* barriers is vital to any achievement, the element of gradience, i.e. gradual, incremental "one-step-at-a-timeness," is also critical to the skillful means of play in the *Kosmic* Life-Game. If we could overcome *all* obstacles easily, we would soon take little pleasure in doing so. *Instant* gratification is short-lived in providing desirable value content. Alternatively, if we could scarcely overcome any obstacle at all, we would soon become discouraged, inhibited, and disinterested, as active players.

As already noted; to maintain the game, we need to play, *and* win at it, in proportionately scaled and confrontable *increments of betterment* which are achievable, manageable and acceptably rewarding. The concept of *gradual* and staged confrontation of targeted sub rational material is also crucial to Holosophy counseling with its progressively managed dialogue process and cognitive milestones of erasure.

The unwillingness to *attain gradually*, i.e., the sub-rational

> "A man cannot be too careful in the choice of his enemies."
> Oscar Wilde, playwrite
> "The true object of all human life is *play*."
> -- G. K. Chesterton, author

Chapter II – Lila; The Life Game Paradigm

insistence on having it *all*, or doing it all, or being it *all, right now,* actually reflects an unwillingness to play the game, which, like all games, requires finite and overcomable barriers: achievements-enabled by, and requiring rationally *deferred* gratification. An irrational insistence on obsessive immediacy of goal realization rejects all incremental and temporal game elements or agreements, by unethically shortcutting these as a participant, and with commensurately *shortened* or reduced *satisfaction.*

Obsessive "urgency to achieve" or to gain advantage, opens the door to failure to participate fairly or to contribute on a *level* playing field. This in turn leads to no-exchange, which further devolves to broadly harming and ultimately even descends to neurosis, insanity and criminality.[71] The intolerance of rational achievement *gradients*[72] is a gateway to *dis*ability and ethical decline, with resulting player game abdication. It signals, the sub-rational re-enactment and imposition of the case-contour's memorial "self," and therefore by tacit default, *exclusion* from the actual game itself[73]

---

[71] The criminal has a severely disabled capacity to both perceive and agree to abide by the social "Rules of the Game" most of which involve deferred gratification and recognition of gradients and equitable exchanges.

[72] Rational advance toward accomplishing *any* goal is composed of "managed gradients" or increments of betterment. However, subliminal and persisting responses to trauma can form hidden sub-rational standards for achievement which can *never* be met, e.g. the "approval" of a dead father. Therefore, in such a case, no increment of betterment is ever "good enough"; *assuring* failure, which in turn, creates a scarcity of actually fulfilled needs, and inevitably an obsessional impulse to falsely value and fulfill them.

[73] It is apparently a Cosmic, rather than Kosmic "landscape" that is described. It would therefore exclude any reference to the "possibilities" of the *non*-material, e.g., consciousness, value, ethics, *meaning* as distinct from information, free will, and any numinous "Ground of Existence."

Chapter III - Dialectical Idealism

Chapter III
Dialectical Idealism: Extending the Kosmic Game-Matrix

> "Surely any God worthy of the name could pretend a limitation or incapacity for the purpose of Divine Recreation, and without violating its omnipotence."
> -- Holosophy Canon
>
> "The emptying of memory, though not as great as a state of union, yet because it delivers souls from much sorrow, grief and sadness, besides imperfection and sins, is in reality, a great good."
> -- St. John of the Cross, mystic

III - Dialectical Idealism
EXTENDING the KOSMIC GAME-MATRIX

We have suggested throughout that human beings are, in essence, Holons, or spiritual beings, *distinct* from, but *using* bodies, brains, minds and personalities to interact on the physical plane for the purpose of *Play*. But how exactly do we, *as* Holon *users*, endow and control these usefully convincing *tools* of Kosmic enthrallment? What do *we* actually *do* to make our arms embrace a child, to use minds to imagine a new work of art, recall the sizzle of a steak or the smell of a rose?

How do *we* manage to express ourselves as alternatively gregarious and fond of music, or shy and indifferent to song? In short, what *are* the essential capacities of a Holon, this unit of self-actualizing consciousness? To get some sense of an answer, we might re-examine more completely the concept of the Holon as a creative or *originative*[1] *non*-material individuality.

To exist as an individuated entity, to be a unique *unit* or *agent* of consciousness, a Holon must first have a stable point of view; a *selective* awareness of *this* moment, space, or object, and *not*, simultaneously, of *all others*. *It* must be able to *choose* a

---

[1] Perception could, in the deepest sense, be considered *constrained imagination.* Constrained by what? By the spontaneous and *interpretive* act of apprehending the game-defining, but innate background agreement and *context* of Holon's Consensus Thralldom, always benevolent or "rationally" paradoxical, as are all primal and generative conceptualities. One must be the "deceiver"; *and the* deceived at *once to be a Kosmic game participant.*

> "I do not paint things, I paint the differences *between* things."
> -- H. Matisse, artist
>
> "Theatre takes place all the time wherever one is, and art simply persuades one that this *is* the case…"
> -- John Cage, artist & composer

Chapter III - Dialectical Idealism

unique and distinctive contextual *basis* for a particular, volitional, viewpoint of *origin* for "being; doing, or having," of one, or a *specified* array of things, to the *exclusion* of all *other* things. *That* is the *volition* which *frames* and endows life-game experience.

Without manifesting *through* this innate self-actualizing categorical duality[2] of "self-*not* self" which allows each Holon's selective *viewing* perspective, it would remain merely a *potential for* a realization; only a *possible be*-able, without real *being;* an *un*actualized latency for individuality, contained within the infinitely specifiable *potential* possibilities (7th domain) that, when projected, *actualized*, and optimized, make up the gaming matrices of Kosmic Reality.

As a suggestive, but imperfect analogy, try to again imagine a drop of water as part of an ocean. You can easily *conceive* of an ocean being made up of many drops, but without a knowing selection of the observational parameters which *define* a single drop -- space, mass, density, time, location, etc. -- in other words, without a specifying or dimensionally delineating point of emergence distinct from the ocean's total aqueous background, it is impossible for *that* drop to exist as a discrete entity; it only *pre*-exists *in potentia*…as yet *un*manifest, but then as an emergent *actuality,* through a somehow *quantum-selected*, formative, and *projected* combination of being one and *not*-being *all else* - it becomes *a* drop!

---

[2] Duality: the innate categorical capacity for twoness or dichotomous manifestation; wherein the epistemic (concept), reified, "becomes" the ontic; (existence), in simpler terms; from the innate conceptual and categorical realm is brought forth as a whole; a distinct "this" vs. all "not this" existent; or a *something* enclosed by, but differentiated from, everything *not* that thing. The ultimate mechanism for quantum "wave-form" collapse, *as* many physicists maintain, is a *selective* conscious actualization.

> "A 'verbosopher' is one who mistakes language for existence."
> -- Anonymous
>
> "Repeating a word again and again shows that, in itself, without a use in a situation, it becomes meaningless."
> -- Ludwig Wittgenstein, philosopher

Chapter III - Dialectical Idealism

In a somewhat similar sense, and in order to enter and play the *Kosmic* Life-Game, the Holon apparently *perpetually* instantiates in a *knowing* act of creation, a kind of nonmaterial *conceptual* linkage to the physical universe[3], which it adopts and maintains as a "window," or a framing and *accessing view*point. This *meta*-physical portal is a channel of actualization for the Holon's unique, innate character and persona, as a *self*-determined agency or *observer/participant*.[4] The Holon assumes a viewpoint of origin and identity, *through* which it then projects, and acts upon, its personal Kosmic game-perspectives and goals.

The definitive reservoir of being and action or *personal presence* of each Holon; which both distinguishes it from other Holons, and from the mere *possibility* of existing, *is* its unique and *intentional* self-actualized focusing of awareness or attention.[5]

In summary, a Holon is *selectively* aware of some things, and unaware of others[6], within an enthralled, but *self*-generated and necessary *recreational verisimilitude* of tacit participation in the shared context of *any* particular game. Simultaneously, each being is involved and *consensually* active within the full play-spectrum of *all* domains of the Kosmic mythic journey and the

---

[3] *Potential intentionality* is senior to manifest intention as a specific choice, therefore, the Holon is "self-chosen," i.e. not a *result* of an enactment of choice within a time-stream of causes and effects, but from its own innate time *creating* potentiality for enduring self-actualization.

[4] "Observer participancy" is a description given by a great modern physicist to the central role of consciousness in the generative experiencing and inhabiting of the physical world.

[5] In the Shakespearian sense of having given itself, "a local habitation and a name"

[6] That *selective unawareness* is the suspension of disbelief or "useful credulity"; subliminal and seamless "*whole*-making"; or "artful pretense" that characterizes the essence of the generating thralldom, or tacit and benevolently *designed* recreational display, of the Kosmos.

> "Through my scientific work I have come to believe more and more strongly that the physical universe is put together with an ingenuity so astonishing that I cannot accept it merely as brute fact."
> -- Paul Davies, physicist
>
> "There are only two ways to live your life; as though nothing is a miracle, or as though *everything* is."
> -- Albert Einstein, physicist

Chapter III - Dialectical Idealism

benevolent recreational display of emergent Playerhood.

Postulation: Metaphysical "Movie Making"

Postulation is not a commonly used word, but it is the most precisely descriptive word we can use in this context. In our usage, postulation means manufacture, creation, or *bringing into being* through sheer creative intent or *volitional cognitive projection*. It is not synonymous with "thinking" thoughts, or mental-images, which are in actuality things *created by* postulate.

Nor is postulating an effortful activity, although it can have *degrees* of manifest and direct effects *on* the external world. We cannot effectively try to will or intend. A postulate is an intentional non-material *bringing-about*, and is never a *result, a part* of, or caused by, the reality or process which it creates and commands. Postulation is like the role of a movie projectionist: whose knowing, willful, *intent* to select and show an amplified image *precedes* and is causally independent and distinct from, *any* concurrent thinking, action, or *process* involved in so doing.[7]

Perception: The Playing Field as Imaginal Constraint

Perception is more typically thought of in conjunction with the mere *receiving* of an effect on awareness or attention, but Holosophy holds that perception is actually of the same *supersensible* order of *postulated* act as a creation or *rendition*, because, using our cinematic metaphor, it is always edited, cut

---

[7] Consciousness, the *source* of postulation, is not defined by or contained in any process, just as the *moving image* on the screen is not directly contained in, or part of; the individual frames of film.

> "We *build* our world-models from strange raw materials; signal-processing tools designed by evolution to filter a universe swarming with information into very few streams of incoming data."
> -- Frank Wilczek, physicist
>
> "Perception is a creative act of *selective* filtration emerging from a contextual "grid" of archetypal alternatives."
> -- Holosophy Canon

Chapter III - Dialectical Idealism

and *imaginally* fused together to achieve a final sensory completeness. It is a *projected* and continually re-framed reification of that same innate knowledge-essence that is the primal source of *all* Kosmic existence[8].

We selectively perceive each infinitely varied instance of the color *red* only by *knowing*[9], first innately, categorically, and in a perceptual *context*, what *redness is!* We perceive a foreign object -- a point of light skimming across the night sky – only to the degree that we can *constructively know* or bind together cognitively its gestalt[10] as a *whole,* that is greater than the sum of its seamlessly combined *primal conceptual components* or qualia: point of light, track, skimming, sky, night, etc., *equals* "Shooting Star!," a creative *cognitive fusion* of inference and attribution.

Consequently, we seem *not* to readily perceive that which we are not already potentially *willing* to allow ourselves to know or confront.[11] Perception and postulation then, are both essentially epistemic or *knowing* acts of creation, or significant *forming*; for to postulate and perceive anything, a Holon must, in a deeper sense, be *able* to *extract* it selectively from an infinite conceptual background of *potential knowing.*

---

[8] Here we owe a great theoretical debt to Plato. Holosophy concurs with the philosopher, A. N. Whitehead who considered *all* western philosophies mere "footnotes" to Plato.
[9] Knowing could be considered the *intentional* capacity for *attributed* meaning to selectively appear from an innate realm of conceptuality, the same innate capacity that enables us to volitionally see a particular "red" without contingent reference to any prior perception, "framed" by the categorical familiarity of "redness," but *enabling* the selected *primary* appearance of a precise *shade and hue of red and no other qualia.*
[10] A *whole* which is greater as *itself*, than the integrated sum or *fusion* of its *conceptual* component parts.
[11] Many experiments demonstrating the distortion or modification of perception based on peripheral conceptual a*ssumptions* and *pre*conceptions have been conducted confirming perception as a rendition, a *framing,* creatively enacted by consciousness.

> "A "Whole" is that which has a beginning, middle and end."
> -- Aristotle
>
> "I have simply wished to assert the reasoned and independent feeling of my own individuality within a *total* knowledge tradition."
> -- H. Matisse, artist

Chapter III - Dialectical Idealism

It can then *project* that innate and ordered knowingness as a perceived, *externally manifest* attribution, requiring, often subtle, *contextual* re-formation of its private filtered universe. Perception must be spontaneously attuned, as well, to the diverse magnitudes and countrapuntal dimensions of a larger *co*-orchestrated musical background; the *shared* playing fields, or domains of the Kosmos.

When we refer to Holons, i.e. *ourselves,* we mean spiritual beings whose primary and essential capability is the bringing about, or the actualizing, of *meaningful* eventuality, through pure intention, qualified by informed context, to a projected, *intended result!*

In the *Kosmic* Life-Game, Holons manifest or "actuate" postulation and perception most basically as existential sequences of emergence, persistence, and closure, or *action-cycles.* A term[12] which we will continue to use to denote the most fundamental, *useful*, and descriptive characteristics of both cosmic and Kosmic *events.* The most primal, formative, and *unitary* existential attribution, a beginning, continuing, and completing…a creatively known, elicited, and *rendered* eventuation.[13]

A few simple examples; within a context of a *knowing* familiarity and *intending* to read, one picks up a book, scans its pages, and puts it down. Intending to word-process a letter, one boots up the computer, selects the appropriate program, types in the draft, checks for spelling, and prints out hard copy. In cooking, from the concept to the executed meal, one follows a

---

[12] The word *cycle* is derived from the Greek "kairos" or "coming into a new state of "being."
[13] The capacity for relevant and context-specific imaginal knowing*ness,* as distinct from replicant or mentally *pictured* memorialization, or a *process* of representational "feedback."

> "The primary physical nature of reality is at once *both* corpuscular [particulate] and undulatory [wavelike]; "which" we perceive depends wholly on our *selection* of an experimental setting."
> -- W. Heisenberg, physicist
>
> "The triad is the *form* of the completion of all things."
> -- Nichomachus, philosopher

Chapter III - Dialectical Idealism

recipe. These are all simple action-cycles[14]; but in a larger sense *all* life-events *are* algorithmically actuated. Life is not a disjointed and chaotic blur, but an ever-progressing, orderly *continuum*; seamlessly framed, sequentially *imposed*, perceived, and volitionally enacted; *ideally* as a logical pattern of linked, and purpose-driven events, punctuated by a *cyclically* accomplished *intent*.

Action Cycles: The Dynamic Tapestry of Play

The concept of action-cycles has been touched on in various historical contexts as a basic unitary element of existence, from the ancient Vedic hymns to the sciences of our own times. For instance, in some cognitive disciplines the term "transactions" is used to refer to the basic units of personal interaction with *others*. We, however, use the terms "action-cycle" and exchange[15] in Holosophy because they provide a broader context; one that more usefully describes *all* actions, not just those involving other people, or a generic *blur* of things happening, but each one a selective "*micro*-kosm"; a *primary* unitary recapitulation *and* building block of the *total* Kosmic Game-Cycle structure.[16]

Action-cycles and/or exchanges then, are the primary event-units of activity that make up our *play* in the *Kosmic* Life-Game. They

---

[14] Consider also the triadic grammatical primitives of *all* language e.g. subject, verb; object, and be, do, have; which suggests a common source or "deep structure" of linguistic, and archetypal pattern-logic behind the cognitive orderliness of grammar, and the event cycles of common experience. If we add "knowing" as the "fourth" innate *source* from which the triads of being, doing, and having *derive*, we can perhaps reconcile the ancient polemic duality of the triad (3) *vs.* the quaternity (4) as the fundamental existential archetype ("three" for the Cosmos; "four" for the *Kosmos*).

[15] The word, "exchange" is used in Holosophy to *emphasize* the more fundamental, reciprocal, and *cyclical* nature of *all* transactions as *intentional* consecutive acts with *mutually* attributed source and receipt points.

[16] Here we refer to all ontic or reified eventuality, from the smallest to the largest parts of existence.

> "The mind, works on the data it receives much as the sculptor works on his block of stone."
> -- Wm. James, philosopher
>
> "Substance is *ens* (action), that subsists *per se* (in itself)."
> -- G. W. Leibniz, philosopher

can contain any combination of postulations and perceptions, but each cycle comprises a space-time *continuum;* established by conceiving an act, and *then,* executing it to have a seamlessly consecutive beginning, middle, and *end* or completion.

The content and logical order of event-progression can be usefully reduced to some variation of the following algorithmic (and manifestly triadic) sequence, which contains a *fourth* but often overlooked and omitted, but *implicit* contextual background of the creative, determinant, and *knowing* participation of the Holon:

ACTION-CYCLE: (CREATE) → **(1)BEGIN** (CREATE) → **(2)CONTINUE** (CREATE) → **(3) COMPLETE** (CREATE CESSATION).

A tennis swing as a total act, for example, is a *triadic* cyclical continuum which is observed as comprised of (1) "intent to swing" (*create*-begin), (2) "forward movement of arm" (*create*-continue), "follow-through" (*create*-continue), and (3) "cease swinging" (*create*-complete), with each of these components smoothly integrated and accomplished to form the total and completed cycle, ended by a punctuating and defined closure, i.e. no(further)-creation[17] of *that cycle* (event or exchange).

The linked event-sequence of cycled actions are in fact creatively *managed* by the Holon, who, although not *part* of the physical process, acts as a kind of "invisible captain" directing and controlling its intended path and purpose.[18] Ideally, there are

---

[17] "No creation" is in fact the same fundamental capacity of the Holon which enables it to "cease to create" (erase) *all* sub-rational mental imagery.
[18] A *linked* series of small cycles still falls within an *overall* intended and managed cycle of a *completed* purpose...

> "The first word ah, blossomed into all others, each of them is True."
> -- Zen Poem
>
> "*Beauty* is what ultimately binds us to an object, person, existence, memory, *or belief.* Its full *re*-creation and contemplation can, through volitional erasure, *also release* us from that bondage."
> -- Holosophy Canon

Chapter III - Dialectical Idealism

no mentally-pictured and distracting images sub-rationally inserted to insulate, and thus *prevent* the Holon from direct, full, and immediate creative execution of each individual action-cycle. (Each enacted as part of the completed sequence of *intentionally linked cycles* that comprise the totality of an accomplished act, goal, or aspiration.)

Further, as earlier noted, the Holon's formative "non-creation" surrounding this or any action-cycle, *frames* and distinguishes each particular event-sequence. Michelangelo stated this truth eloquently when he explained how he sculpted the David; "I simply removed [uncreated][19] everything that was *not* David," a seemingly paradoxical integration of doing and *not* doing.[20]

However, since all *primary* existence categories are dichotomous (dual in nature), *non*-creation is, itself, in the deepest sense, also a determinant *creation,* and as such implicitly frame's each cycle's "boundary condition"; and is necessarily imposed and managed for any creative *act* to be uniquely specified, and realized as an integral part of the enchanted connective-tissue of existence.

In visual terms, *Kosmic* Life-Game action-cycles are like those in the motion-picture of a swinging racquet in our tennis example. Each discrete part of the cyclical continuum or "link of meaning," whether it is the impulse to swing, the tightening of one's grip, the focusing of the eyes, or the drawing back of one's

---

[19] To impose and *extract* an imaginal form upon the marble is to knowingly *subtract* all but *one* of a potential infinity of forms, *and* to declare it "finished," a constructive *closure* of execution.
[20] Apparently such *regulating* dichotomies are the transformative linkage from the *Conceptual* 7th domain, to the emergent *combined* conceptual assemblages or qualia, of *physical* perception (6th domain).

> "The least initial deviation from the truth is multiplied *later*...a thousand fold."
> -- Aristotle, philosopher
>
> "Love is infallible; it has no errors, for all errors are the *want* of love."
> -- William Law, mystic

Chapter III - Dialectical Idealism

arm, is a distinguishing *created* part of the total event sequence; a distinct decision to "be, do, or have" (*something* and *not* something *else)* in each single frame, or operation, regardless of how conscious or apparently "*un*conscious" that decision is.

Of course, one operant-frame of an extended creation is scarcely noticeable. Like a single frame of the movie film, it does not "persist," but flashes on and off *almost* simultaneously. The instant one perceptually *creates* or "brings about" cognitive linkage to the next frame, the previous one ceases to exist. It is only when similar, yet distinctly different action-cycles are projected in a series, like the sequential frames of the celluloid film[21], that there is a created illusion, or co-participant *apparency,* of a seamless and *intentional* persistence…a triadic unity (with conscious intent as an implicit *fourth* element) or *rendering* of a *conjured* eventuation; the action-cycle.

As one might expect, an action-cycle is most effective or successful when it is *consciously determined*,[22] i.e. intended or caused; when the projected intent to be, do or have, (or not be, not do, or not have) is *knowingly* volitional and conscious, and when it is followed by sequential actions which serve and accomplish only *that* intent[23]. This is what is meant by concentrating, or being focused, as an ace tennis player is mindful of the game *in progress*, and little else, while playing a

---
[21] Human perception apparently operates at approximately 25 instantiations or "frames" per second; on which the cinematic frame-sequencing and duration was practically based, i.e. an experimentally "constrained" *process* of photon *information* which correlates with the Holon's imaginal capacity for projection and integration of actual form.
[22] *Not* "self" consciously, with a redundant image of "self" injected as a disabling insulation from the *integrated immediacy* of an authentic creative act.
[23] Even when *the* intention accomplishes a multitasking result, it is still unilaterally *intended.*

> "The concept of a clock enfolds *all* succession in time…In concept, the sixth hour is not "earlier" than the seventh or eighth, although the clock never strikes the hour save when the *concept* biddeth."
> -- Nicholas of Cusa, contemplative
>
> "The "before and after" and *flow* of time are game-enabling *constructs* of consciousness."
> -- Holosophy Canon

Chapter III - Dialectical Idealism

match with a *directed* and undistracted centeredness.

Quite often, of course, we can consciously interrupt or "park" an action-cycle[24] to attend to something more pressing. We may momentarily suspend a household task to attend to a crying child, stop reading a report to answer the telephone; or pause in watering the lawn to talk with a neighbor. As long as the interruption is *aware* and intentional (or purposeful), and we either consciously resume what we were doing (the parked action-cycle, in progress) or choose *not* to resume doing it, *there is no problem.*

One way or another, when we have *consciously* completed the pending cycle; we have, with awareness, created its beginning, middle and end - bringing it to *closure*. It is only when we *sub-consciously fail* to impose an ending, or interpose a post-traumatically *inserted* ending, without realizing it, that the cycle escapes control and becomes *subjectively* problematic.

In our common experiences, much such sub-rational restraint and tension comes from the usually mistaken assumption that a burdensome or difficult to express thought, feeling, or action will *not* be understood, or otherwise accepted, and is *withheld* un-expressed, and never brought "to closure," often leading to post-traumatically *charged* reactivations.

These *incomplete* communication "cycles," or conflicting intentions of, at once, saying and *not* (resisted) saying, form

---

[24] A remarkable capacity of consciousness enables us to concentrate exclusively on a *selected* sensory input, e.g. a particular conversation, (sometimes referred to as the "cocktail party phenomenon"), in the midst of many potentially conflicting sensory inputs.

> "Why are you unhappy? Because 99.9% of what you think
> and everything you do, is for 'your*self,*' and there *isn't* one."
> -- Wu Wei, Taoist philosopher
>
> "Move on!"
> -- Zen Admonition

Chapter III - Dialectical Idealism

hidden cyclic impediments and disruptions, like a redundant double-cycle of driving with a foot on the brakes; doing one thing while at the same time, sub-rationally doing another, also fails to complete, remedy, or *erase* any resulting impasse, conflict, or upset; while covertly maintaining the disabling persistence of the *incomplete* cycle with its unwanted and conflicted experiencing.

Problematic Cycles of Action: Redundancy in Action

Obviously, sub-rational problems can arise when we fail to consciously control, and *complete*, an action cycle; when it is *mis*intended or interrupted below the level of our consciousness by the pain-enforced superimposition of another *opposing and counter-intentional* action-cycle; i.e. by a hidden, fixed and conflicting, "out of phase" *mental* re-activity. In other words, such *false* problems arise when an action-cycle in the present is redundantly overlaid with a mentally pictured, *mis*-valued *equality* of trauma-based *opposing* intentions which *conflict,* resulting in a convincing but false equivalence, or apparent stuckness.

This forms a false "balancing" of the *opposing* intentionalities, perceived as an unchanging and worrisome present condition[25] which demands, *while at the same time* covertly *resisting,* a solution. The importance of eliminating this superimposed and sub-rational balancing act to the restoration of

---

[25] Fixed or conflicted attention, e.g. a "worry" is not a *thing* externally situated (an *actual* condition) it is a *mental* construction, and *always* based on the Holon's unwillingness to confront and *own* the hidden and mis-valued "half" of a falsely balanced, stuck or "clotted" intentionality, which through Holosophy Dialogue can be revealed and *de*constructed or *erased*, causing the "problem" or unwanted, seemingly *external,* "condition" to vanish.

> "The daily floggings aboard this vessel will continue until the morale and attitude of the crew improves."
> -- Royal Navy Orders of the Day -- 1783
>
> "We are forced by our **a priori** adherence to material causes, to create an apparatus of investigation and a set of concepts that *produce* material explanations. We cannot allow the Divine foot in the door!
> -- S. Lewontin, biologist

Chapter III - Dialectical Idealism

rational and *objective* problem-solving through *erasure,* is obvious.

In summary, *all* such unwanted (*subjective*) problems or worrisome conditions in life seem ultimately to derive from unperceived, uncontrolled and sub-volitionally *conflicting* or *double-binding* (falsely opposed and *balanced*) intentions contained in past traumatic (obsessively continuing) action-cycles *imposed on the present.* But to better understand goal-related action-cycles, which are focused on rational and real-time *objective* problems,[26] it is useful to further examine the *Kosmic* Life-Game context of Ethical Exchange.

Exchange: "Coins" of the Kosmic Domains

Exchange of commodity, or giving and getting a valued something *for another* valued something, is a vital cyclical element inherent in any game. One provides services to an employer in exchange for money and benefits. One helps to maintain a household in exchange for the security, quality of life, and comfort it provides. Such exchanges need not be narrowly "equal" to be ethical. They need only to be *equitable and unforced.* A teacher may willingly lend her time, wisdom and patience to a promising student without charge, if she is sufficiently gratified, measured on a higher scale of *qualitative*

---

[26] Problems that are not mental-picture "encrusted" and/or containing conflicted intentions, and are only temporary and *situational barriers* to a goal-related and *consciously* intended result or closure.

> "True meditation is not driven by purpose...
> does the Light ask for *more* light?"
> -- J. Krishnamurti, contemplative
> "All knowledge *is* without cause."
> -- J. S. Singh, contemplative

Chapter III - Dialectical Idealism

compensatory *value*, by the sincere commitment and continuing cognitive growth of the seeker.[27]

What seems *not* ethical and sub-optimum, in the play *interactivity of any game* is the demanding or exacting of something for *nothing*[28]: a malingering employee, a gouging profiteer; a child refusing to help at home, a student neglecting his studies; a potential political constituency promised unwarranted subsidies or entitlements; a de-based currency: to cite a few common examples. Such unwillingness, to exchange, *in extremis* underlies criminality, for it disrupts, in *some* measure large or small, an entire *rational* social fabric based on free and equitably-valued exchange and transaction.

The play-*viability* of the Life-Game is a vital and dynamic balance and equilibrium that essentially involves *valued,* (in coin, commodity, service or betterment) and lawful *exchanges* of *valued* things resulting from completed cycles of action (goods, services, or *any* existential requirement for play) which represent productivity[29], *between and within* the various sectors or domains of life.

Players who allow or encourage disproportionate, unbalanced, or inequitable exchange, are also responsible for the contra-survival disorder which results: The employer who fails to either

---

[27] Charitable giving, although it does not exact a direct exchange does receive indirect benefits on that *higher* scale of value, from any greater incremental betterment imparted to all the domains affected.
[28] Making a profit on a transaction is not something for "nothing" since the efforts, risk assumption and intelligence of the "seller" are themselves, valuable commodities and count as exchangeables in the transaction. Profit is not theft.
[29] Tangible evidence of incremental betterment i.e. needed and wanted "exchangeable" consumables, including anything one domain provides another, to enable or enhance general Kosmic participancy, welfare, and/or higher qualitative contemplation and activity.

> "When Henry David Thoreau lay dying, he was asked if he had made his peace with God; he answered, "We have never quarreled."
> -- A friends report
>
> "Anytime you become *willing* to experience the void, it is available."
> -- Ken Wilber, philosopher

coach or dismiss, the noncontributing or counter-productive employee, effectively *fosters* the harm caused, as does the spouse who "looks the other way" when his or her partner abuses the children.

It can also be observed that when an individual or group either *takes,* without a balanced *quid pro quo* of *giving,* or is given *to* without expectation of any contributing, personal, situation-enhancing exchange, or, alternatively, the *prohibition* of such exchange, e.g., a government's prevention by statute or taxation of the free choice and exercise of the cyclical-activity (work) necessary to produce a valid and desired service or commodity; that individual or group will decline, physically, mentally, or ethically, and usually in all three *inter*dependent aspects.

Congruently, wherever an individual or group appears to be in chronically poor physical, mental or spiritual health, i.e., obsessively victimized by persisting unwanted conditions; there will be found a personal history of the harmful and unethical[30], imbalance of exchange, both in the effected area of life, and between it and *other* game-domain sectors of existence.

Ethics as Optimization: Wisdom's Rational Choices

Ethics, could be considered, as a system of qualitative principles for estimation and initiation of *objectively rational[31] valuation and*

---

[30] Ethics in Holosophy presupposes the rational capacity for making free choices that ideally implement increments of betterment, e.g. optimally balanced exchanges within the Kosmic fabric of play, those that contribute to short and long term survival; reduction of pain and disease; enhanced living conditions; increased ability and awareness; and the general well being and balanced quality of life overall.

[31] "Rational" in this context could be defined as relevant, maximally informed discernment and knowing postulation toward primal *game-inception* referenced i.e., *primary* and *objective* standards of survival-related activity, contemplation, and enjoyment involving all domains.

> "And I suspect, for me, the way is like the weasels, open to time and death painlessly, noticing everything, remembering nothing, choosing the *given,* with a fierce and pointed will."
> -- Annie Dillard, writer
>
> "True compassion is *ruthless.*"
> -- Zen Saying

Chapter III - Dialectical Idealism

choice necessary for enacting what is "good" (optimum) or "bad" (suboptimum) in any game *co*-postulated and played, by consenting Holons. The *objective* Ethos of any game is apparently founded upon the primal and willing *agreement* of its players to play within an enduring rule-bound, and *hierarchically value-referent,* Kosmic continuum, mutually shared and *endowed* by all; the *primal* freely chosen and enduring fealty to which, undergirds *all* subsequent commitment to making *rational* choices.

As an example, implicit in this system of agreements might be the reasoned prioritizing of the *total* game-at-large over self, generally making the welfare of the preponderance of the games activity-domains senior to the welfare of only *one*…What is ethical could be defined as that spontaneous and informed calculation or estimation; which results in action (or inaction) for the greatest good (qualitative enhancement) for the greatest number[32] of *domain* aspects of play, i.e., a value-objectified[33], deeply *aware* and rationally exercised power of choosing, to bring about optimized alternatives – a value *calculus* of incremental betterment.

Since decisions which best reflect the welfare of the greatest number tend be those which are *most* informed, i.e., those which use the maximum amount of accurate information and *familiarity* with *each* domain in spontaneously estimating its application to the relative enhancement of the *total* game.

---

[32] Contrast this with the traditional utilitarian concept of the greatest good for the greatest number of *people*…*one* or two domains entered into the calculus rather than the full Kosmic complement of *eight*…

[33] In holosophy, ethics and values are *objective* by reference to the earliest "pre-cosmic" consensual *standards,* upon which are based, and which later guide, free action and choice…Mere *subjective* ethics is completely localized and situational, having no deeper Kosmic reference, foundation, or standards for objective optimization…

> "The objective world rises from the Mind itself."
> -- The Buddha
>
> "Everything is made of emptiness, and form is *condensed* emptiness."
> -- Albert Einstein

Chapter III - Dialectical Idealism

Ethics is, then, incremental game optimization through informed and *rational choice*; each choice ideally maximizing at once, the welfare and quality[34] of *all domains*, in its *Kosmic* dimensional impact and, as modified by each Holon's natural, and *current* endowment of ability and awareness as a player.

Therefore, a *Kosmic* ethos exemplifying actual, deeply *shared*, and *primarily objectified meta*physical standards cannot be reduced to mere subjectivity or *relative* situational mores, to a sterile propriety; a narrow correctness; or an officious legality. A small business owner *may* operate "correctly," strictly within the letter of the law. If, however, he considers *only* his personal welfare, his *total* ethical awareness could be said to be minimal. By contrast, another who considers herself, her staff, her community, her industry *and* also her extended environment, might be considered *gradiently* more ethical in comparison.

Altruism, or *enlightened* self-interest, unlike the isolating sterility of a gross egoism, involves an agreed-upon *multiple* life-domain reference for decision-making; true altruism *is* possible,[35] merely because an act entails benefits to *self,* and perhaps to slightly lesser degree, a broader spectrum of life and existence, does *not* devalue or diminish it to mere self-service.

The informative relevance of all (including self) dimensions of

---

[34] By quality is meant *awareness* of, and intent to enhance and realize the spectrum of values inherent in, and manifestly associated with, the archetypical ideals of Truth, Beauty, the Good, and the Numinous; which have served, inspired, and *guided* human choice and behavior through the ages. (see Truth Functions in appendix 1.)

[35] One might say that compassion is the ability to confront the suffering and adversity of *others* with an empathically distanced helping, but also an *engaged* and undiminished equanimity; a *knowingly* heightened *rational* and *loving* intentionality, contrasted with sympathy, which is often a sub-rational and *mal*-emotional *co*-experienced resonance with another who is perceived as "victim"; a disabled, self-reducing, *in*effective reaction to circumstance that "confirms" and justifies the *non*-responsibility of all concerned as responsible *players.*

> "Cause is intention, extended."
> -- Holosophy Canon
> Meaning isn't just in things, but in *between* them..."
> -- Norman O. Brown, historian

Chapter III - Dialectical Idealism

the Life-Game in making any decision, entail and exemplify a rational and deeply rooted *ethos;* a rationally applicable *calculus of betterment* i.e., volitional optimization with *full*-spectrum Kosmic context and standards, embodying an intrinsically proportionate emphasis on higher purpose, aesthetics, and spirituality.

Justice: Benign Umpiring

To retain their endowed interest, games must contain some consistent interpretation and enforcement of limiting rules and boundaries; e.g., an *umpiring* mechanism that ensures just distribution of rewards for rational rule observance, as well as penalties for irrational violation or non-observance.

Innately and by nature, Holons, however, are *basically* good[36], and tend (minus the sub rational case-contour) to naturally *self*-impose those corrective measures necessary for guiding and limiting behavior; *and* to selectively establish and define the scope and standards of cognitive optimization and its calculus.

Individually a Holon also tends to *spontaneously* correct his or her mistakes and favor just amends or restitutions, as well as acknowledge contributions to, and betterments of self *and* Game with compensatory gestures, and re-visioning of life-priorities.

In a rational game with consensual laws and justice systems

---

[36] "Evil," by contrast, is distorted, exaggerated, or *misdirected Good,* and is therefore fundamentally *parasitic* in nature because its power and force is derived from the primary and underlying, but sub-rationally alienated, Goodness, a pristine good formatively inherent in the original, and consensual, rule-making of the Life Game. But, "evil," even as a de-valued *good* has therefore a de-based but "borrowed" and often rationalized "value."

> "There are realities existing apart from our sense perception, and problems and conflicts where these realities are of greater value for us than the richest treasures of the world of experience."
> -- A. Einstein, physicist
>
> "A trifle consoles us, because a trifle upsets us."
> -- Blaise Pascal, contemplative

Chapter III - Dialectical Idealism

serving as enlightened *umpires* of Play, the playing field is kept essentially level, with full and adventurous opportunity for all, *earned* by, and consistent with, individually attained levels of consciousness, ability, and causation.

If one could consider metaphorically, the elemental and *extreme*, forces of nature--wind, fire, flood and earthquake, to be dramatic natural examples of planetary checks-and-balances (barrier-conditions affecting play), it would seem that they tend to lie at the outer *human* play-limiting perimeters of the *Kosmos* and only temporarily and locally effect its more ordinary or normative play perspectives. An erupting volcano, a natural but devastating hurricane, or a massive flood might be considered from a *lofty* perspective, as an extreme *but perforce Kosmically instructive* global boundary condition, perhaps providing an elevating context of comparison for increased insightful *valuing* of the more benignly challenging exigencies of daily life.[37]

Humankind as a whole tends to balance, contain and "filter," its play activity to stay within the limiting confines of the game's civilized rules of engagement; i.e. *created* rules, involving the known rewards, penalties, contesting forces, opposition, and the primary and enduring purposeful self-actualization, fundamental to any game.

Obviously however, an unbalanced and oppressive enforcement of rules is sometimes irrationally imposed on one or a group of

---

[37] Such higher "cosmic" perspectives are perhaps also useful in anticipating the rare cataclysms of meteor, asteroid, and solar, impacts on the planet, which in theory, an advanced and fully optimized earth civilization might scientifically counter or neutralize.

> "God sleeps in the rock, dreams in the plant, stirs in the animal, and awakens in man."
> -- Sufi Teaching
>
> "Physics is a reflection of the divine Ideas of creation. Therefore, physics is divine *service*."
> -- W. Heisenberg, physicist

Holons by another. While such harmful external force and duress may be unjustly inflicted upon us by others, we can also observe that we often covertly invite or inflict it upon *ourselves,* in a far more subtle, *un*consciously purposeful, and self-sabotaging way -- a kind of *selective sub-rational proclivity for "quid pro quo" to "expiate"* specific injurious effects caused to *others*.

It is this, the invited "retributive reflex," which, as we have observed, identifies and underlies all *sub rational* patterns of behavior; because it is an aspect of the redundant imposition of the *case-contour* (surrogate "self") by the Holon, to subrationally enforce by trauma-induced replication, its own primary[38] and native ethical nature or *character*.[39]

Aesthetics: Qualitative Gateway of the Infinite

In Holosophy, aesthetics is closely related to ethics. In the broadest sense, it refers to the constructive, *idealized*, and emotive, appreciation of the *beautiful,* i.e. the highest qualitative and harmonious relationships *among* the greatest number of *value-*adding *Kosmic* game selections, decisions, and actions taken; as well as, the creation, contemplation, and communication of, qualitatively significant and instructive forms, symbols, objects, archetypes, ambiguities, and ascendantly *ideal,* kosmic scenarios.

These aesthetically endowed or value-significant creations at a minimum, give pleasurable intimation of, but also dramatically

---

[38] The Holon uses the case-contour to "feign goodness" by imposing sub-rational limitation to "insure" that it *is* good, which of course it already is, innately and *without* such additive restraint, disability, or falsification!
[39] The sub rational mind, or "case contour" is actually a traumatically installed *copy* of the actual pattern of existence, which is then compulsively re-endowed and falsely enacted as the *actual* Kosmic template.

> "The concept of existence, however, cannot be relativized, without destroying its meaning completely."
> -- Kurt Gödel, logician
>
> "...a very great more truth can become *known* than can be proven..."
> -- R. Feynman, physicist

Chapter III - Dialectical Idealism

invite awareness of, and *celebrate*[40], a higher vision of harmonious coherence -- an innate but generative Order that manifests as a vast Holoarchy of *cyclical* play-activity, descending from, and, ascending *within*, the same ultimate and enthralled sensorium, which Plato called "the moving image of the *Infinite*"-- the Kosmos.

For example, consider the aesthetic value, or comparative excellence of a diamond. It depends on an agreed upon *standard grade* of quality for its color, clarity, and cut, considered together with its carat weight. A small, dull diamond is of lesser value, no matter how well it is cut. A large, fiery diamond cut to perfection can take one's breath away--as can, *a fortiori,* a sudden revelation or epiphany of an innate but immediately accessible, spiritual Order; a sublimely transcendent Goodness, Beauty, Truth, or Divinity.[41]

The *Kosmic* Life-Game *is* ultimately the consensual experiencing and enjoyment of aesthetics[42] and *gesture;* each instant of player participation is ideally, an act of deeply metaphoric and *optimized recreational display,* a celebratory cosmic enactment, of the Kosmic essence. Solving life's routine problems is the ordinary coin and fabric of *play (ars practica),* which, when *fully* discerned and *integrated*, leads inevitably to the higher expressive realization of the *spirit* of play.

This is ideally projected in the enactment or *displayed*

---

[40] Joyous epiphantic anticipation of non-dual awareness. Beauty and value are the primary "conceptual-coils" of connectivity, that both bind *and* separate, at once, the Holon and its creations.

[41] The 7th domain apparently "contains," as conceptual *potentiality*, an objective standard for truth and value, which makes quality levels distinct and consensually appreciable, and "outranks" mere opinion. *This* is what differentiates *objectively*, the *beauty* of a Shakespearean sonnet from the mere tropisms of lavatory graffiti. (see Truth Functions in Appendix)

[42] Aesthetics seems to use as its cosmic vehicle, a much higher and more refined energy spectrum or wave length associated with the transitional 7th to 6th domains connectivity to formative content and *manifest* creativity.

> "There seems to exist a 'principal' of maximum diversity which ensures that the laws of nature and initial conditions are such as to make the universe as interesting as possible."
> -- Freeman Dyson, physicist

> "Platonic existence as I see it refers to the existence of an objective external *standard* that is not dependent on our individual opinions nor upon our particular culture."
> -- Sir Roger Penrose, physicist

Chapter III - Dialectical Idealism

optimization of, the total Game, through the transformative *gestural* intent embodied in *each moment* of rationally chosen action *(ars spiritus)*. The Holosophy Programs assist in gradually restoring to the active creative imagination, access to higher realms of aesthetic sensibility resulting in *acts of creation* that have too often been sub-rationally reduced to the narrower and exclusive dictates of trauma-driven "survival" compulsiveness, and wastefully trivial self-indulgence.[43]

In Holosophy, the word "gesture" is more fully defined as an elevated, qualitative, but almost effortless actualization of meaningful expressiveness, an implicitly intended, often seemingly ambiguous,[44] celebratory enactment of individual or group play-enhancement through art, graceful action, and/or metaphoric intimation.

The *Kosmic* Life-Game unfolds then, with a creative, knowing, but also a playfully *concealed* and co-limiting thralldom of tacit complicity among the Players, which each game-optimizing *gestural* increment of right action makes aesthetically, ethically, and *meaningfully* evident, as a vast and marvelously intricate consensuality.

This seminal and revelatory concept is embodied in and central to, the full spectrum of Dialoguing Modalities of Holosophy, which obviously owe much to the inspirational wisdom traditions of both East and West.

---

[43] It was the philosopher Bertrand Russell, who defined television waggishly as "chewing gum for the eyes."
[44] Ambiguous in the sense that the best art and poetry exploit a choiceful *multiplicity of meaning* from within finite representations of language or form. The highest metaphysical realms of meaning are not fixedly or symbolically limited, as the transformative intimations of art seem intended to remind us.

> "Clarity is gained through breadth."
> -- Niels Bohr, physicist
>
> "Einstein's Dilemma: each photon in a pair, when experimentally created and then separated, seems to behave as if it *knows* instantaneously what is happening to the *other* photon, somehow *entangled*, even if there is a light-years distance between them…"
> -- Holosophy Canon

As has been emphasized, the *Kosmic* Life-Game, as do all games, has ultimate and consensual rules of engagement. The better a player *understands* and personally re-*endows and affirms* these pre-established standards for betterment of the *totality* of domain play, the more extended are his or her options for playing skillfully and successfully.[45]

A Holon's personal capabilities and awareness at any stage of the Game, can evolve (improve) or *de*volve, (deteriorate), variably, within the scope of play. Commitment to the primordial and enduring archetypal structure or *soul*-encoded dialectical game pattern itself, however, remains inviolate. (Apparently, by prior and sustained agreement; and, for the duration of the Kosmic Game Cycle, its rules obtain.[46])

The Creation of the Game: Maya Modernized

Holons *exist*. Our player-perspectives *exist*. The vast multi-domain perceptual "field" of action cycles which Holosophy terms the "*Kosmic* Life-Game" *exist*. But exactly, *how* was this grand consensual assemblage of Holon existences *itself* brought about? It is not the intent of these commentaries to *fully* explore the precise nature of any primal Kosmic event which may have occasioned (or perennially *sustain*) the creation of the universe

---

[45] As has *also* been emphasized, it is the covert and compulsive mental re-imposition of this primal commitment, sub-rationally reified by the Holon as the case-contour, that characterizes *all* aberration.

[46] Providing *objective* standards and stable points of reference and agreement, which may be consulted in making rational choices, and value judgments. There's "no disputing taste" *except* by discerning access to earlier agreed upon, historical "wisdom-forms" of value representation, which underscore the implicit legitimacy of primal but enduring (therefore objective) standards of *comparative* valuation.

> "Let's just stick to the facts, m'am."
> -- TV's Sgt. Joe Friday
>
> "Truth is a pragmatic and imaginal balance of logical coherence and observational correspondence, a warranted assertability that guides and accommodates play!"
> -- Holosophy Canon

Chapter III - Dialectical Idealism

as we know and perceive it, or the sub rational departure from the natural Kosmic error-limit devolution which characterizes all human aberration and suffering which dialoguing evidence suggests is associated with a response to some ancient profoundly traumatic cosmic event (see Chapter 4).

We can however, perhaps gain some small insight into its *localized* apparency or "presentational immediacy" by looking a bit more closely at the theoretic *nature* and capacities of its most self-evident and immediate *designer,* by default, *the Holon itself,* acting as both a generative and limiting sensorium, an attributing entity without any objective, measurable *"quantity"* as itself, a "pure witness," whose cognitive "channel" of selectable Kosmic options *frames and elicits all* that is experienceable.

We have defined a Holon as an irreducible and immanent, but *self-actualized* unit of consciousness; a creative essence-viewpoint whose sole existential activity is "postulation and perception". Since it is also assumed that *reified* postulation and its perception or resultant occasions *are* external "reality," then an *individual* Holon cannot "be" *both* non-material perceiver/subject, *and* the substantive objects, perceptions, or processes, that are both created and *projected.*[47]

In other words, there is a primary *conceptual* distinction, between the *first domain* of the Holon as immaterial observer-

---

[47] Consider any entity whose functional properties match the input/output and processing complexity of the human mind/brain. Would such an entity by virtue solely of its complex computational aspects possess emergent *qualitative* and *cognitive* features? E.G. is a termite colony, the Brazilian economy, or the library of Congress, *conscious,* i.e. "aware" of *being* aware because of its mere quantitative complexity?

> "Sometimes it proves to be the highest understanding not to understand."
> -- Gracian, philosopher
>
> "In the beginning there was nothing and the Lord said, 'Let there be light' and there was still nothing, but now you could *see* it…"
> -- T. Pratchett, physicist

Chapter III - Dialectical Idealism

viewpoint[48] and the projected and *observed* perspectives of the other external and palpable domains of play. It follows then, that *what* we see is a direct function of *how* we, as Holons, creatively *frame* it; i.e. we are not mere unwilling effects of the natural world, we are "victims" only of *how* we view (or distort) it through an *interpretive* lens of our own devising.

If only one Holon is perceiving, and postulating a particular identity, activity or quality; that identity, and its *manifest* nature will persist only as long as that Holon's attention and intention is projecting it; or, more accurately, only as long as the Holon is *endowing* an actual existence as *a privately observed* cycle of cognitive-closure or "quantum wave function collapse." Recall the earlier analogy of the motion picture. A single point of view is like the films projected image with only one viewer. It has actuality *as* itself, but no reality beyond its own uniquely projected viewpoint. I*t lacks agreement.*

To make something *real* enough to persist, there must be *multiple* viewpoints comprising a *mutual* perspective, i.e. the sequential *co-creative alteration* of one actual and immediate, but transient *truth*, into a co-*observed*[49] continuum; a kind of complicit fabric of pretense, i.e. an enthralled progression of multi-perspectival alterations or *relative* observational *un*-truths.

---

[48] Any, redundant mental-image the Holon has of "itself" however, as a substantive "thinker" or as *part* of the mind or brain, and not the final, witnessing and *generative* "abstract-ego," should be differentiated, perceived, and *erased.*

[49] Observation is here considered a joint action of intricately created co-participancy or "*reality*" extracted from the background of statistical or numerical possibilities or "potential" by the player-holons involved, e.g. in physics the "principle of uncertainty" asserts that all observation "causes" alteration by the minimal "quantum of energy" of interaction required to perceive it's "continuity."

> "Those who believe in the reality of a world of spirit, the poet, the artist, the mystic, are at one in believing that there are other domains than that of physics."
> -- Sir James Jeans, physicist
>
> "Every man's world picture is, and always remains, a construct of his *mind*, and cannot be proved to have any other existence."
> -- Erwin Schrödinger, physicist

Chapter III - Dialectical Idealism

These, like a fine tapestry, are woven together into a unified and substantial *attribution* of common experience, but where each *separate* and distinct *thread* of truth states by its differentiation the *apparent* and therefore *working untruth* of the whole.

Apparently, also in the *physical* cosmos (*not* the Kosmos)[50], a fundamental rule is that two things cannot occupy the same space, thus any fact of existence cannot "continue" to also be the *same* fact. It is altered by each *new* moment, a separate instantiation of each fresh observable; a duplicative progression of *working* "untruths" for, as Heraclitus put it: "no one can step into the *same* river twice," although we usually pretend it *is* the same river or perceived object.

There must be the innately coordinated "untruth" of two or more projected and converging points of view--at least multiple Holons co-creating and "editing" the "movie," in "real-time," by perceiving it and tacitly postulating it together (but each from a *different angle* of actual[51] viewing) in order to "share" the generalized *un*-truth that enables *persisting* common experience.

It follows then, however paradoxically, that each uniquely perceived existential and sensory distinction is *ultimately* "true" or actual for *one* Holon, but "false"[52] or *relatively* unreal for others. The "necessary *un*truth" of mutually perceived

---

[50] An unlimited number of concepts, like a "multiplicity of *angels*," can "dance on the head of a pin" since "they" as *concepts*, apparently have no extension in space or *substantial* existence as objects.

[51] "Actual" refers to the uniquely primal or native point of view, which when altered and combined, through time and collective nuancing, becomes a "real" agreement-consensus.

[52] Obviously anything known or presented by only one Holon is relatively unreal until it gains "real" currency and traction by the "reality-filter" of a multi-perspective "averaging" alteration. Each holon's perspective is only a "slice" of the complete "whole baked loaf" of perception.

> "The word *information* in this (information) theory is used in a special mathematical sense that must not be confused with its ordinary uses 'information' must not be confused with *meaning*."
> -- Warren Weaver, cyberneticist
>
> "Information *content* is distinct from mere information *carrying* capacity."
> --- Holosophy Canon

consensual alteration, with uncertain "origination" and ownership, is needed to obtain a shared, persisting, synchronized, and *convincingly apparent* playing field with the requisite subliminal unanimity for *all* observers: Reality is a co-creative *agreement*.

Reality: Consciousness *Uses* Process: "Its" from "Bits"

To better grasp the concept of reality and perception as creatively shared *agreement*, let's revisit our original "mind = computer" analogy. Mathematically, information is numerically represented as an *encoded* meaning*ful* quantity of symbolic elements, it is *not* meaning *itself*. A basic numerical *1 or 0* ("something" or *nothing*) is used as a symbolic element of information called a "bit."[53] Combinations of bits are organized via computer "programs" to form representational images, e.g. the arranged pixel-graphics on a monitor or *the spaced dots of light on a* TV screen.

Information is thus an it (meaning) from bit (process), a neutral and *non*-cognitive *vehicle* or conveyance of an *encoded* symbol to which is *attributed* meaning *by consciousness*. However, each "bit," in fact, is itself, in the same existential sense, *already* an "it," since it is *itself* tacitly assumed and perceived as a primary, *unit*ized and attributed, conceptuality, i.e. a

---

[53] A "bit" is in the material sense, a simple on/off switch which holds one of the two values of the basic binary code of information, e.g. a transistor when "on" = 1, when off = "0". These ones and zeros combined in further complex configurations to form the programs, processes and output of computers of all types. Combined and *interpreted* by a conscious "operator," but without *meaning*, per se until de-coded, i.e. *given meaning* by the de-programmer!

> "A neural network (in attempting artificial intelligence) can't do *logical* reasoning because it *calculates* probabilities, but can't understand what those numbers really *mean.*"
> -- Marvin Minsky, neuroscientist
>
> "Every event or occurrence is fundamentally...a *subject*..."
> -- Holosophy Canon

Chapter III - Dialectical Idealism

created symbol, or kind of a cloaked knowing,[54] applied in *representing, or reifying,* any encoded meaning. The programmer uses a string of combined bits to form a perceived "it" or whole, fundamentally a mechanically conveyed *conceptuality!*

In quantum-mechanics mathematical symbols and equations are endowed with scientific meaning to represent the extraction[55] of the "real" from the merely probable i.e., to predict and describe actualization through *a process of conscious observation,* which somehow creatively extracts the "*its*" of space, particles, energy and cycles, from the hidden quantum "*bits*" to manufacture the *physical* world.

In other words, quantum mechanics enable the conveniently seamless *conversion,* (or "reduction") through acts of *conscious* and interrogative measurement of an unseen background of *wave form* potentiality, into a *solid,* but also subliminally *filtered, and endowed* "objective" reality.

However, the unitary "bit" and its aggregate product of "its," are *both,* in fact, *themselves* only symbolic conceptual projections by *conscious* Holons; creatively extracted gestalts or qualia[56], arranged in a consensually ordered and emergent

---

[54] It is *meaning,* that symbols of any kind merely represent, and that when reified as ordered conceptual assemblages, can then be further used in art and science to explore and celebrate the *essence* that a projected existence makes manifest. But the *meaning* is always distinct from the *manifestation*, requiring an interpretive consciousness of "abstracting" by a conscious agency.

[55] For example the quantum physics view that conscious observation and measurement, "extracts" reality from a merely *potential* cosmic background as earlier referenced.

[56] Qualia: a clear and irreducibly *whole* and distinct element of perception, e.g., redness, sweetness, hardness, etc.; an emergent integrated and combined unitary meaningfulness, reified, or made *beable as perceived phenomena.*

> "We now know demonstrably, that the moon is *not* there when nobody looks…"
> -- David Mermin, physicist
>
> "History will be kind to me, since *I* shall write it."
> -- Winston Churchill

Chapter III - Dialectical Idealism

pattern of *existence*; a process of reified algorithmically projected *meaning*.

In Holosophy a symbol is considered fundamentally as a "concretized" cognitive *triad*, or threesome; a *conceptual* combination of (1) specified knowing, i.e. the idea or *meaning* necessary for it to *be* a specific "it." (2) A capacity for physical transmission or communicative mobility to do it. And finally (3) a perceivable referent, mass, or *thingness*, to contain or embody it;[57] and make it usable, reachable, and *hav*able.

An example from mathematics: first the concept of a simple unitary *be*able or *number*, which in combined forms, are expressed as equations or complex *symbolizations*,[58] of a formalized and logically lawful *aggregate* conceptuality. These symbolic and densely *encoded knowings* are then used to *represent* or describe the wing of a butterfly; the trajectory of a space-craft; the numerical constants of a universe, or perhaps to *symbolize,* the core thematic matrices of, an entire Kosmos.

Naturally, the greater the agreement or number of converging (*bits*-mixing, and modifying) points of view, the more lasting and substantive will be the resulting complex of "its," as above. *One* molecule of hydrogen and oxygen, for example, is invisible, hardly there. But the "it"-forming *many,* joined together, make the aggregate, *real* multi-perception of an ocean, the *workable, un*truths of a persisting agreement.

---

[57] A word can even be *touched* to convey its meaning, as in Braile: the tactile language of the blind.
[58] In computer language the binary code of "1"s and "0"s.

> "Process, Pattern, and Perception are all cognitive concretions or reifications of the distinct and determinant Agency of consciousness below which they supervene."
> -- Holosophy Canon
>
> "Listen: there's a hell of a good universe next door! Let's go!"
> -- E.E. Cummings, poet

We can, then, usefully deduce from these and other theoretical considerations that the *qualia*, or reified conceptual gestalts of space, time, energy and matter; derive essentially from tacit co-observations, or, cumulatively integrated *knowing* agreements between conscious Holons.[59]

Life is then, a co-creation of multiple co-enthralled consciousnesses that has been brought about through *descending* orders of Kosmic change and complexity…from a primary non-physical generative *potential* for life[60], to a "constructive illusion" that all Holons co-experience as the sensory basis for the multi-domained game of *Kosmic* "Reality."

Selective Unknowing: Thralldom as Theme

To maintain playerhood and participation as *homo ludens,* "Man as Player," with convincedness and authenticity, a native capacity for *selective un*knowing is necessary. To bring this concept into a more practical perspective, consider again the possible metaphysical "origins" of *any* object of creation as the emergent expression of a seminal series of *managed,* sanctioned, and rule-guiding *un*truths; a fabric of benevolent and reality-enabling *pretentions.*

---

[59] Some current physicists theorize that the cosmos is a kind of holographic projection from densely encoded information or "bits" on a mathematically described universal "horizon" that forms the framing boundary for our collective awareness; a somewhat familiar ancient hypothesis in modern dress.

[60] For example, the accessibility of a dialectic "Kosmos" or the Holon's consensually pre-established, archetypal blueprint or "soul-code," for game creation and projection. We also find that the sub rational mind's observed persistence and power results from the trauma-based alteration, and re-enactment of this template in the name of redundant "survival."

> "It is impossible to travel faster then the speed of light, and certainly not desirable, as one's hat keeps blowing off."
> -- Woody Allen, comedian, auteur
>
> "No amount of human having or human doing can make up for a deficit in human *being*."
> -- John Adams, president

Chapter III - Dialectical Idealism

Although an experience may have begun as the seemingly arbitrary actualizing postulation of a single Holon, expressed through imagination and *then* communication; all came to *final* fruition, solidity or "reality," through subsequent agreements and *co*participation among *many* Holons, who *chose*, as above, in a co-conscious *patterned* unison, only those *filtered*[61] and determinate *knowings* which best accommodated, and also subliminally perpetuated the Kosmic Game itself.[62]

Reality as we know it, is apparently *not* a purposeless "fait accompli," not merely a vast and overwhelming materiality, however entrancing, persisting, and mysteriously presented as merely an "ad-hoc" event. Our universe is obviously *not* an accidental, inimical and relentlessly imposed *cosmos*-only habitat…without *any* inherent design, meaning or value.

History, for example, is not just a fixed serial memorialization of facts. Although a past event can be mentally *re*stored, its cognitive *frame* is ever fluid. Interpretation is all; an adult can look back honestly on a childhood peccadillo, and *realize* a freeing, but long denied, personal accountability; whereas, before, only a festering context of guilt, or hateful *vindication,* was felt and *acted-out* compulsively.

In fact, reality is *only* what *we* create and agree on. It is a reflection of ourselves, of *our* on-going power of rational choice

---

[61] As in earlier references, a kind of "cognitive filtration" is required to create and occupy the "acting illusion" of Kosmic Play, a filtration that imposes the necessary volitional constraints of a "Kosmic blueprint."

[62] The same mechanism, to chose a quotidian neurological example, that enables a cross-eyed person to *see*. Each eye is presented with a visual field that is askew compared to the other, the perceiving *subject* "orders" the brain which cannot integrate them stereo-optically, to "switch off" one or the other input alternatively and selectivity to *un*-blur perceptions.

> "Be not anxious for the morrow. For which of you, being anxious, can add one cubit to his stature?"
> -- The Bible
>
> "Blame or sub-rationally *critical* mis-assignment of causation, is the corrosive and energetic force that insures victimization by sub-rationally enacting the mental-image encapsulation of the Holon."
> -- Holosophy Canon

and the experiential continuum that choices make manifest. The ultimate context for the *meta*-physical agreements, which undergird and form the nature of reality, is an a*ctuating* but innate *duality that* extracts and projects the finite from the infinite. A primary *something-nothing* cognitive distinction is necessary for the dialectical display of "thoughts-made-substance." These emergent conceptual *assemblages* as perception, *reference* the higher Kosmic domains; but are projected locally, through the creative-window and lens-like, *duality*-integrating agency of the Holon.[63]

Dialectical Idealism: Holon as Observer/Participant/Player

"*Dialectic*" is a word that conveys the ancient concept of an unfolding, cyclical, dynamically structured and natural cosmic *order* of events, foreshadowed in the Vedic hymns 10,000 years ago, later in the Upanishads, then in the yoga-sutras of Patañjali; the verses of Nagarjuna, and also appearing in early Greek philosophy and mythos. Heraclitus, for example, saw reality as a flow of perpetual conflict and change, ultimately forming its own opposites.

Socrates later used *dialectic*[64] *argument* to resolve the tension and contradiction of ideas in apparent opposition, to reveal the hidden truths obscured by false logic. Plato further envisioned the process to achieve what he considered the highest, level of knowledge; the concept of "Zetema" or *quest for Truth,* in

---

[63] Infinite Potential as the highest or 8th Domain seems to manifest itself "through" the Holon to experience "Itself" as total *Kosmos*. Thereby displaying for our participative contemplation, the loftiest of metaphysical paradoxes: Infinity achieving an eternal *transfinite* enrichment of *Itself.*

[64] Dialectic in the related sense of a purposeful and revelatory pattern of logical *discourse.*

> "Consciousness is the ground of being, manifesting as the subject *that* chooses; and experiences *what* it chooses, as it self-reflexively collapses the quantum wave function."
> -- Amit Goswami, physicist

> "Our mission is to gain true discrimination of the contraries; first as contraries, but then as poles of unity."
> -- Herman Hesse, novelist

Chapter III - Dialectical Idealism

which the idealized and generative forms of existence itself, are revealed as immutable truths, *related* to each other in an innate but ordered realm of Ideas, of which, the "real" world is a mere gross reflection.

Benefiting from the insights afforded by these enduring wisdom traditions, a *living Kosmic* dialectic then might be considered as a *creatively* ordered pattern and telic (purposeful) progression of opposing *ideas* reified[65] in existence, as a dynamically cascading historical process of eventuality.

The philosopher Hegel combined these early and seminal ideas of a progressive cosmic *event*ualization, into a triadic formalism which attempted to logically extend the ancient Heraclitan opposites to achieve a *new* dialectical-historical process or *synthesis*, integrating what is *true* and valuable in a continuum of evolving and self-reconciling polarities.

Unfortunately, neither the Hegelian dialectic nor its more modern variations have any place for, or emphasis on, a creative, *alive*, event-*causing* and broadly determinant Holon *individuality*, that could be a central and localized *agency* necessary to *frame* the unfolding dialectic order of things and most importantly, no insight into the dialectic as possibly containing a soul-encoded template for a universal *game*; or existence itself, *as* that *Game,* which the Absolute could be playing; with, and through, multiple endowed individualities, as quasi-divine unitary constituents of *Itself*.

---

[65] The word "reify" is used in Holosophy to mean the process of giving, non-material concepts substance and perceptual reality, i.e. "*ideas* made *flesh*" or given "local habitation and a name" as Shakespeare beautifully describes it.

> "All the *way* to heaven... *is* heaven..."
> -- Catherine of Sienna
>
> "Energy is eternal delight."
> -- William Blake, poet
>
> "*Any* experience is mystical, and therefore *indescribable.*"
> -- R. D. Laing, psychiatrist

Chapter III - Dialectical Idealism

The total sensory order of the Kosmos, as re-visioned by Holosophy, is governed by a consensual and rule-bound conceptual patterning in that, percepts themselves, are inferential *constructions,* emerging a priori, from a deeper and non-material categorical realm of ordered Knowing. Existence is *demonstrably* a projected representation of that innate formative template-context or a kind of pre-planned Kosmic matrix[66], or an enabling habituation for the infinite diversity of life-form Playerhood.

In this larger sense, Kosmic history and its progression as a Game, unfolds guided by what might be termed a *dialectical-*algorithm; a purposeful schema for events and cycles that operates as an "enchanted loom" *weaving* the Kosmos as a value-laden tapestry of endless *theme and variation* for divinely sourced play-activity and opportunity.

The dramatically differing version of existence that, for the most part, modern Western philosophy presents, is a rather dreary and sterile universe of natural cosmic events driven mindlessly and inexorably through tension, opposition and conflict toward an evolving but ultimately *meaningless*, "naturally-selected" but *purposeless*, existence of brute and insensate material phenomena[67] and its reductive biologic *epi*phenomena...us!

By contrast, Holosophy takes the dialectic-*idealist* position that

---

[66] Holosophy has taken certain neologistic license in translating the *"cosmic* code" into a richer Kosmic variation.
[67] *Incidentally* bereft or *minus*; freedom, responsibility, value, spirituality, immortality and *Kosmic* consciousness...

> It is difficult for the matter of fact physicist to accept the view that the substratum of everything *is* of mental character. But no one can deny that the *mind* is the first and most direct thing in our experience, and all else is remote *inference*."
> -- Sir Arthur Eddington, physicist
>
> "Being...is the *active* seeing...of *knowing*."
> -- Holosophy Canon

the innate rhythmic pattern of dynamic polarities that under-girds the Kosmic-historical process, emerges as triadic event-cycles *projected* by Holon agent-participants which in turn, *by agreement* forms a *designed*, rule-bounded, landscape of limitless opportunity for self-determination, choice and multi-domain play.

It is this intrinsic Kosmic blueprint, that encodes and *guides,* but does *not* compel the dialectic unfolding of the pattern. The profound recognition of, and *chosen* commitment to, that guiding source is the essence of each Holon's unique *psychic-grid* of authentic self-actualization, or *character*.

It is through an ancient and traumatic intervention, resonating with the actual pattern of the Kosmos, that the Holon is deceptively influenced to *redundantly* replicate or "armor " its true character with *sub rational* mental-imagery; which is then *worn*, i.e. sub-rationally endowed, imposed, and *obeyed* as the hidden, parasitic, and *true-self*-limiting *sub-rational* "ego" or case-contour.[68]

Limiting the Infinite: The *Domains* of the Kosmic Life-Game

As discussed in the previous chapter, all games require assumptive boundaries of space, information, and capacity to both enable and contain, or ethically *limit* play: *external* boundaries to delineate and enclose the game as a whole, and

---

[68] It is this *displacement* of the Holon's strongest and most enduring *natural* impulse *to play the game*, that, *copied* and distorted under episodic duress, descends to the sub-rational demand for mere biological continuity, or "*SURVIVAL.*" It is of course, also the Holon's authentic character that is the model on which the redundant and reactive "self-surrogate" case-contour replicates and from which it "evolves" to parasitically characterize and *compel* the *actual* Holon's aberrant behavior.

> "Small minds discuss people, average minds discuss events. Great minds discuss ideas…"
> -- Socrates, philosopher
>
> "In matters of philosophy, the average quantum mechanic is about as preoccupied as the average garage mechanic…"
> -- E. Squires, physicist

Chapter III - Dialectical Idealism

internal limitations and rules to both define and restrict, the sub-games and volitional *moves* within them.

The game of football, for example, is played in a large rectangular field, within which, are touch-down objectives established by goal posts, while its *sub*-game of making first downs, is played within yard-markers. Chess is played on a checkered board, where its moves are confined to certain of its configurations. Golf is played on a wide and arranged expanse of intricate landscapes, while basic player actions, i.e. drives, are confined to fairways and putts to greens. All delineate and contain the agreed upon targeted location or terminus for the object of play.

To vastly extend the analogy, the *Kosmic* Life-Game, although almost infinitely varied and complex, nonetheless, has natural and distinguishing area boundaries, each with a unique categorical and existential integrity, as part of a total innate blueprint or dialectically designed *order*.

Observably, these appear to comprise eight basic and usefully distinct *domains* or sectors of play: and can be generally and pragmatically described as those of (1) personality, (2) family/procreation, (3) group/community, (4) humanity, (5) biology, (6) cosmology, (7) conceptuality, and (8) infinity. All aspects of life, all aspiring, playing, excelling and evolving -- can be seen as *designed* [69] with conceptual integrity, to fall typically, logically and *usefully*

---

[69] Holosophy uses the word to mean the intentional and orderly conceptualization of an ideal scene used to guide and accomplish a *purpose*…

> "In Emptiness there is no time, no space, no beginning, nothing-ness, it is what makes all things possible. It is a zero full of infinite possibilities, a void of inexhaustible contents."
> -- D. T. Suzuki, Zen Roshi
>
> "To fall in love is to create a religion that has a fallible God."
> -- Jorge Luis Borges, essayist/novelist

Chapter III - Dialectical Idealism

within these generic interactive perimeters or *domain*-sectors, as follows:

1st Domain:

Self or Personality, reflects the urge of Holons to manifest as categorically *distinct* self-determined individualities or unique and endowed *windows of access* to other domains, as distinct from the infinite *un*manifest potential from which *all* domains *emerge*. Everything that is uniquely *personal* is a 1st Domain component: one's character, one's appearance, one's taste in clothes, food and art, one's style, skills and talents; one's unique position and perspectives in and of the Game -- one's point of view, where one *fits in*, and how one uses any role and rank being assumed. Any expression of one's uniqueness as a *self-actualized subject,* basic personality, identity, or personal *agency,*[70] as different from another's, could be considered a primary aspect of this domain.

2nd Domain:

Family and Procreation, reflects the urge of Holons to manifest through reproductivity or procreation. It obviously includes basic sexual orientation, one's mental and physical expression of it, along with the pleasurable[71] engagement in

---

[70] Defined as an individual *capacity to act* in pursuit of *rational* self-interest, but with broader *Kosmic* implication; as a vehicle of access and exchange…

[71] Here defined as *survival*-related enjoyment experienced in a *Kosmically* contextual frame, i.e. a *spectrum* of sensual, emotive, conceptual, and esthetic perceptics or qualia "received" in *exchange* for action and contemplation which ideally promotes the use of one's endowed faculties for optimization or greater good of the totality of domains and is enjoyed commensurately.

> "My aim is to teach you to pass from a piece of disguised nonsense to what is *clearly* nonsense…"
> -- L. Wittgenstein, philosopher
>
> "In other living creatures ignorance of self is nature, in man, it is vice…"
> -- Boethius, contemplative

Chapter III - Dialectical Idealism

intimate partnerships, the bearing and rearing of children, and most directly, the optimal maintaining of congenial and familial relationships which support these activities.

While the primary focus of play is ultimately to produce and support progeny to *continue the Game*, there are nonetheless alternative sub-games which also seem an important part of the activity: the sublimation or use of sexuality for authentic spiritual purpose[72], for example, or a childless union for a sake of expressing deep commitment and love, as well as the post-procreative unions of advancing age.

The Second domain, Elements of a *Rational* Scenario:

Let us take a closer and more extended look at goal-directed involvement in this, one of the more prominent, if also problematic and affliction-beset game-domains of existence. Virtually every human being has a natural desire for enjoyment in families, romantic intimacy and commitment. A *winning* pursuit of this goal could mean, first of all, pleasure in searching for and finding a suitable partner from among many rationally suitable possibilities, then freely and happily choosing to be with that consenting person.

Once committed to a mutually sustained relationship, winning at it would mean being willing and able to communicate with one's mate on any subject that one chooses, at any time one chooses, under any appropriate circumstances, with confidence,

---

[72] For example, the practices of Tantric Buddhism or Karezza, et al…

> "Marriage has *many* pains. But celibacy has *no* pleasures!"
> -- Mark Twain, author
>
> "No man is a hero to his wife's psychiatrist."
> -- Eric Berne, psychiatrist
>
> "Sexuality is a door to the Infinite. Open it!"
> -- Tantric Prescription

Chapter III - Dialectical Idealism

trust and comfort; and being equally willing and able to listen to, and *understand* what the other has to say.

Further, it would mean being willing and able to confront and solve together whatever real (objective) problems life presents (or are *selected*) in establishing and enhancing a stable family and marital unity with creativity, fairness and compassionate good nature.

Ideally then, winning at intimacy and commitment would mean *knowingly* choosing to be with the other to create and sustain a *mutually* pleasurable[73], erotically meaningful, responsibly supportive, and, more importantly, in a broader sense, a Kosmically *purposeful* relationship, i.e. one that results in ethical, joyful and transformatively *co*-actualized productivity[74] in all aspects of the domain.

Contrast this ideal (optimal) scenario[75] with a sub-rational gamut of un-wanted no-win, "game with victim" situations:

> *Dreading the pre-marital (or any) "dating" process or avoiding it altogether; finding fault with every potential partner, or feeling convinced there are no suitable partners available; "falling" into obsessively casual intimate relationships with people one doesn't really care deeply about; committing, or tolerating, injurious gender or child-related abuse of some kind; making or sustaining a marital commitment prematurely or unrealistically, or entering*

---

[73] Of course, one does not suddenly abandon any relationship for *trivial*, sub-rationally superficial pressures of need or self-interest, as any presence of "sub rational indicators" would suggest in any such case.

[74] "The actual pattern" or blueprint of the life game apparently contains a pathway for entry; transformative transition *through* the game cycle; and the possibility of "exit by enlightenment." Cognitive Optimization assures that optimum game progress is not impeded by sub-rational barriers to rational choices that implement it.

[75] Although *ideally* Kosmic (all domain) optimization can be the elevating standard for *guiding* choices, as a practical matter, the limitations of the human condition require us to often "settle" for a "best effort" paradigm for optimizing choice; based on the individual level of awareness and ability. Apparently such truly rational, and pragmatic, if *imperfect*, choices represent the evolving but authentic ethical expression of our higher nature as beings, using our ultimate self-endowed potential as Kosmic entrants.

> "That reality has turned out to be quantitatively more extravagant than we supposed, suggests that its *qualitative* features may be equally beyond our suppositions."
> -- Houston Smith, philosopher
>
> "Computational states are not *within* physics, they are *assigned* to physics."
> -- J. Searle, philosopher

Chapter III - Dialectical Idealism

a relationship out of despair, neediness, loneliness, guilt, apathy or spite; feeling too afraid, embarrassed, inhibited or angry to truthfully communicate; ignoring "problems" in relating, or hoping they "go away" by themselves; committing violations (overt or covert) of the partnership agreements; irrational co-dependency; "losing" one's temper frequently or harboring deeply concealed resentments; behaving stubbornly, demandingly, or fixed in uncompromising rigidity, or unforgiveness; and, overall, failing to genuinely love the other in the truly heartfelt and "best efforts" ethical sense of the word.

to mention but a few of the average problematic afflictions visited upon an obsessive or *sub-rational* second domain…

It does not take much further reflection to realize that, if individuals feel they *can* make a rational choice, they will certainly choose a more ideal, i.e. *winning* scenario. Who, in a "right," i.e. rational, non-reactive (non-obsessive) *optimal* mind-set, would willingly enter into, or obsessively maintain, a negative, unhappy, or basically counter-productive relationship? But in fact, such *sub*-optimum belief and behavior is all too commonplace.

If asked, however, *why* they compulsively stay in an unsatisfying, abusive, or co-dependent relationship, or conversely *why* they dread making *any* commitments at all… they will usually tell you it's "because of" such-and-such, or so-and-so (i.e., an imposed and seemingly "unchosen" *reaction* to something or some*one* they have been, or are being, "hopelessly" influenced or effected by) and *never* because, at some level, they *knowingly*,[76] choose and covertly, *sub*-rationally, require it.

---

[76] Even if that knowledge is hidden under an overlay of selective unawareness, e.g., the case-contour's sub-rational "pictured" *mockery* of the authentic "unknowing" thralldom of Playerhood…

> "God is man, Purified."
> -- J. Krishnamurt, contemplative
>
> "The body is an implement of the soul, and the soul, of God."
> -- Jacob Boehme, mystic
>
> "We're all in this together, by ourselves."
> -- Lily Tomlin, comedian

Chapter III - Dialectical Idealism

3rd Domain:

Group/Community, reflects the creative societal urge of Holons to manifest in, and *as*, friendships, groups or extended collective organizations such as teams, schools, companies, societies, associations, clubs, or local governments, and to plan, organize, extend and optimize through mediums of exchange, any group interaction to increase constructive work- potential for the greater good and maintenance of *extended* social, and therefore optimally Kosmic, order and purpose.

4th Domain:

Humanity, reflects the creative urge of Holons to manifest *globally* as humankind, as each and *all* planetary races in the aggregate, with "world-concerned" survival and coordinated quality-of-life goals for each unique and contributing ethnicity…and that are consistent with the greater aspiration -- the optimized welfare of *all* human beings, as part of a larger, organized, and cooperative *bio*-cosmic *project and Purpose.*

5th Domain:

Biology, reflects the creative urge to care for and optimally utilize the physical body; and to more fully perfect the *general* health and welfare of the *bio*-cosm's life *forms and symbiotes,* and to sheppard, conserve, and rationally and *cosmically* extend, the life-energy, forms, and ecology of the planetary bio-sphere with ever-expanding and *optimized* bio-diversity.

Chapter III - Dialectical Idealism

> "Meaning is the *beingness* of knowing."
> -- Holosophy Canon
>
> "Ethics is essentially the ability and willingness to make rational choices for the greater good..."
> -- Holosophy Ethics
>
> "...just as the ignorant being attached to actions, act, so should the 'Enlightened', being unattached also act...to maintain order in the world."
> -- The Bhagavad Gita

6th Domain:

Cosmology, reflects the creative urge to manifest through, possess, utilize, and enhance, the physical, or any *theoretical* alternative universe,[77] as a *cosmic playing field* of matter, energy, space and time, in all of its microcosmic and macrocosmic potentia and diversity of game-related *havables;* its emergent objects, energies, places, forces, forms, cycles and events, ideally experienced and utilized in the framing *value*-context of the higher domains.[78]

7th Domain:

Conceptuality, reflects the *pre*-creative or *potential* intent and capacity to manifest through projected and *specified* formative knowings, and conceptualities, within defined and distinct but still innate *category*-potentials. (E.g. when these natively abstract significances are made *manifest*, they *appear* within each domain category as the *things* of that uniquely reified or materialized domain). The epistemically reconciled, non-dual Source of all manifest paradoxical duality, it includes, as well, any *discarnate* spiritual beings and all other aspects of the non-corporeal realm such as *imaginal* creativity, aesthetics, values, ideals, psychic abilities and dreams, i.e. ultimately formative non-material *Meaningfullness,* that when postulated and

---

[77] It might be interesting to hypothesize, that the "black-hole" singularities of our own and also of putative (but as yet *un*observable) "multiverses" might in fact, be inverted "portals of entry" for higher domains to exit from, and "enter" into *manifestation*...

[78] Which might include as the highest of purposes...the freeing of *all* holons "trapped" in the consensus *trance* of cosmic materiality...and the ultimate transmutation of "physical" existence into a creative and *novel* display of idealized and Kosmically-optimized and idealized novelty and futures.

> "God is a pure working...removed from creatures."
> -- Meister Eckhart, theologian
>
> "You would not seek Me, if you had not *already* found Me."
> -- Blaise Pascal, mathematician & contemplative

Chapter III - Dialectical Idealism

specified, is an actualizing *subtraction* from a higher *potential infinity* of possibilities, and thereby enables and *becomes,* as *reifying conceptual combinations*, *(any)* projected and perceived *Kosmic* existence within the six domains "below."

8th Domain:

Infinite *Potential,* the Ultimate Ground *for all* Knowing as *meant*, being, doing and having, *within and between* the domains; the theoretically unlimited and unspecified "*Source* of sources." It is pure non-dual, *primal* Knowing*ness*.[79] The *un*qualified essence of *all* knowing, and *not* knowing. The ineffable "neither the one nor the many" paradoxicality, that is yet *epistemically precedent* to all, and ground of all, *specified* conceptual description, or knowing *about* - (7th domain).

It contains the ultimate *Potentiality* for all entification[80] of all other *manifest* domains. Without expressing itself *as* any one, or being itself *completely* definable or delineated as any conceptual particularity, It *is* the Infinite, and finitely subtractable[81], Potentiality *for all exchangeable specificability,* consideration, and manifest existence. It can be conceived in the contemplative sense, as the imminent and supercedent, Enabling Ground of all the other domains, including even assemblages of

---

[79] The intrinsic *capacity of knowingness* to know *about,* is not yet itself an *object* of knowledge. All verbal descriptions of the 8th domain are necessarily "about" what can only be *Known as" That"* without an object; or an Ultimately Reconciled Duality as an ultimate, *non*-objective; contemplative awareness.

[80] A word used in Holosophy to describe the elements of all existence as potential *subjects* rather than mere objects.

[81] Finitude is the *subtractive* power of an Infinite Potential to endow all specified and projected Conceptuality. Not as pantheism (God *as* Cosmos) but panentheism (God as *more* than Cosmos).

> "Desire is the cause of all suffering."
> -- The Buddha
>
> "Desire is the *pictured* need to have: an obvious *resistive and energizing* component of suffering. But, a rational, optimal, *requiring* is not desire, and is therefore free of its sub-rational consequences."
> -- Holosophy Canon

Chapter III - Dialectical Idealism

sub-deities, and *their* concerted Kosmic *knowings*, as Non-Duality It*self*, *and* all Otherness, *at once*.

Errant Domains: Confusions and Blurred Distinctions

Since human beings are complex, *composite* beings (Holon-Mind-Body), our urge to experience the quality of life, ideally expresses itself within *each* of the *many* separate but related domain aspects. In fact, however, solving real *self*-determined problems efficiently, evidently requires doing so in a rational, optimized, and coordinated manner.

Such goal-directed activity involves, to an optimizing extent, a degree of awareness and consideration of *all* of the other domains simultaneously. Even though, in an individual's primary character and life goals, there may be a tendency to be more goal or *telos*-focused, and expressive, on one or two of them in particular. An athlete, for instance, may focus on the 5th Domain, an artist on the 7th Domain, a politician on the 3rd (*and* hopefully, also 4th) Domain, and so on…

The *Kosmic* Life-Game seems to consist fundamentally of the potentially usable, valuable or consumable *inter*-domain *exchanges* of each domains unique constituent parts; commodities; or services. This comprises the *interactive play activity* of experiencing and overcoming *barriers* to such exchange, as required, to maintain the dynamic flow of *optimized* give and take; between, and within, *all* Domains.

> "If the object did not have the nature of awareness, it would be without illumination. As it was *before* it appeared, *awareness* is the essential nature of the object."
> -- Upaladeva, contemplative
>
> "Blaming, as contrasted with rational discernment and judgment, endows, sustains and implements all 'evil' purpose."
> -- Holosophy Canon

Chapter III - Dialectical Idealism

To broadly illustrate: the first domain gives a particular self-defined venue or *window* of emergent actualization or *agency* perspective, for elements of the remaining domains to be perceived and acted upon. A body *provides* a biological (5th domain) unit of expression, nutritional care, sensation, and action and *receives* a unique conceptual (7th domain) identifying recognition-factor, as a conceptually *meaningful* vehicle of game activity.

The 8th domain *gives* the *ultimate* ontic *and* epistemic[82] power and potentiality for meaning and existence to *all* things, *conceptual or material*, and *receives* a Kosmic-spectrum of "*Self*"-portrayal on all seven remaining domain "stages" for infinitely possible actualization. The 6th domain *gives* physical embodiment and substantiality to the conceptual realm (7th domain) and *receives* from it the order and formativeness of archetypal essences that can be made manifest as the various-forms required by the larger, progressive dialectic *play* activity, of the *total Kosmos*.

The practical significance of recognizing and distinguishing *between* the various domains and their exchangeable components has apparently much to do with Ethics and success in the *Kosmic* Life-Game. Obviously, there are rules of conduct, conditions, and items of existence unique to each domain; certain *definitive*, forms, limitations, and meanings that should not be confused with, or sub-rationally *transferred* to other domain sectors.

---

[82] Ontic refers to beingness, or existence in the deepest sense. Epistemic refers to knowing in every shade and degree. The 8th domain is infinite potential, but a *potential*, infinite, or otherwise, is not yet a Game until manifest, *displayed*, and cognitively optimized.

> "*Things* are *meanings*, combined and compacted."
> -- Holosophy Canon
> "There is no *right* higher than that of the Truth."
> -- Indian saying
> "When you *love,* you can do what you *will.*"
> -- St. Augustine

Chapter III - Dialectical Idealism

For example, while it is appropriate to think of one's spouse, parents, relatives or children as family, it seems inappropriate (and ultimately counter-productive) to think of one's company as a genetic family, with the same expectation of nurturing entitlement, patriarchal (or matriarchal) authority, or extended *familial* care and commitment.[83] A company is not a family.

Another example: anthropomorphism or idolatry confusing life forms (5th Domain) or physical objects (6th Domain) or personalities (1st domain) with the transcendent and *un*manifest infinite-potential that is more properly characterized, *ideally* by the purely numinous and *supersensible realization*, of an ultimately ineffable Supreme Being (8th Domain).

The blurring of distinctions between domains and their interactions or item exchanges is not always so obvious, but it is extremely common and is in fact a primary indication of *sub-rationality*, and conveys the attendant lack of a differentiation, necessary for an ethical sensibility.[84] Most human beings, for instance, chronically fail to distinguish between created mental-images or *brain*-encoded synaptic information (5th and 7th Domains), and themselves as Holons (1st Domain[85]).

We mistakenly assume that the beliefs, feelings, attitudes and ideas we *project* and experience *are* us, and that whenever *they* are challenged or threatened, *we* seem challenged or threatened.

---

[83] That is not to exclude reasonable concern for and support of, one's employees.
[84] Legal and moral codes can be seen to be designed to reflect and maintain rational separations between domains to allow, expedite, and optimize their exchanges of viewpoint data, and commodity.
[85] That which is looked *at* is never what is *looking.* The Holon is not itself a *process* whether synaptic or "neuro-transmitted," each of which, however closely Holon-"identified" or "close-in," are ultimately viewable and *changeable (erasable) as* they *effect* consciousness.

> "There is the endless power of men to hypnotize themselves into unawareness in the presence of a challenge."
> -- Marshall McLuhan, futurist philosopher
>
> "The second-rate 'superior' minds of a cultivated age are usually in exaggerated opposition to its *spirit*."
> -- John Stuart Mill, philosopher

Chapter III - Dialectical Idealism

Similarly, we often fail to distinguish between our brains, our bodies and ourselves;[86] and distort our perceptions accordingly. "My *brain* can't comprehend," or "*I* am sick," versus the perhaps more accurate observation, "My body is *sick*." We can also identify ourselves with our jobs or company (or any activity) and if we lose them, we suffer a seeming lose of "self"; a little death, as it were.

In fact, as already discussed, virtually any *chronic* problem which arises within a particular playing domain can be seen on closer inspection to involve a distorted perception or blurring of distinction preventing communication and beneficial *exchange* of specific domain elements and intentions, *or* proper identification of and separation *between* domains.

An individual who claims, "I am afraid of heights," for instance, is likely experiencing a confused *dis*array of sub-rationally "blended" domains, e.g. confusing the 1st Domain (the individual self or Holon) with the 7th Domain ("pictured feelings" of past fears, and compulsive conceptuality about falling), and the 6th Domain (the actual gravity and spaces of the physical universe.)

Thus false perception and valuation displaces actual domain item-discernment, creating *unwanted* "subjective" or mentally *pictured* barriers to exercising an accurate *Ethical Calculus of Optimization* to choose rational and purposeful exchanges, instead of the joyful fulfillment of overcoming the natural and

---

[86] Consider the "hoarder" who perceives things as part of his body; or the skeletal bulemic who still sees "herself" as too fat. "The *fundamental* false identification is, of course, the "is of identity." The sub-rational confusion of mental-*images* or symbols with the *things* they represent… (See Appendix IX)

> "Knowledge we could never attain, remaining what we are, may be attainable in consequence of higher powers, and a higher life, which we may *normally* achieve."
> -- Wm. James, philosopher
>
> "Though human souls are immaterial particulars, they are not substances."
> -- St.Thomas Aquinas

Chapter III - Dialectical Idealism

objective obstacles to goal-related domain exchange activity (productivity).

Generally; such a domain category-error and its resultant distortion of identification and selection, inevitably leads to further irrational choices and unethical behavior (the two being synonymous).[87] A kind of gradual and detrimental *abdication* of the full range of cognitive optimization options and choices necessary for the ethically committed and empowered "game-commerce" of Kosmic playerhood.

In the "fear of heights" example given, such irrational (and unethical) behavior may involve something as relatively trivial as an agoraphobic refusal to go up to the higher floors of a high-rise building. Irrational, because tall buildings are generally safe for the millions of people who live and work inside them; *unethical* because the behavior is (originally chosen, even if under duress), unnecessarily, and to an actual finite degree, *harmfull,*[88] limiting ones power of choice and therefore reducing the range of *possible* pro-survival options. One may need to enter such a building to work to support a family; to keep an important appointment or to deliver a vital service -- or only to join in family vacation fun while visiting the big city.

---

[87] Another typical example: sociological studies indicate that most prostitutes consider *all* sexual relations including marriage (2nd domain) as essentially *commercial* transactions (3rd domain) and rationalize their "choice" of profession accordingly.

[88] A degree of sub-rational displacement of the Holon by the "case-contour" is a result of actual but *hidden volition* which leads to inaccurate and imprecise estimations of effort and prediction, which in turn lead to errors in action and judgment which tend to *harm other players* and to compensatory, and harmful, self-restraint.

> "Consciousness is a *partner* of matter, not an *activity* of matter."
> -- H. P. Stapp, physicist
>
> "By limiting through subtractive specification the infinitely possible; the finitely actual is created."
> -- Holosophy Canon

Chapter III - Dialectical Idealism

The sub-rational suppression of these normally viable options, on one or more domains, because of the compulsive enactment of sub-rational indicators effectively eliminates them as data in making decisions for selecting the interactions and exchanges necessary to realize a *greater* good. Therefore, by default, such "forbidden" options lead to further irrational omissions and avoidance, and other ultimately *volitional* consequences, i.e. *repetitive sub*optimum and therefore *un*ethical (harming) action or *in*action and the final sub-volitional seeking of compensatory damage to self as *expiation* for harm caused others.

Universes: Kosmic Windows of Illusion

Within the context of each or all of the *Kosmic* Life-Game playing fields or domains can be observed four basic types of "universes"[89] or (Observational perspectives useful in making domain distinctions and choices) (1) One's Personal Universe, (I, Me, Mine); (2) Another's Universe, (You, He, She); (3) The Shared Social Universe (We, They, Us, Ours); and (4) The Co-Perceived Physical Cosmos (It, It's). These primally distinctive, and addressable *awareness*-frames are usefully defined by projected and grammatical pronoun-referenced points of view, both *within*, and *of*, the 8 domains.

One's Personal Universe consists of any given viewpoint (created perspective) an *individual* Holon is willing to have. Thus it includes possibilities of, not only that which one is aware

---

[89] Universes are defined here as perceptual "slices" or *consciousness perspectives* encompassing one or more of the Kosmic domains which emerge into manifest form and existence from the innate "Kosmic Kodex," or are thematic and dialectic archetypal variations within the 7th and 8th Domains.

> "A robot can be said to give a speech only in the way a pencil can be said to write a play."
> -- anonymous
>
> "Everything that deceives may be said to enchant."
> -- Plato

Chapter III - Dialectical Idealism

of, but also that which one *has been* aware of in the past, and that which one is willing to *become* aware of in the future. It is the infinite-potential context for postulation, perception and action (play) focused through the particular lens or window of each Holon's individuality. By the same token, *another's* universe consists of any given point of view *that* individual is willing to have and act through, together providing the fundamental game element of opponency; a context for domain interaction as *play*.

The shared universe consists of the *con*sensual, *co*incident, and *co*-existent "averaging" of viewpoints that enable, define and constructively limit, the interactive vistas or domains shared by all Holons as players, and thereby enables interactive *Kosmic* Life-Game experiences. One could refer to the totality of such shared universes as "reality," or our individual imaginings combined, and *agreed upon, and shared* as a reciprocally *enthralled* perspective.

However, the higher visionary capacity of the Holon can *transform* reality into cognitively optimized novelty. i.e. the rationally optimum playing of the game, *informed* by the relative importance of available data from all of its domains. With optimized discernment qualified by *capacity*, (of all four universe perspectives), they can be integrated to achieve imaginal *ideal scenes,* or higher, more enlightened and optimally envisioned, Kosmic goals and aspirations.[90]

---

[90] Or betterment viewed as "rational pragmatics," acting with *best efforts* to achieve *incremental* ascendance on a rising scale of multi-domain oriented quality and value, but "settling" rationally, as human beings, for a practical "viability estimate" of betterment, that is based on real capacity, is achievable *and* excludes *no* domains.

> "It seems that the human mind has first to *construct* forms independently, before we can find them in things."
> -- A. Einstein, physicist
>
> "The descent or *involution* of consciousness must take place before any ascent or evolution can occur."
> -- Sri Aurobindo, comtemplative

Chapter III - Dialectical Idealism

The "it"ness of an external shared universe at large, is not to be confused with the local *superficially* averaged consensus-view of the polled majority, however much they may outnumber the lone voice and perception of an actually more rational visionary. In the 1400's, the world was "Officially Presumed Flat," notwithstanding previous insights of the early Greeks and the observational effrontery of a *globe*-certain Christopher Columbus.

It was Columbus incidentally, who noticed as an example of *sub-rational mass agreement,* the interesting fact that, during his later voyages, the local natives readily perceived his *confrontable* (to them) *small* boat landings on their shores, but would not "see" the *it* of his much larger *ships.* Also, interestingly, during World War II, native New Guineans who had never seen aircraft made "gods" of the previously unknown and *unreal* (to them) cargo transport *"it's"* which flew over their villages.

Today, all too many groups, be they composed of irrational fanatics, or ideologues of *any* description, call reality the traumatically imprinted subjective "core-beliefs" which they sub-rationally assume and project, to insulate themselves from the rest of the world. Like mass-hypnosis, fanaticism, or similar excesses, such false *un*-reality is simply an aberrant "consensus trance"[91] in miniature; *subrational* and *entranced* variant of the vast and extended Kosmic thralldom…actually just a mere

---

[91] It is reliably reported by researchers that a group of "Peruvian Shamans" apparently together *see and share* identical visions after ceremonial ingestion of a psychedelic substance, perhaps accessing the native and natural capacity of Holons to achieve the perceptual unanimity of an enthralled temporarily shared, psychic unification.

> "Sitting silently, doing nothing, Spring comes, and the grass grows by itself."
> -- Haiku
>
> "When I think of God, God also thinks of me."
> -- Jacob Boehme, mystic

Chapter III - Dialectical Idealism

narrow and delusional *fixed frame, or* recurrent trauma-born *belief* system, expressed as a "post-traumatic" suggestion.

Holosophy Dialogues target and reveal the *sub*conscious but actually *selective un*knowing that clouds that expanded vision. Indeed, as has been emphasized, the *most* basic obstacle to rationality, is the Holon's confusion of its authentic *character* or own universe with the case-contour's[92] false replication and *close-in* mental feed-back of post-traumatic memories of distorted past belief-systems and perspectives.

The failure to make necessary distinctions between domains and consequently, the sub-rational failure to make sufficient differentiation *between* the four interacting *universe* perspectives, (which *disables* capacity for erasure), inhibits the ability to make the *reality*-based *personal* choices necessary for full ethical game participation, or to erase post traumatic *copies* of *real* Kosmic experience, perspectives and events…

In other words, transformative, cognitive distinction between the real *factually* objective and logically-coherent universe perspectives, contrasted with their trauma-based subjective "factoid"[93] mental image surrogates, is vital to a sustained, and enhanced quality of life.

---

[92] As variously referred to; an individual's unique core reactive configuration or false persona; an "alter-ego" formed of traumatically imprinted experiences and viewpoints (false identities) which when activated, submerge and command the Holon's true character and individuality…

[93] A fashionable literary trope, used here to mean a sub-rationally distorted "fact"…A view typical of post modernism is that any true description of reality is nothing but a subjective and relativistic social construction. Applied to post modernism, the idea that all truth is *only* subjective, would indicate that post modernism itself has *no objective* truth value.

> "The new situation in physics has so forcibly reminded us of the old truth that we are both onlookers and *actors* in the great drama of existence."
> -- Niels Bohr, physicist

> "The *quibit* because of its entangled extra-dimensional capacities, more effectively simulates (as informing symbol) the infinite context-potential of consciousness, than the mere "bit."
> -- Holosophy Canon

Chapter III - Dialectical Idealism

It is this urge to re-discover, comprehend and utilize for higher purposes, the deepest meanings of our shared Kosmos of domains, that motivates all sincere scientists, artists and truth-seekers. Those who choose the path of ascendant personal-integration, and cognitive *optimization,* however that ultimate wisdom-path may be named, interpreted and followed, are potentially fully realized participants in the eternal, *Kosmic* game-cycle.[94]

---

[94] Sir Roger Penrose, physicist and Platonist, has recently theorized something called "Conformal cycles" in which the cosmos has an internal cyclical impulse to re-create itself. This re-creativity would be theoretically consistent with a primal game-seriality intent which Holosophy postulates as descriptive of a larger *Kosmic* purposeness. Holosophy differs, however from traditional Platonism which postulates the existence of *un*created primal and supersensible, universals or *ideal forms* from which all existence is derived. Holosophy holds that there is an *aseity*, or *self createdness* capacity inherent in all Holons and necessary for individual freedom of choice and responsibility. By contrast, an ascendant deity that is total and *sole* creator of *all* individual existence, agency and choice, would seem to negate logically and epistemically any *innate* responsibility of its creations for "their" choices. Holosophy's concept of deity is not limited by specified definition apart from *infinite potentiality* which exceeds any limiting qualification except perhaps those of ultimate Value…Truth, Beauty, Goodness, Justness et al, a celestial *value-system* which is both rational and sublimely reasonable, but also seems inconsistent with such a divinely imposed but seemingly sub-optimum and condemnatory "freedom." "*Divine"* aseity remains of course, a property reserved for any infinite potentiality that is truly and ultimately consistent with *Kosmic optimization and* recreational Play activity across the eight domains. (see Appendix II and XV for further discussion)

Chapter IV
Life-Gamesmanship: Ability, Disability and Limitation

> "All the world's a stage."
> -- William Shakespeare
>
> "A games *createdness* requires space that can both access *and* confine: water that can quench thirst *and* drown: fire to warm *and* scorch flesh: mentality that can accurately discern *and* experience error."
> -- Holosophy Canon

IV – Life Gamesmanship
ABILITY, *DI*SABILITY AND LIMITATION

Life's Melody: "Do, Be, Do, Be, Do…Have!"

As with *any* game, participation in the *Life*-Game necessitates a spirit of play, a willingness and ability to be, do, or have anything appropriate in the context of play at any given time, and to *not* be, *not* do or *not* have what is not appropriate. An actor, for example, must be willing to alter and advance his characterization of a role as the play unfolds, rather than perform un-nuanced, and by rote; giving a 'canned' rendition, performance after performance or worse, draw content or interpretation from a *different play entirely.* Similarly, in the third domain, the corporate game for example, a newly promoted manager must be willing to flexibly assume new responsibilities and perspectives, and abandon any limiting tendencies or inapplicable viewpoints held from a previous position or situation.

Also, implicit in the spirit of play is proper control, or the *smoothly accomplished* intent to begin, continue or complete any relevant or necessary action-cycle with precision. Both the actor and by analogy, the corporate player must be able to *start, change and stop* their performance at will. They must have causal power over their actions, i.e. be able to bring about or withhold *effects;* speak or remain silent, move expressively or remain still, as well as *receive,* and be responsive to the intended

> "Tell your boss what you *really* think of him and the truth shall set you free."
> -- Unknown
>
> "He who bends to himself a Joy, does the winged life destroy. But he who kisses the Joy as it flies, lives in eternity's sunrise."
> -- William Blake, poet

Chapter IV - Life Game

input and effects of others; take cues and direction, listen and respond meaningfully to the needs, intentions, and actions of their fellow players; as is the case in *all* games, 'local' or *Kosmic* in scope.

Traditionally, the 'Golden Mean'[1] has proven also to be a wise prescription in matters of optimal behavior. It would seem that, when there *is* balance and symmetry between cause and effect in experience, the Life-Game is interesting and fun. When there is imbalance--too much cause and too little effect, or conversely, excessive effect and not enough cause--the game becomes tedious, demoralizing even painful. For example, a student who is intellectually advanced beyond the level of his studies has *too much* cause over them. He will be bored until he finds material which has some desirable effect upon him--i.e., material which sufficiently interests and *challenges* him, gives him barriers to overcome, and provides an ideally proportionate game to play.

The office worker who cannot offer even a mildly dissenting opinion, or act independently, has too little cause over her situation. She will not be job-satisfied until her ability to create *some* positive, and *winning* increment of situational effect on others is restored. It is the inability to create or receive a wanted

---

[1] An ancient Pythagorean concept of ideal numerical relationship which states that the division of a segment into two parts 'is golden', where the desirable middle is between the two extremes, one of excess the other of deficiency, linking it to Eastern philosophies that considered the whole is reflected by or contained in the part, and with an emphasis on harmony, balance, and a need for aesthetic proportion and optimally ideal symmetry in all things including *self-actualizaton* (Holosophy additions and modifications added).

> "Any idea seriously entertained, tends to bring about the realization of itself."
> -- J. C. Pearce, author
>
> "To an awakened consciousness, red flowers *bloom red.*"
> -- Zen Saying

Chapter IV - Life Gamesmanship

effect, or to *cease* creating or *counter* receiving an *un*wanted effect--i.e., the '*sub rational* inability' to be a capable and *authentically ranking* player in the Life-Game -- that constitutes *dis*ability.

The distinctions between *ability, inability* and *disability* are important and bear emphasizing. An *ability* is a demonstrable capacity to 'be, do, or have,' which one can exercise or withhold *at will.* If an individual has learned to effectively *use* the words of a particular language, he or she has the ability or *power over* speaking it, and can confidently bring about intended linguistic and communicative effects.

An *inability* is the normative lack of an ability to be, do or have due to some legitimate limitation, such as insufficient learning, training or practice. An English speaker who has never learned to speak Spanish, for example, has an *in*ability regarding the speaking of Spanish. Though he *could* learn to speak it, he is currently unable to grasp it instantly, the capacity exists potentially but is latent and un-realized.

Contrastingly, a *disability* is a *sub-rationally commanded* incapacity or *dis*-empowerment, which one often fatalistically (and falsely) attributes to some assumed natural flaw, or genetically pre-determined[2] personal 'can't be,' 'can't do' or

---

[2] Modern genetic research has increasingly shown that genome endowment per se, is insufficient to fully account for the range and nuanced capacities of the human being…e.g. the genetic structure of the chimpanzee and humans is 98% identical; does that 2% account for the magnitude of difference? A builder is generally guided by a blueprint, but is not *created* or *endowed* by it.

> "There are maximum security prisons, those with bars and guards, and minimum security prisons with fixed ideas, assumed victimhood and sub-rational and confining horizons."
> -- Holosophy Canon

> "The differences between a conjurer and a psychologist is that one pulls a rabbit out of a hat and the other pulls habits out of a rat."
> -- Anonymous

'can't have' condition, even though others have obviously overcome similar conditions. For example, if, in a corporate business context, an executive observes that he perspires, stutters and often feels nauseous when addressing his colleagues in the boardroom, he could easily regard his ineptness at public speaking as an inborn or 'natural' shortcoming, *'I'm lousy at giving speeches…I just don't have what it takes.'*

Such an individual might even come to assume that he is afflicted with some constitutional or genetic incapacity in the area of public speaking, instead of the more obvious failure to develop his natural talent created by a sub-rational and 'resistive' mental prohibition to *not seek and apply gradually, the learning efforts necessary to attain it.*

Factually, it is rarely a 'congenital' inability to speak that is affecting him; he possesses both the mental and physical capacities for speech, and is usually perfectly comfortable speaking; one on one; to others. What *is* lacking is the reactively suppressed willingness (*dis*ability) to master and *demonstrate,* in normal confidence-building learning increments, a relaxed and natural capacity to address and *appear* before groups or audiences.

Typical personal *dis*abilities in the *Kosmic* Life-Game can be symptomatically physical, mental or emotional in nature and can manifest 'challenged' behavioral deficiencies within any of the eight domains. Following are some common representative

> "I am big! I contain many contradictions."
> -- Walt Whitman, poet
>
> "The cosmos is a *Kosmic* residue."
> -- Holosophy Canon

Chapter IV - Life Gamesmanship

examples that also are associated with, or variants of, the sub-rational indicators[3] and conditions mentioned earlier.

I. Disabilities Regarding Self: general *dis*ability to communicate; consistent indecisiveness; compulsions; aversions; phobias; low self-image/esteem; criticalness, persistent lack of energy, intention[4] and creativity; timidity, unwilling to hold a position; tendency to confuse self with projected mental images, any persisting doubts as to personal identity capability or authentic selfhood.

II. Disabilities Regarding Family & Procreation: conflicts with gender orientation; inability to relate; dysfunctional sexual compulsions or incapacity; risk-intensive sexual practices or choices of partners; fear of intimacy, or rational commitment; persistent problems with children; poor relations with family, domestic violence, obsessive dominance or withdrawal.

III. Disabilities Regarding Group & Communities: aversion to joining, participation, or managing; poor team-player, disloyalty; no political sensitivity, subversiveness; obsessive counter-intention; sustained doubtfulness as to group membership; being an obsessive 'loner'; lack of candor; friendlessness; chronic victimization, fanatic radicalism or protest.

IV. Disabilities Regarding Humanity: racism; disdain for

---

[3] See Appendix V
[4] Intentionality = Holosophy defines as the degree of capacity for goal-directed attentiveness, focus, and conclusive action and resolution, i.e. ability to 'bring about' an effect predictably, expeditiously and with definite *finality*.

> "When the triple world is surveyed by the Bodhisattva, he perceives that its existence is due to memory accumulated from the beginningless past, but wrongly interpreted."
> -- Lankavatara Sutra
>
> "Man is a God in ruin."
> -- R. W. Emerson, essayist

Chapter IV - Life Gamesmanship

people; sustained pessimism about mankind's future; fixed ideas about the limits of the human condition, lack of extended global awareness, of, or concern about, potential impacts of own actions on world issues…disinterest in, and/or assumed inability to influence or effect, planetary or cosmic futures.

V.   Disabilities Regarding Biology: hygienic disregard of own body; chronic psychosomatic illness, neglect of potential pollutant or toxin-related disease factors, neglect or misuse of rational growth and marketing of vital global nutrient commodities; poor nutrition, allergies; addictions; broad ecological unawareness; fixed exclusion of anything but a strictly allopathic medical remedy; neglect of, aversions to, or unwarranted abusiveness to, animals, plants, life forms, or their symbiotes.

VI.   Disabilities Regarding Cosmology: critical of material wealth, ownership, or rational exchange; can't *have,* conserve, or improve physical things; chronically insufficient money or assets; not 'enough' time, energy, or space; aversions to places or things; vandalism, neglect or abuse of environment or possessions; preferring *dis*order; insensitive to any implicit meaning behind the contingency and order[5] of natural events. Perceiving the *physical* universe as unalterable, unfriendly, or

---

[5] The Jungian theory of 'Synchronicity', defined as "any apparent coincidence that inspires a sense of natural wonder or particular significance…a perceived *connection* between persons or events without *obvious* causation."…Holosophy extends this useful line of contemplation to reference through the cognitive 'hints' or intimation provided by such 'meaningful coincidence'; the underlying and profoundly interconnected, and encoded *fabric* of a consensual, co-oriented, and *playful Kosmos*…'clothed' existentially in the quantum 'non-locality' of *cosmic* events…always a revelatory portal to the implicit *Kosmic* coded signification which *shapes* contingency…

> "Every man who takes refuge behind the excuse of his passions, who sets up a determination to account for his actions, such as heredity, his nature, his circumstances, his society; is a dishonest man…"
> -- J. Paul Sartre, philosopher
>
> "To mis-habitually *avoid* awareness of personal causation or volition is the Holon's *primary* mistake…"
> -- Holosophy Canon

Chapter IV - Life Gamesmanship

inimical; or conversely, as the *only* existing domain.

VII. Disabilities Regarding Conceptuality & Spirituality: dullness, literalness, poor concentration and/or differentiation; resistance to learning; susceptible to confusion, fixated on dilemmas, and disabling paradoxes; closed-mindedness; inhibited imagination; generally insensitive to poetic, esthetic, or philosophic quality, value, or appreciation; disdain for methods or ideas of increasing personal ability or awareness; fixated ideation; feelings of hauntedness; possession; can't create; tends to confuse *concepts* with words or words with 'things', and encoded or symbolic 'information' with *meaning*; goalless; having obdurate contempt for anything not rigidly and reductively materialistic or 'scientific.'[6]

VIII. Disability Regarding Infinity: Since the 8th Domain, considered the realm of an ultimate generative ground of Being, *is* Infinite Potential without any additive, qualifying, expression or description, we might make implicit reference to *dis*ability in this area as; e.g. religious fanaticism, intolerance and zealotry, in all its diversity of forms; a general insensitivity to the epiphantic, mystical, or numinous; a resistance to any higher contemplative awareness, no certainty of, or intimations regarding, any innate Knowingness; 'suchness'; or the non-dual source of all cognitive specification.

---

[6] Since awareness or 'knowing' undoubtedly *exists,* as our most primal and immediate degree of certainty, existence *without* consciousness seems all the more incomprehensibly presumptive. The attribution of apparently seamless continuity to qualia or gestalts, which themselves are always abstracted assemblages of elemental and *dis*-continuous conceptuality, seems a curiously, convenient and tenacious 'mystery' of consciousness.

> "There are no 'equal signs' in nature."
> -- Holosophy Canon
>
> "Addiction is *sub*-rational *mis*-habituation covertly empowered by the case-contours false 'self'-equivalence, to the Holon's subliminal and authentic commitment to *automatically* experiencing the Game."
> -- Holosophy Canon

Defining *Dis*ability: Beyond Reduction-Biased Norms

The presence of ability, or the extent to which one is willing and able to demonstrate effective doing, participate, exercise power and *succeed* or constructively achieve, within each of the *proportionately emphasized* (optimized) eight Kosmic domains, is a basic indication of one's *willingness* to play the Life-Game.

For example, an individual Holon with a fully *self*-actualized personality (1st Domain), a healthy body (5th Domain); an able and constructive conceptual capacity (7th Domain); a commitment to stable intimate relationships (2nd Domain); a capacity for productive group membership (3rd Domain); a proprietary respect (not a self-diminishing reverence) for the physical universe at large (6th Domain) *and* an actively contemplative awareness of *each* domain's relation to an ultimate Infinite Potentiality of Being (8th Domain); exhibits a very high intent and capacity to *play*.

It is this type of *Kosmic*ally realized individual whom we intuitively respect and admire most in society, for he or she embodies an attainable, if idealized, norm of *full* engagement in the Life-Game, free of *sub*rational impediments and with decisive and proportionate awareness of, and *actively constructive* integration, between and within, *all* Kosmic domains.

Chapter IV - Life Gamesmanship

> "Several studies have shown that nutrient absorption from food is correlated with the degree of *liking* for the food."
> -- Holosophy Canon
>
> "Compassion is the chief law of human existence."
> -- F. Dostoyevsky, novelist

By contrast, a person who is sub-rationally life-disabled[7], feels incapable of participating or succeeding on one, or usually more of these game-spheres or domains of the Life-Game. An extreme example would be an individual who has a *dis*abled, and introverted personality (1st Domain); who resists or obsessively forms intimate ties (2nd Domain); or friendships and participancy (3rd Domain); who cares little about the human race (4th Domain); who, while distressed by a tendency to chronic illness, avoids proper hygiene, nutrition, and exercise (5th Domain); who disregards the care and conservation of personal possessions, or the broader physical environment (6th Domain); who lacks or dismisses any aesthetic, poetic, or 'higher' *conceptual* sensitivity or value appreciation (7th Domain); and finally one who has no sense of the numinous; or *meta*-physical awe about the ultimate non-dual source of all Kosmic consciousness (8th Domain).

Ability: A *Kosmic Re*-visioning

'Post hoc, ergo propter hoc.' Latin for: *After this, therefore in consequence of this.* This logical fallacy, i.e.; considering a subsequent event a *result* of a preceding one merely because of the temporal and material event-sequence, is very relevant to the error of considering that *all* human behavior is 'nothing but' *the result of prior* physical and *emotional* conditioning and/or earlier or current 'brain states.'

In fact, and by observation, human beings have the often-

---

[7] Mere impairment, as from an accident, is not disability in the *sub*-rational sense, as would be say, an addiction or obsession.

Chapter IV - Life Gamesmanship

> "The deeper layer (of *personal* unconscious) is *universal*. It has contents and modes of behavior which are more or less the same in *all* individuals."
> -- C. G. Jung, psychiatrist
>
> "Man is the dwarf of Himself."
> -- R. W. Emerson, essayist

overlooked ability and creative capacity to *respond* without reference to past mental-imagery, but with innate self-determined *familiarity*[8] to the present impacts and stresses of life...*How* they respond varies significantly, based on their understanding, background and ability to confront. However, decisions made *under* stress to "solve" a perceived threat to survival, tend to become compellingly mis-habitual. A person then becomes addicted to the *pictured* feed-back of these *past* traumatic belief-imprints (i.e. irrational and fixed solutions to stress).

Diminished awareness and with it, access to *familiarity*[9], then increases the Holon's further sub rational usage of these behavioral patterns with *false* survival-value (*fixed* 'rightness') and the resulting obsessive 're-use' of them to obsessively *simulate* rational choice.

In this way, a creative, self-generated but also fixed and irrational mental *response* gets *mis*-habituated through repeated use. Each *re*-enactment is also innately *volitional,* but with gradually diminishing awareness to the point where one has 'knee jerk' reactions to similar situations *apparently* disconnected from the early, now 'forgotten' decision and its associated traumatic event, with continuing, but submerged, and compelling importance.

---

[8] Since all images require 'prior' *knowledge* to be recognized, it follows that *image-less* knowing is the 'vera causa' or true source of memory, or the *applied* and selective imaginal representation of what is *already* 'known'; but without the cumbersome and redundant *internal* use of symbols to replace or 'assist' conceptual understanding.

[9] Holosophy's definition and *use* of the term entails a non-material cognitive repository or 'source' of specifiable meaningfulness, from which the *pre*-symbolic *knowings* that, combined, and attributed, give form and substance to *all* perception, are derived.

Chapter IV - Life Gamesmanship

> "The only difference between a wise man and a fool is that the wise man *knows* he's *playing*."
> -- Fritz Perls, psychologist
>
> Things deprived suddenly of their putative meaning, the place assigned them in the ostensible order of things make us laugh."
> -- Milan Kundera, novelist

This is not to trivialize real abuse or stress in early childhood but what is being overlooked by many 'modern' therapeutic approaches is that the Holon is in fact a *spiritual* agent and is *always and ably,* exercising power of choice even if that choice is currently denied, hidden, or subsequently 'forgotten.'

The proof is that when the being fully recovers (through Transformative Dialogue Technique) the memory and awareness of having sub-rationally exercised that power of choice to *create* the early charged belief-formation or personality disorder, the associated *behavior diminishes and dissipates.* The result is a choiceful *cessation*[10] by the Holon of all traumatically 'enforced' re-enactment, and the return of the Holon's capacity for a *knowing,* optimal causation and restored *domain differentiation awareness,* freely motivated by an idealized *future* and independent of any earlier and stressfully compelling mental-imagery.

For example, a child is beaten and *decides* in the moment, the "best way" to handle this threat to its survival, is to "feel nothing" and then "get even." Such irrational decisions made under stress often aquire subsequent command value. The individual tends to *re-apply* these belief decisions (automatically) when faced with new but 'similar' situations.

Depending on the depth and power of the solving response the pattern becomes, through repetition, fully *mis*-habituated, fixed

---

[10] The Holon's capacity for the selective and volitional *cessation of causation* of any self-reflexive mental *picturing* or compulsive imagery and imagining, would seem to be the *metaphysical* essence of *all* transformative meditative practice, the ultimate *re*-empowerment of the *de-*victimized Holon's true Kosmic identity.

> "I'm nobody! Who are you? Are you…nobody too?"
> -- Emily Dickinson, poet
>
> "Tell me, where dwell the thoughts, till thou call them forth?"
> -- Wm. Blake, poet

Chapter IV - Life Gamesmanship

and seemingly *in*voluntary. But did the abuse itself *cause* the behavior…or is it the result of the person's original, volitional, *response to it,* and then, its hidden but self-caused and continuing mental image *re*-imposition *by* the Holon itself?

What do the studies regarding these effects of childhood abuse *really* establish? That certain 'current' negative behavior is *associated* with[11] but not necessarily "caused by" the early stress. Of course, the typical reductionist interpretation does not recognize any unique personal *agency* or power of choice as a factor. However, it is demonstrable that there *is* a formative and *creative* exercise of *ability to choose,* even during a traumatic event.

Through applying a transformative and uniquely 'multi-vectored' unburdening Dialogue Protocol that gradually restores *full* access to these *primary scenes, and* that application reveals that the original response *was* volitional, as is the subliminal *continuity* of that response projected into the present! The client, when realizing this, is spontaneously and with typically *amused* insight, *enabled to cease to create* the original irrational response.[12] This *erasure* or volitional 'extinction' of the

---

[11] Correlation is *not* causation. Do pixels *cause* images, or groups of particles *cause qualia*, or does quantity contain or denote quality?

[12] A note on the typical client-responses associated with erasure: What is normally experienced when an *authentic* erasure, epiphany, or subtractive realization occurs, is a momentary (but sometimes protracted) feeling of well-being or even mild euphoria. It is as if one 'gets' the metaphysical "Kosmic Joke" of a revealed pretense of '*not knowing*', i.e. realizing, with a burst of amusement the absurdity of the Holon's contrived and locally '*denied* familiarity' with its own native creativity; as well as the relief and *joy* in that larger Discovery. In fact, the cascade of insightful inferences characteristic of a successful Dialogue, has even come to be somewhat aptly called the 'giggle *path*' one that usually results in a spontaneous and insightful laugh at the revealed absurdity of pretense: the presence or absence of which *can* be a useful diagnostic indicator of whether actual volitional *vanishment* of the targeted obstacle has occurred.

Chapter IV - Life Gamesmanship

> "Two leaps per chasm are fatal."
> -- Chinese proverb
> "Consciousness is *not* the mere computability of discrete elements of a process."
> -- Holosophy Canon
> "Nature loves to hide."
> -- Heraclitus

aberrant, 'pictured' patterns of belief and behavior, *at their traumatic point of origin,* is the essence of all Holosophy *re-habilitation* through dialogue or re-education.

Actually, most modern helping disciplines seem to implicitly presume that people can in some measure *change* their minds about their past experience. (How else could they improve?) Holosophy, in particular, holds *further*, that the ability to *change* one's mind (and therefore behavior) must be based (with a certain hierarchic logic), on the assumption that *one made up one's mind to begin with!* Again, this can be confirmed with a vivid certainty of recall, through a wide variety of Holosophy Cognitive Applications.

Once free of disabling sub-volitional automatic-responses we can be *appropriately* emotionally responsive, *but* with a viewpoint that is newly and more deeply framed by the innate, and compassionate[13] awareness that *all* beings are *ultimately responsible* for the mental condition they're in. Nothing less is demanded by the facts, or by any society's practical and reasonable justice system and ethos, than the need for actual and primary personal accountability.

To again pose the basic question considered in earlier chapters; *Why* do such sub-rational *dis*abilities occur? If we are causative by nature, if ultimately what we are, do and have derives from what *we* postulate and perceive, why is it in a

---

[13] Compassion is a higher and truer level of 'resonant awareness' of both shared *and* personally responsible, causation, within the Kosmic fabric of play.

> "There is nothing left to you at this moment [satori] but to have a good laugh."
> -- Zen Master
>
> "There is nothing of which everyman is so afraid as getting to know how enormously much he is capable of doing and becoming."
> -- S. Kierkegaard, contempletive

deeper sense, that we seem too often unable to create the effects we want, achieve our aspirations, or live without needless suffering and tribulation?

The *ultimate* answer lies in the cognitive research discovery of a *very* early *traumatic distortion* of the archetypal dialectic template, or thematic *pattern* of existence. The Holon's sub-rational but *creative responses to that profound stress* were deceptively[14] 'grafted-on' and sub-rationally endowed as a mentally-pictured surrogate for the Holon's natural *Kosmic* Life-Game pattern or Code of *self*-imposed Life-game-enabling limitation.

More immediately, it is a matter of ability to perceive and postulate *gone awry*. To better understand how this *dis*abling mechanism operates, we will in the succeeding chapters attempt to revisit in more detail the distinctions between the Holon or essential being, and its *projected* computational vehicle, the mind[15] and consider how the Holon *agency*-consciousness, with *its* mind and *its* brain form a rational, limiting, hierarchical, and coordinated instrumentality for expanded execution of life-game tasks and objectives.

---

[14] We must be mindful here, of the Holosophy principle that *any* 'sub-volitional' act or response contains *as its genesis*, the Holon's own innate ability to postulate a *response* to any challenge or situation.

[15] Here we continue to expand and deepen the *sub*-rational causation hypothesis that the aberrative repetitive power of traumatic experience comes from *only* having *survived* it (see page 15); to the deeper and more generalized view that traumatic command value is sub-rationally derived from the Holon's *own* assertive recreation of game-sustaining limitations, *through* the 'case-contours' redundant mockery of the Holon's own necessary and volitional game-participatory *self-limits* of ability.

> "The greater good is often the *lesser* evil."
> -- Holosophy Canon
>
> "Though error is not evil itself, it can bring evil in its wake."
> -- Gerald Shroeder, physicist

Chapter IV - Life Gamesmanship

    Let us further explore in the next chapter the insidious, uncontrolled and self-sabotaging mechanism of the Holon's hidden, "brain-correlated" and *disabling re-use* of selective traumatic mental-imagery and the associated and fixed identities it contains to mistakenly solve the challenges of adversity, both to *ensure* its own survival as a player, and even more basicly, with seeming, but misplaced trauma-born relevance, the continuity of the Kosmic Game itself!

Chapter V
Consciousness: a Triadic Mysterium, Holon, Mind and Brain

> "I do not seek...I find!"
> -- Pablo Picasso, artist
>
> "To make biological survival possible, Mind at Large has to be funneled through the reducing valve of the brain and nervous system. What comes out at the other end is a measly trickle of the kind of consciousness which will help us stay alive on the surface of this particular planet."
> -- Aldous Huxley, author/essayist

V - Consciousness: A Triadic Mysterium
HOLON, MIND and BRAIN

It has already been suggested in multiple contexts that the essential Being, Spirit; or *Holon* is a *non*-material entity clearly distinct from the body, mind, and brain it *uses*.[1] If the mind is likened to a computer program (or software), the *Being* is the *user* that creates, understands and inputs programs that manipulate and extract data, but is not *itself* merely the mechanism, the data, or the program that is projected, *processed and applied, or the biological "hardware" that supports it.*

As spiritual beings (Holons), we *use* our minds for some things, but not for *all* things. For example, our minds are apparently not required for us *to be aware*. How often have we searched mentally for a *known* but "missing" word or datum? While the mind is thinking, or seeking to retrieve or locate something implicitly *known* but not yet *represented*, *we*, while waiting for its appearance, remain *aware,* and therefore independently and *knowingly poised*, and distinct from, any *prompting parade* of objects or thoughts. Consciousness *is* that innate, but conceptually *capacitative* quality, of each separate witnessing Holon that makes the ability to postulate and perceive all substantive *things*[2] -- *including the functional mind*

---

[1] The self-absorbed "thinker," however, *if* only a mental copy of the hosting Holon, is actually "itself" an erasable and redundantly pictured egoic "*thought-process*" and *not* the authentic non-material source and *projector* of all thought, including "self"-consiousness.

[2] The great physicist and mathematician John Von Neumann postulated the logical necessity of an "abstract ego" as the final and ultimate "observer" that completed the causal chain of observational steps that reduced the cosmic "wave-form of probability" into an *experienced* actuality and event.

> "I think our consciousness is not just a passive epiphenomenon carried along by chemical events in our brains, but is an active *agent* forcing the molecular complexes to make *choices* between one quantum state and another."
> -- Freeman Dyson, physicist

> "An optimist thinks that this is the best of all possible worlds. The pessimist is afraid that's true."
> -- Anonymous

Chapter V - Consciousness: A Triadic Mysterium

– possible.

Similarly, as has been emphasized consistently, we do not *need* the mind's externally projected images, mental products or spatial perspectives, to conceptually *know* i.e., meaning is metaphysically senior, as a *potential* signifier or attributor, *before* it is represented by an *image,* however acquired, or *searched* for.[3]

To illustrate: for a moment *conceive* of what "beauty" is; what "goodness" is, what "truth" is; or what *responsibility* is. Did you *first* observe or consult, with a mental-image or process[4] to confirm whether you understood the selective and infinitely nuanced applicability of these concepts? Familiarity, i.e., the intrinsic well-spring of *meaning* or contextually specified knowing, *precedes* any word, symbol, or image that is projected to *represent* it and "*remind*" us of its precise connotation.

You may have learned as a child the *words* which usefully represent or communicate underlying concepts and which were understood to have *meaning* in various contexts. But you as the essential Being, can intuitively grasp or *recognize* the abstract cognitive multiplicity of these concepts; their contextual significances or *meanings* because, as Plato[5] famously demonstrated; *You* already inherently *know* (i.e., have an imminent and *meta*-physical *familiarity* with) them...and can

---

[3] The senior and controlling awareness that we *have* a destination, is not a part of the selective "step by step" *searching process* of the journey as a whole...as knowing *intent,* is senior to the conscious increments of sequenced attainment of *objects* of knowledge.

[4] It is assumed by some that the source of all conscious thought is actually the *unconscious* "processing" of and by brain-states... resulting in the effective *elimination* of any conscious *agency*; the very thing *essential* to recognize and extract or "de-code" qualitative *meaning* from quantitative "information" or process...at *any* level.

[5] Refers to Socrates extracting by simple questioning a geometric theorem from an uneducated slave, in Plato's, dialogue "The Meno."

> "Perception is constrained imagination."
> -- Fransisco Verella, neuro-scientist
>
> "Mind as we now see, has the power to alter biological matter significantly; that three pound lump of gelatinous ooze within our skull is truly the mind's brain."
> -- Jefferey Schwattz MD, psychiatric researcher

(and *do*) *conceptually endow* the appropriate linguistic symbols with apt, *shareable,* meaningfulness; an ultimately *prior knowing!*

Awareness, potential knowingness, and the *selectable* knowings of *familiarity,* are interchangeably linked as cognitive qualities, emanating from the same innate realms, and are choicefully accessed and interpreted, as above, *by the Holon* to optimally respond to each distinct situational requirement. The mere external *form*, grammatical arrangement, or sound of the words doesn't "contain" the infinitely varied contextual and *implicit meaning* necessary to understand, convey and *apply* them *explicitly.*[6] Semantics is *not* syntax, nor word the thing.

Life-Game *Imag*ination: The Purpose of Mind

As non-corporeal Holons, we operate *from* the conceptual or spiritual plane. When we assume bodies, we also require an interesting faculty and *means* to operate on the physical plane. The mind is apparently *used* to form a nexus of *"re*-minding" imaginal convenience within the spectrum bounded by these two planes of existence. It serves to assist Holons (as incarnate beings) to interact and communicate, in an effective but confined and *enthralled* human proximity, with, and within, the *represented physical* universe.

---

[6] Sufficient evidence and demonstration of this un-definable background *matrix* is that the very concept is comprehended. It would seem difficult to "*know* about," and communicate what and *how* we think, using only thought *forms* themselves; images without epistemic context – a context that to accommodate infinitely nuanced meaning must itself be infinite!

> "The good of man is the active exercise of his soul's faculties in conformity, with excellence or virtue."
> -- Aristotle, philosopher
>
> "Cortical activity is spontaneously re-mapped as the minds selective attentional patterns of activity *change,* and are shown as *acting* on brain."
> -- Merzinch and deCharms, neuro-scientists

Chapter V - Consciousness: A Triadic Mysterium

The mind might be likened to a kind of refined, bio-electric *search-engine* operated by the Holon to automatically monitor, reflect and more importantly, *limit* perception and knowing. It provides the *reduced* scope of awareness[7] of the events and domains necessary to be and remain an enthralled or suitably tacit and "*un*knowing" Kosmic game-participant.

Seemingly, and by analogy, we *use* mental-mechanisms to perceive, analyze, codify, and file bits of data or referential mental-images about our surroundings; to assist in physically communicating with other beings; to command the autonomic functions of our bodies; and to analyze, decide and *compute* survival options.

There is also the assumption that, *like* the computer, we use our minds as "difference-engines" or assisting estimating *vehicles,* to learn and re-apply *survival* behavior, and to process the bits of data-input that comprise our perceptions and experiences; filing them in mental-image "storage," for future use as the basis for all action and decision.

Ultimately, however, the mind-computer analogy is flawed, since an automatic, algorithmic (rule or menu-driven) *process*; which is all a computer (hardware) *or* its program (software) is capable of, as earlier observed, only produces electronically *structured* "bits" or grouped symbolic permutations of en-coded *ones and zeros* or, in the brain, a *bio*-electrically on-off firing of neurons, or chemical and molecular *processed* messaging of

---

[7] The mind *and* the associated *brain* combine to act as an efficient reducing "valve" for limiting *total* perception in order to accommodate Kosmic participation by the Holon…

> "*Life only* avails…not the *having* lived…"
> -- R. W. Emerson, essayist
>
> "Ultimate Cosmic finality is seen by modern science in the form of "black holes," which turn out not to be "eaters" or destroyers of information, but storage containers for its retrieval and possible *re*-minding re-use?
> -- Holosophy 6th Domain Conjecture

Chapter V - Consciousness: A Triadic Mysterium

neuro-transmitters.

Somehow, *meaning* is a deeper qualitative thing, on a larger *conceptual* canvas, contributed by a *knowing* Holon *using a mind*, who must conveniently and selectively replicate, *de*code, and extract *that* knowledge which is distinct *from* its referent symbology[8], and from the *quantitative information* conveyed by it!

The mind and its particular brain vehicle, or *bio*-computer, serves as a kind of programmed "*reducing* valve" for selectively framing the omniscience or the *total cognitive familiarity* of "Mind at Large" i.e., the potentially *unlimited* awareness and ability of the 7th and 8th domains. The Holon, as player/*agency,* requires a *benevolent pretense* of limitation, and uses the mind as an ideo-cognitive engine to manage that tacit perimeter. It does this in order to convincingly display itself, functionally, from *within* a localized *game*-sanctioned scope and boundary, which also enables a *trans*actional gaming-potential[9] between domains.

There is, then, a fascinating difference between the conceptual or qualitative knowing of the Holon and the quantitative image-based computable modality, of the *mind*: While the Being simply *knows, conceptually*, what it can conceive, it also *links* itself creatively to the projected mind which *processes*

---

[8] Symbolic in the sense that any image or mental object, i.e. an element of a computation is a potential "information" or en-coded data *carrier*, a vehicle for attributed meaning, but *not* the meaning *itself.*
[9] A *believable* and authentic seeming "presentational immediacy" or a convincingly consensual playing field, that permits the full range of exchanges that characterize the essence of Kosmic Play.

> "All materialist explanations are promissory; all the *hard* questions are consigned to an endless future for answering."
> -- Sir John Eccles, neuro-scientist
>
> "For man has closed himself up…till he sees all things thru narrow chinks of his cavern."
> -- Wm. Blake, poet

Chapter V - Consciousness: A Triadic Mysterium

information, i.e. knowledge quantified and trans*formed* into symbols in the form of "pictures," or mental-images with distinct and *assigned* cognitive values, made meaningful *upon translation.*

Consider again, what is "beauty"? Against what background is "it" defined and *made* meaningful? Usually one does not question or confirm with an interior monologue whether or not one "understands" a particular *use* of the word, or *wordless* apperception *of* "beauty," (or *any* abstract idea). You *knew* in the moment, what it *means* now, or was for *you*, because you spontaneously endow its *conceptual* representational capacity with the framing context of higher epistemic *familiarity.*

One may, however, also have created and viewed a fleeting *imaginal*[10] "picture" of something beautiful, like a rose, or tried to envision a "way" to define and describe beauty, but even these ordinary habits of "thinking" are *already* symbolic and communicable representations of *meanings,* to which we must have *prior conceptual access* and *attributing capacity,* in order to refer them selectively, to *things.*

That is the difference. The Being (Holon) *already* knows; the mind *pictures* that knowing. The mind is the presentational stage or "theatre" for the conceptually formed bits, "dots" or "pixels" of projected mental processes to *appear.* The Being connects, combines, organizes, and thereby perceives them, giving them *meaning.* And

---

[10] Imaginal, in that its playfully conceptual "substantiality" is evanescent *not* redundantly persistent. The mental "substance" involved is perhaps a *useful* transient application of the scaled-down original ability of the Holon to *create* perceptible, *solid*, but *non*-particulate *imagined* universes.

> "Saying that consciousness is completely brain dependent is like saying that a TV signal and image must be "caused" by the TV set because it disappears when the set is turned off."
> -- Holosophy Canon
>
> "The invariable mark of wisdom is to see the miraculous in the common place."
> -- R. W. Emerson, essayist

Chapter V - Consciousness: A Triadic Mysterium

through an act of intentional creativity, ideas are thus made "flesh" and given substance. Existence is fundamentally reified knowing.[11] Semantics is therefore distinct from mere syntactical "processing;"[12] a kind of "mental matrix." (An ordering and selective filter for the enabling the *balance* of perception and *non*-perception, needed to embody, dis*play* and communicate *useful knowing*…i.e., Kosmic optimization of the Game.)

What Does The Brain Actually *Do*? Correlations vs. Causation

Let us revisit in somewhat more detail, the researches, of one of the first scientists to observe *in vitro,* and purportedly, *in* the *actual* brain, the mind's mental-image processing, Dr. Wilder Penfield of Montreal's McGill University. Penfield, a neurosurgeon, discovered as early as 1951 that if he stimulated (during brain surgery) the live, exposed brain with an electrode, he could *force* imagery clearly derived from the patient's memory. He then proceeded to do this with hundreds of patients over many years. These recollections were usually comprised of vivid eidetic percepts: i.e., actual and vivid sights, sounds, tastes, smells, tactile sensations, and emotions:

> *In one case, a so-stimulated patient could "see" a "7-Up Bottling Company (and) the Harrison Bakery." Another patient saw "a man and a dog walking along a road near his home in the country." Yet another heard a song being played, as if by an orchestra.*[13]

---

[11] The 7th Domain defines and represents the contextually specified capacity to know and thus "bring" about the localized substantial habitation of the phenomenal world (6th domain) or cosmos.

[12] Semantics here refers to *meaning*, the conceptual and qualitative essence of what is *known*. Syntax refers to how meanings are *organized* and logically structured as grammar or symbols, e.g. in a sentence to *simulate* existential order.

[13] None of the subjects, however, ever felt *connected* personally or *volitionally* to the stimulated memory images as would be the case if memorial activity is *identical* with mere cortical brain states.

> "The brain functions as an organ of *limitation*, to restrict conscious awareness of the external world to what is practical and useful."
> -- Henri Bergson, philosopher
>
> "Do ideas "exist" *outside* of the human mind, or only *in* the human mind, or when no human mind *existed?*"
> -- Werner Heisenberg physicist

Chapter V - Consciousness: A Triadic Mysterium

Dr. Penfield soon found, however, as had neuro-scientist K. Lashley earlier, that surgical excision of the exact brain-matter stimulated, did not remove the correlated "memory," which was apparently *not* localized in *any* specific brain tissue. These seminal experiments, and many since, have suggested that the mind somehow records experience[14] not only in the form of still "photographs," but also in the form of entire "movies" or real-time episodic event-sequences that are apparently *not* functionally or structurally identical with any specific *part* of the physical brain.

When Penfield's patients were brain-stimulated to remember, they seemed actually to *relive* incidents as if they were occurring in the present moment; but if the brain tissue site of the stimulation was *not* the origin of the eidetic images as had been confirmed experimentally, what was?

Dr. Penfield's work also seemed to demonstrate that consciousness itself, is *correlated*[15] with, but not essentially *caused* by, memory, mental states, *or* the brain. Despite years of varied and persistent attempts, he was, by his own observation, never able through electrical or surgical means to reach or touch, what he considered to be, the *central core* of any patients awareness, or persona; leading him to speculate at the end of a long career, that the illusive *"mind"* and its projected *mnemonic* imagery was perhaps remotely-viewed from a source *outside the body*!

---

[14] It must also be noted that it is an amazing but often overlooked fact that perception is composed of the *synchronized* integration of *many* distinct senses into a *creatively* coordinated "whole;" we smell and touch *what* we see and hear and taste…*plus* an additional *fifty-odd* perceptic capacities…*all* integrated!

[15] By "correlation" is meant a pre-established harmony, resonance, or inter-activity, but not a "one to one" identity, or "causal closure chain."

> "Atoms are not things."
> -- W. Heisenberg, physicist
>
> "When we see a tree and *call* it a tree we think this sense experience is final. But the sense experience is only possible when it is *conceptualized.* A tree is not a tree until it is inferentially subsumed under the *concept* tree*ness..*"
> -- Holosophy Canon

Chapter V - Consciousness: A Triadic Mysterium

More recent research conducted by British neurologist John Lorber, already referred to in chapter two (the case of the student with *no* brain), would seem to further suggest this, as do accurate (and confirmed) "unconscious" memories recorded during operations; also those recovered from patients revived after having been brain dead (*no* electrical activity of the brain) for as long as twenty minutes, and even from revived cold-water drowning victims with completely suspended electro-cortical brain activity, for as long as one and a half hours![16]

Even if these, and many other, similar research anomalies did not exist, it would seem, *prima facie*, physically (if not logically) impossible for the brain to "store" routinely, *and instantly* cognitively search, *recognize,* file, and cross-*reference* the billions upon billions (if not *trillions*) of "bits" of data that are *theoretically* required to account for what is perceived, recalled, and evaluated by the computable mind in even just a few *minutes* of life (including the vast implicatory relevances of *contextual* knowing); let alone the mental activity of a lifetime, and, of course, even putative *pre*-existences, encompassing *many lifetimes*[17] and obviously with *different,* brains!

It is estimated that the mind, at *whatever* level of consciousness may functionally account for it,[18] records unitary

---

[16] It is interesting to consider also that memories of previous incarnations, if valid, could not conceivably be attributed to a particular *present brain* which did not then exist nor, in fact, could cosmological origins *require* brains, if *dis*-embodied *consciousness* "predates" them, a challenging concept for science and cosmogony in general.

[17] Detailed memories of such "near death" experience, i.e., *no* brain activity, have been recovered and validated, indicating that "something" was very much *still* conscious during such periods of "brain death" or trauma-engendered incapacity (see appendix VIII).

[18] Eg., as a vehicle to facilitate and accumulate the emergences from the background "collapses" of the *possible* quantum events to the *actual* "known" perceptions and "observables".

> "Observers are necessary to bring the universe into being."
> -- John Wheeler, physicist

> "Anecdotal accounts of patients having sudden and total death-bed lucidity including those suffering from Alzheimer's disease are numerous in the medical literature."
> -- Holosophy Canon

perceptual events or "snap-shots" at the equivalent rate of twenty to twenty-five *pictures* or perceptic "bits" per second, just like a motion picture camera (which was *designed* to simulate human image-perception) records single frames.

The brain, as noted in Chapter II, may be *used* by the Holon, with a presumed *quantum-linkage* to the mind, to *somehow* filter, reference, or mechanistically manipulate these representational "bits" of information, for limited everyday use[19] but it does *not* originate or *store* this raw en-coded data *or* the *de*coded conceptual thought processes, or *knowings* of its users.

As with the computer, the recording and storage of information is ostensibly a *syntactical* or "processing" *function* of the mind, *interpreted semantically* (as meaning) by the Holon. The question also arises again, as to just *how* the mind (considered as a mere supervening *veneer* of brain/states) could, independent of any conscious and *knowing* agency or operator, *perform* the essentially *epistemic*[20] searching process for *choosing* memories, data, words, etc. (not even considering relevance, *context*, or *nuance*) This.is beyond the cognitive *processing* capacities of *any* computer, real, or proposed, since it requires *infinite* contextual data capacity!

In stark contrast to the Holon's varied capacities to originate conceptual knowledge, the *computer's* presumably brain-based

---

[19] Interestingly, human and ape brains and genes are remarkably similar in size and configuration. The *vast* differences in cognitive capacity would seem to hardly result from the relatively *small* amounts of additional but still similar brain tissue.

[20] Epistemic: relating to knowing as a capacity in the deepest sense as contrasted with mere programmed matching of already coded "information." See "epistemological"…

> "Just get to the root. Don't worry about the branches."
> -- Zen Saying
>
> "The word is *not* the thing. The map is *not* the territory. We must always be "*conscious* of abstracting.""
> -- A. Korzybski, General Semantics

Chapter V - Consciousness: A Triadic Mysterium

filing searches are basically *programmed* systems that mechanically *match* "electron-configurations" or binary checker-board patterns of "ones and zeros" (*not* qualia, gestalts, or abstract *meanings*) in its silicon encased software-bit "memory."[21]

The computer operates as has been emphasized, only syntactically (as a physical process) and is not "conscious" of abstracting and doesn't *know* or interpret what it is finding *semantically as meaning,* only the *conscious* witness-*user* (Holon) knows *what* it wants to find; *directs* the search, and recognizes *when* and *if* the programmed searching *mechanism* has "found" it i.e. has merely *matched pre-selected grids!*

Searching as a fundamentally *meta*physical, and noetic[21] capacity is obviously *not,* the presumed to exist semantic and "intelligent" function of a physical and brain-bound electro-chemical *process. A* process which, however complex its circuitry, does *not* have, in principle, the cognitive, *meaning-*intensive, and interpretive (non-computable) *familiarity* capacity, of a pure and *knowingly* conscious Holon-agency.[22]

Memory: The Mind's Kosmic Library

While Dr. Penfield did demonstrate that memories are in

---

[21] So called "parallel processing" or "quantum computing," i.e., multi-layered and simultaneous calculation of data input, however *vast*, still requires a *recognition* and matching of the *qualitative* aspects of experience, or *gestalts*... which even the *hyper*-complex qu-bit recombination of ones and zeros, without the conceptual or *meaningful interpretation* of consciousness, cannot provide; but can *simulate*, with an *operator* to cognitively optimize!

[22] Apparently a Holon remains an imminent integral persona even when possessing *multiple* brains: a young Chicago woman believed she was normal until an MRI scan revealed that she had three small but fully formed and functional brains. She lives a normal life as a bakery clerk, with no apparent evidence of "multiple" personalities. "*Weekly World News,"* November 12, 1996, pg. 35

> "Some dance to remember. Some dance to forget. We are all just prisoners here, of our own device."
> -- The Eagles, Hotel California
>
> "The mind merely *displays* the varieties of limited *knowing*…"
> -- Holosophy Canon

Chapter V - Consciousness: A Triadic Mysterium

some way *correlated* with brain-states, and also *somehow* stored outside the brain, as illusive and apparently *eidetic*[23] mental-pictures; the work of a long list of contemporary researchers further suggests that the mind's vast storehouse of such memories, *however* accomplished, includes mental-pictures of *every moment* of our lives.

One such investigator, Dr. David Chamberlain, of the Pre- and Peri-natal Psychology Association of North America, has contributed a great deal of research to support the existence of this faculty. Using hypnosis, Chamberlain has assisted many patients to vividly recall not only memories of childhood, memories of birth; but *pre*-natal memories of incidents which apparently occurred while in the *womb*! Here is one example:

> *My client Loretta remembered something that happened while she was still in the womb. Her mother was standing on the deck of a boat, holding tightly to a railing, trying to steady herself. "She's looking at an island. There are other people looking over the water, listening to someone tell them where they are going, explaining to them about the island. My father is standing by my mother, worried about her. He wants to know if she is all right. The rocking of the boat is making her sick. She sat down and is rubbing her stomach. I feel the motion on the stomach, the rubbing. My mother was rubbing me, and she was worried If I was all right. She was relaxing me by rubbing."* [24]

Obviously, the client's mother and father were surprised to hear this story of an event that took place during the third trimester of a pregnancy! They said, however, that she had correctly reported their outing on a sightseeing boat, something they had never told her about. Even if they had, it would not

---

[23] Refers to mental images of an event containing the full range of its sensory and three dimensional perceptual content, an exact representation or "copy" of *experience*.
[24] Chamberlain, David B. "The Expanding Boundaries of Memory." ReVision, Volume 12, Number 4, (Spring, 1990) pg. 14

> "Karma is never the *cause* of enlightenment."
> -- Shankara
>
> "*Sincerity!* If you can fake *that*, you've got it made."
> - Groucho Marx, comedian
>
> "Clusters of 1"s and 0"s, or the dots of a screened image; as, and by themselves *mean* nothing."
> -- Holosophy Canon

Chapter V - Consciousness: A Triadic Mysterium

adequately explain the empathy, perception and apparent detailed accuracy, or the emotional *relief* she found in the recounting of her experience.

In addition to such confirmed accounts provided by his own patients, Chamberlain's many reports of *intra-uterine* memory include the observations of other researchers:

> *Australian psychiatrist Graham Farrant (1986) discovered in repeated primals that his mother had attempted to abort him. When he telephoned his mother and asked about it, she denied it, but after he described to her how she had taken a bunch of pills and gotten into a hot tub, she broke into tears and said, "You couldn't know this; I never told anybody."* [25]

While Chamberlain cites many cases of pre-natal memory, we find numerous others have observed and investigated what appear to be, the experiences of *previous lifetimes.* We have already mentioned the extensive research of Dr. Ian Stevenson, who has carefully and with robust rigor, investigated literally *thousands* of personal accounts of reincarnation. Dr. Bruce Goldberg, a licensed hypnotherapist, is another credible researcher (among many) who reports dozens of such cases in his book, *Past Lives, Future Lives.* Such credible and expert investigative reports are burgeoning.[26]

Consciousness, Flawed Perfection: A Summing Up

---

[25] Ibid
[26] A few examples from a long list: David Cheek, MD, a surgeon, has conducted and published many accounts of early "unconscious" traumas restored to fully abreacted memory; (including those from "unconscious" patients during major surgical procedures and confirmed by personnel present at the time) another surgeon Bernie Siegel, MD has recovered similar "forgotten" memories from patients as has Stanislav Grof, MD who has *re*viewed memories of pre-existences in many of his patients.

> "The only past that *can* be changed (erased) is the one that is still, mistakenly, kept "in" the present."
> -- Holosophy Canon
>
> "Are these *real* poems or did you make them up?"
> -- query, at a reading…

Chapter V - Consciousness: A Triadic Mysterium

One of the main themes of this book is that the mind, and the psycho-physical and emotive continuum it facilitates, is *used* to link the Holon with the wider *condensed* "substance-mentality" of the 6th or "physical" domain of the Kosmos. Implied in that connective role is a dedication to preserving the highest survival perspectives and well-being of the essential instrument of play the body, and its symbiotes (5th domain). The mind implements this mission in different ways, depending on the degree and levels of its *user's* awareness and ability.

What inferences we can reasonably draw from the consciousness research discussed so far, strongly suggests that an instrumentality of the mind, ordered and controlled by the Holon, "photographs" and records all of its experiences, both of this and previous lifetimes, in the form of mental-pictures, and that all of these *created* representations, however hidden, traumatic and painful, are potentially available to us as memorable content.

However, as we have stressed repeatedly, while the mind may somehow record and store *and use* these pictures continuously and precisely, it does *not*, depending on its state and degree of awareness, always do so rationally and effectively.

The Conscious Mind: of Wholes and Holons

As has already been considered from various heuristic perspectives mental-pictures, i.e. the functional "processing units" of the conscious mind are not themselves, as *objects,* conscious.[27]

---

[27] Panpsychism, which attempts to resolve the traditional philosophic difficulties associated with "mind vs. matter" dualism, holds that all physicality is to some finite degree *conscious* (however rudimentarily) as an object enacting

> "A hundred thousand lemmings *can't* be wrong."
> -- An anonymous "idea fixe"
> "90% of the Politicians give the rest of us a bad name."
> -- Henry Kissinger, statesman

Chapter V - Consciousness: A Triadic Mysterium

We (Holons) are conscious *of* them while *using* them much like an operator "uses" a computer's software and CPU.

This *analytical,* or rationally and consciously *managed* portion of the mind, operates during states of wakefulness, and accomplishes its pro-survival mission primarily through *assisting* the Holons' conceptual or contemplative reasoning.[28] It analyzes what it perceives by comparing present data input with relevant knowledge of the past, and *conceptual* estimations of the future, to form *globally* i.e., Kosmically, optimized decisions and conclusions.

When we look at a tree, for instance, the brain *correlated* and assisted, conscious mind actually "perceives" within a limited field of vision, a *selected* and complex *mosaic* of minute, discrete picture-symbols (reified knowings). These, when *put together*, or observed, are selectively *joined* like dots of light on a computer screen, to "form" the *projected* perceptual object or gestalt (whole) which, perceiving Holons, in a co-interpretive act of thralldom, tacitly, *agree* to *name* and recognize, as a particular "tree."

We as Holons, *choose*, but in the ordinary state of consciousness, and using the mind, *habitually* attribute and give an *enthralled* order to, a formative *rendering "template"* for, the *totality* of emergent qualia:[29] tall + bark + branches + leaves + *n* = tree, i.e. a combined aggregation of seamlessly represented *meaning*fulness, *combined* to

---

subject, i.e. an "active occasion" per A. N. Whitehead. Holosophy adds the theoretical developmental potential inherent in every such "object" to become through increasing such *awareness,* a *volitional* subject.

[28] The mind can contain "computational" automaticities set up by the Holon to assist as "shorthand" calculation-support in the "background" of awareness and typically used to "expedite" the more ordinary, immediate, and *habitual* but sub-rationally unencumbered "*knowings.*"

[29] A word referring to the "gestalt" or unitary *wholeness* of a perceptic element, expressed in modern philosophical terms as, "redness," "hardness," "roundness," i.e., reified ideation or "qualities" made substantive or *quantitive.*

> "The triad has a special beauty and fairness beyond all numbers, primarily because it is the very first to make actual the *potentialities* of the monad (oneness)."
> -- Iamblichus, philosopher

> "The world thus appears as a complicated tissue of *events* in which connections of different kinds alternate, or overlap, or combine, and thereby determine the texture of the whole…"
> -- W. Heisenberg, physicist

Chapter V - Consciousness: A Triadic Mysterium

form a projected field of *co*-existential but "constrained" imagery, or the *Reality* of appearance.

The *more* detailed grouped, and organized, symbols or percepts the conscious/mind automatically combines, presents, and perceives, the finer more nuanced distinctions the Holon can make. It can provide the perceptic basis to tell the difference between seemingly *identical* twins, discern subtleties of taste discrimination between fine coffees or vintage wines; observe that the *"same"* individual is at times callous and unfair, while at others, is kind and just and, as a higher priority, more optimally begin to notice the *freeing* differentiation between distorted sub-rational indicator imagery and the more positive and reasonable quality of *natural,* un-aberrated, and *differentiatively* cognitive human experience of rational *familiarity*.[30]

Have you ever noticed while driving, an indistinct object in the road up ahead, and wondered whether it was a piece of tire or a struck animal? The object in and of itself had no specific meaning until you got closer, and the conscious/mind could perceive and "process" its finer details, to extract and specify real *thingness*; i.e. *unitized,* and combined qualia, for the Holon to further interpret and *make* meaningful.

If the preceptic data the conscious/mind is "processing" is accurate, its decisions and conclusions will also be reliable. If it makes mistakes, the input data will prove on inspection to have been faulty. For example, if a *fully* aware individual has *recorded and*

---

[30] Combined conceptuality, the generative mechanism of existential appearance, results from the Holon's innate, *creative* ability to specify, interpret, and *infer,* i.e. to optimally *postulate* and perceive *specific* holistic aggregates of manifest *knowing* or *familiarity*, which is short form, imaginal, and "para"-computably or *referenced* knowing.

> "My one regret in life is that I am not somebody else."
> -- Woody Allen, comedian
>
> "Fixed belief or *conviction* is the residual "certainty" imprinted by creative, but sub-volitional response to *impact*."
> -- Holosophy Canon

stored directions to a party, follows them to the letter, and arrives at the wrong location, obviously he was either given the wrong information, or somehow he mis-recorded or misunderstood what he was told, i.e., no *computational* error was made.

The *computability* of the conscious/mind is ultimately rational (and error-free). It apparently never errs in the *way* it functions. It only *appears to err* when its data, or *interpreting* belief-system, is faulty, missing or *sub*consciously *weighted* by trauma or stress, and *then* *sub*-rationally applied or interpolated, *without* a total, or *real*-time, rational or optimizing context, of factual data –*relevancy*.

The *Sub*rational Mind: Mind*less* Precision

As described in earlier chapters, the *sub*rational mind operates with a tenacious and primitive *survival* telos, or goal-impetus; continuing to function, even when the individual is experiencing extreme stress or trauma-induced reduction of awareness. Attention is then diminished, by degree, to *semi*-consciousness (i.e. groggy, dazed, stunned, shocked or anesthetized), and finally, if the duress is sufficient, is seemingly reduced to a state of complete "unconsciousness."

Paradoxically, however, the *sub*rational, or rudimentary *re-acting* mind is, in fact, by observation and test the final refuge and capacity for a surviving "residual" *awareness*. It is, (consciousness being the core substrate of existence), *never completely un*conscious but always, to some vestigial degree,

> "Memory is the corpse of experience, from which the life has vanished."
> -- Alan Watts, author, philosopher
>
> "To choose is to selectively *direct* contingency; a *downward* causation, ideally independent of any pictured remembrance or frame."
> -- Holosophy Canon

Chapter V - Consciousness: A Triadic Mysterium

aware and capable.[31]

It should again be emphasized that this *primal sub*conscious mental-faculty does not, while minimally aware, have any actual ability to reason, or analyze, or make useful distinctions. Therefore, when it records painful experience without the higher benefit of the reasoning conscious/mind, it acts, very much like an infant, *or* a highly suggestible hypnotic subject; tending to *blindly* accept and obey without question.

Operating to mentally duplicate, store, and incorporate data in a kind of indelible "fail-safe" preservation mode; but *without* the ability to evaluate degrees or *differences,* the "unconscious *sub*rational" mind records literally, *any* idea, data or perception, that is imprinted on it during such a *lived through* engramic event; which is therefore "labeled" *permanently* as having, *fixed-framed value* for future "survival" reference and auto-priority feed-back, simply because it *was* survived.

On the surface, this "crisis-mode" stimulus-responsiveness may seem to be an innocuous tendency, perhaps a helpful one…and apparently even "necessary" to *actual* survival. Numerous self-help books and lecturers advise us to engage in "positive" auto-suggestion, affirmations, or *sub*liminal learning to install, or *implant* what is assumed are "useful" *commands* for programmed, *re*-habituated, or automated, behavioral *success*

---

[31] Research shows that, for the holon, true unconsciousness is only an apparency occasioned by the holon's selective "unawareness capacity" to forget *after* the "unconfrontable" traumatic event, and as "necessary" to rationally limit its' level of experience, and awareness…e.g. Many experiments have been conducted using regression to recover "unconscious" memories from injuries, operations, and even pre-natal incidents of stress with independent confirmation of the data obtained. Notably, regression experiments done with *twins* recovered significant, un-coached and separately obtained and confirmed data-correlation of such events that were *mutually* experienced…

> "We possess *art,* lest we should perish of the truth. Art, in which precisely the *lie* is sanctified."
> -- F. Nietzsche, philosopher
>
> "The atheist finds creation so perfect that he can dispense with a Creator."
> -- Marcel Proust, author

Chapter V - Consciousness: A Triadic Mysterium

e.g. for quitting smoking, losing weight, and feeling more relaxed, assertive, or "success" motivated; *all* are forms of enforced *natural* ability.

But in fact, *utilizing* the *sub*conscious mind's unreasoning stimulus-responsive, almost sponge-like *sub*rational capacity to absorb (and reenact) pain-related imprints, can and does produce, unpredictably negative results, because it *borrows* and *reinforces* the lowest vestigial level of mind, i.e. the very tendency toward pain-associated, mis-habituated and image-dependent *sub*-rational iteration that, with cognitive optimization we seek to *eliminate.*

Ultimately, all such *installed* and limited "success"-behavior, is actually out of the conscious control of the *person,* and is simply substituting or piggy-backing, one habitual behavior with, or on to, another (albeit seemingly positive or preferable) *without erasing* the underlying *cause* of the unwanted condition; a sub-rational and traumatic-born *"safe-solution;"* a pain enforced *belief* structure, on which the "new" habit-behavior is grafted, and which it ultimately *energizes* and strengthens.

The installing of such *replacement* and potentially addictive *mis*-habituation, therefore omits and counters the real *natural* state of fully restored *dis*-habituated[32] or *re-optimized* awareness; and further undermines and devalues the Holon's *native self*-determinism, which is innate and doesn't require any unnecessarily added "positive" reinforcement.

---

[32] Distinguishes the sub-volitional nature and cause of the problem ("mis") with its removal and correction ("dis") through erasure.

> "It's not what we don't know that hurts. It's what we know that ain't so."
> -- Will Rogers, philosopher/actor
>
> "So long as the subjective experience of consciousness cannot be fully accounted for, the explanatory gap between the physical processes that occurs in the brain and the process of consciousness will remain as wide as ever."
> -- Dalai Lama

Chapter V - Consciousness: A Triadic Mysterium

Robotic *Re*enactment: The hidden liability of *"SURVIVAL"*

Considering that the *sub*rational mind goes into survival or *imprint mode* whenever an individual is overwhelmed by more stress, shock, pain or loss than he or she is able to *confront* with *full* consciousness,[33] then in such moments, with the rational, conscious mind partly or completely shut down, the individual enters a quasi-hypnotic state of automation.

Against the survival-threatening backdrop of pain, the robotic *sub*rational mind, now in a fail-safe *life-game preservation*[34] mode, records as inviolate, and *"must*-repeat," *survival* dicta, *all* sights, sounds, tastes, smells, emotions, spoken words, *thoughts,* and even identities, present in the trauma for automatically conditioned future *re*application, to *re-guarantee* the putative "survival" of player *and* game.

> *At the University of California at Davis, for example, psychologist Henry Bennet and his colleagues played audio tapes to surgical patients while they were under anesthesia. The audio tapes instructed the patients to signal that they had heard the messages by pulling their ears during a post-operative interview. Later, when Bennet conducted the interviews, nine out of eleven subjects who were played the tapes during surgery pulled at their ears, though none remembered having been told to do so...*[35]

As has been emphasized throughout, such imprinted percepts--unchallenged, unreasoned, and unfiltered--become the

---

[33] Exceeds the Holon's *personal ability* boundary condition or game "toleration-perimeter" for *consciously* experiencing unconfrontable force, pain, or tolerable magnitude of event.
[34] Not just "self"-preservation, but that of *all* domains of the Kosmic Game in Progress.
[35] Refer to "Siegal, Bernie, MD, Love, Medicine and Miracles" (New York Harper and Row – 1986)...Page 46 (See also the account of a stenographer brought to an operating room by an obstetrician to record verbatim all conversations during the operations conducted...The patients were later hypnotized and the transcripts were verified *word for word*.)

> "Surprise is the rational alternative to outrage."
> -- Holosophy Canon
> "Negation is the highest form of thought."
> -- A.N. Whitehead, philosopher

Chapter V - Consciousness: A Triadic Mysterium

automatic, stimulus-response, *crisis*-survival-data of the *sub*rational mind. Once installed, they can be *re*-activated or re-cued *any* time the individual encounters similar "reminder" events, percepts, or circumstances in the present.

When the triggering event occurs, the *subrational* (*sub*-conscious) mind *commands* the individual, automatically and unconsciously, to re-experience, and *re-enact* all of the original physical sensations, emotions, and *mental* responses, which were experienced and to otherwise behave irrationally, as if the incident, pain, and stress were occurring *now*, and "need" to be *"survived"* again!

"Sticks and Stones" and *Words Can* Hurt

The *sub*conscious mind's ability to "hypnotically" command the mind and body this way is very powerful. If a traumatic event contains a bit of spoken data like, *"This is making my head spin,"* or *"I feel sick,"* it can act through complex psycho-somatic command channels, to *produce* dizziness, or nausea "on demand," as a compulsive *re-enactment* of "survival."

More deleterious and far-reaching, however, can be what the sub-rational mind *does* with a *thought* or postulate, made *during* a trauma, i.e. a decision, conclusion, *belief, or personal rule or "law"* which the Holon may have subliminally *made* (and recorded), prompted by the pain-associated content of, an engram, or traumatic life-episode which, "survival"-weighted, then tends to be obsessively re-enacted and literally "obeyed" as

> "Mere repetition is distinct from and does not insure the rational *continuity* of optimum survival..."
> -- Holosophy Canon
>
> "There is no history, only biography."
> -- R. W. Emerson, essayist

Chapter V - Consciousness: A Triadic Mysterium

an immutable post-traumatic "law" of behavior when subsequently cued by a *reminding* event or circumstance.

> *An actual case in point: "Miss B" a college student-activist is delivering an impassioned but unpopular speech on campus. The gathering crowd begins to jeer and throw things, and finally to break into a riot. The speaker is knocked over and trampled in the scuffle. During this period of intense confusion, shock and pain, the student "decides," sub-rationally, "Speaking out is a dangerous thing to do, even though I know we're right."*
>
> *Without the full benefit of her trauma-diminished and displaced, conscious, rational mind, there is no differentiation as to which situations, or to which audience, or on which subjects "speaking out" is dangerous; so her generalized, irrational conclusion prompted only by the situational and data content of the event, is recorded and imprinted by her subconscious mind, and later "self"-imposed as a fixed, unreasoning and disabling "personal law" for her, a survival lesson "Miss B" learned too well!*

"Command Value": Failure's Warranty

As described above, the student is *not* aware, of course, that this charged belief-imprint has been formed. When normal consciousness is restored, she gradually recovers from her *physical* injuries, and returns to her normal life. Her enthusiasm for making impassioned speeches is tempered after the incident, but she has, as yet, no *conscious* sense of *sub*-rationally *believing* that the ability to "speak out" in *every* sense, is now subject to a *mysteriously* generalized and "unconscious" taboo...

Some years later, the former student takes a position in a large corporation. She feels strongly positive about the company's business model, services, and philosophies, though they are controversial in her industry. In fact her current corporate-related ideas and feelings are very "similar," to the way she felt

> "At exactly the moment that a dog's master gets up from her desk in an office to return home, the dog walks to the window at home and begins watching for her. This experiment repeated on many occasions demonstrates existence of non-local communication."†
> -- Rupert Sheldrake, biologist
>
> "Acting on stress-born beliefs inevitably leads to all the unwanted conditions in life."
> -- Holosophy Canon

Chapter V - Consciousness: A Triadic Mysterium

about her reformist political position in college. One day her senior approaches her with a request to "speak out" to local community officials about the company's innovative waste-management policies.

His routine and job-related request triggers a *flashpoint*. The whole traumatic mix of pain and unconsciousness in the earlier incident of "public" speaking is *re*-activated; prompting an increasing but inexplicable; negative over-*reaction* both to her boss, and even to the *idea* of giving such a talk, that is (to others!) obviously and wildly disproportionate to what's actually involved.

She is not aware, analytically, that the command-value of the underlying imprinted *personal law* buried in her *sub*conscious mind, is being intrusively "grafted"[36] onto her current behavior but, however inexplicable their effects, she certainly *feels* them, emotionally and physically. She becomes increasingly worried, now with a recurrent pressure in her chest and develops a mysterious aching in her muscles.

A *pattern* of "sub-rational indicators" begins to emerge, at first she simply delays with various explanations; giving the talk, but finally gives it under *protest* and botches it badly. In both cases, her impaired judgment and ability to perform, unless *remedied*, significantly affects her current job situation as well as her future career opportunities, and general well-being.

---

[36] The sub-rational "self-duplicate" or mental-image formed ego-substitute "case-contour" is the hidden but Holon *endowed* repository of such obsessive, ability-constraining, but *believed* "lawfulness" and conviction.

> "(In science) if there is no way to falsify or confirm a hypothesis (by observation), it belongs to the realm of metaphysics together with astrology and spiritualism. By that standard most of the universe has *no* "scientific" reality, it's just a figment of our imagination."
> -- Leonard Susskind, physicist
>
> "Eternity is *very* long. Especially toward the end."
> -- Woody Allen, humorist

Chapter V - Consciousness: A Triadic Mysterium

In fact, such stress-born *beliefs* can cause not only obvious disabling *failure*, but also generate chronic *psycho*somatic illness to *sub*-volitionally ensure and implement it. Severe and unpleasant mal-emotions such as anger, fear, and apathy, containing *psycho*-genic tension, can convert to *psycho*somatic illness, and *physical* symptomology.

Unwanted attitudes, addictive behavior, and all kinds of self-limiting post-traumatic physical, mental, and emotional symptoms of distress can manifest as tension-based dysfunction, and pathology. Here is how the *all-survived-meanings-are-equivalent*, "survival-logic" imprinted, belief-system apparently operated in the above case example:

> *The client's "A=B=C=D" sub-rationally monotoned "mind"-set tells her: "Speaking out is a dangerous thing to do, even though I know I'm right, and feel strongly about my position." = "Talking about the company's policies is speaking out." = "Speaking out about the company's policies is a dangerous thing to do, even though I know I'm right" = original incident of conflicted and disabled behavior and injury-related symptoms = re-impose and re-enact trauma to ensure "surviving" it again!*[37]

Mis-Habituation:
A Trauma-labeled "Charge" To *Re*-act

† Sheldrake, A New Science of Life (See References)

To make matters worse, every time an individual *reacts* irrationally to a *reminder* stimulus in the environment, the tendency to do so *again,* is strengthened, because *any* repetition

---

[37] Equating the simple, useful and *controlled* automatic ties of behavior with the *obsessive* uncontrolled behavior-induced and enforced through a re-enacted traumatic experience, results from the paradoxical and sub-rational dictum that the game must be "repeated" in order to be *continued.* Actual and primary Kosmic *continuance* or "the creative advance into novelty" is confused and interchanged with *pictured* or *repetitive* survival, as literal iteration.

> "An adventure is only an inconvenience rightly understood.
> An inconvenience is only an adventure wrongly considered."
> -- G. K. Chesterton, essayist
>
> "In business, pick two: good [be], fast [do], or cheap [have]."
> -- Holosophy Canon

of an *intent*, even if unreasoned, and whether the source of the resulting action or feeling is conscious or not, is falsely perceived as *survival-relevant* and is therefore habit-*re*-enforcing, in a broad and *generalized* sense.

In the case example given, the student-turned-executive, "Miss B" tended to find it easier and easier to respond irrationally to *all* requests or opportunities to "speak out" on any issues she felt strongly about, simply because she had done so *mis*-habitually in the past. The recurrent, now *favored* pattern of communication *dis*-ability, becomes, through repetition, "self"-perceived as *normal* and the individual becomes *failure*-prone.[38]

As her irrational reactions became more and more habitual, prompting more and more failures, she found it increasingly difficult to communicate successfully about *any* important issues at all. Moreover, *in extremis*, she seemed to lose *any* desire to do so; developing a withdrawn, even cynical attitude at social gatherings and business meetings, generally averting eye contact, or frequently becoming remote or distant; reactions imposed as part of a guarded "private-universe" in order to avoid and *resist* sub-rationally the *challenges* of *all* "dangerous" communication.

Again, in such extremes, once this interrelated stimulus-response material is in place, almost *anything remotely similar* can set it off because its source consists of non-verbal, mental pictures hidden from conscious view, and because each bit of

---

[38] The case-contour in "dictating" operation-mode (mis-habitually), operates as the sub-rational *virtual* self...

> "I call *that* creature a rhinoceros" said Adam. "But why call it *that*," asked Eve."
> "Because" said Adam, "it obviously *looks* like a rhinoceros, that's why!"
> -- Anonymous
>
> "Any fool can make a rule."
> -- H. D. Thoreau, essayist

Chapter V - Consciousness: A Triadic Mysterium

occluded "reminder-data" carries equivalent weight in terms of *believed* "survival" significance. One percept in the stored episodic picture sequence is *equal* to every other percept, even if it is entirely different, and being *falsely* equal, distorts the present, real-time event, when cued (triggered) by a similar *reminding* circumstance.

As in the above real-life *human*-trauma exemplar of the introductory "leopard and antelope" example given in Chapter I:

POLITICAL SPEECH = PAIN = LOSS = BUSINESS PRESENTATION = COMPANY = IMPORTANT ISSUE = FAILURE = *SURVIVAL!*

It is *as if* the elements of this, traumatically re-signified pictorial complex are *all* the same.[39] Given the right "cue-ing" circumstances, the experienced presence of any *one* of them can activate, trigger, or *sub*consciously *remind* the person of all or any of the others, resulting in a confused, conflicted, and *compelled re*-action to a *forgotten* "menace" from the past.

Stress, in general, can prompt an individual to be more susceptible to this triggering stimulus-response mechanism, because whenever the conscious, rational mind is diminished, or out of sorts, to some degree, the hidden material of the *sub*rational mind is *more* likely to intrude into one's life, and interrupt otherwise rational, healthy, normal interactions and even physical well-being.

We have repeatedly emphasized, that when such stressful or

---

[39] At base, a sub-volitional and displaced *mockery* of the Holon's native capacity to *combine, reify, and perpetuate,* conceptuality into necessarily seamlessly *whole* fabric of "Kosmic Qualia" and *combined* quantum constituents.

> "The function of the mind is essentially to *re-mind* the Holon of what it selectively *needs* to know to limit and legitimize its Kosmic participation."
> -- Holosophy Canon
>
> "Limits are conceptuality constrained."
> --Holosophy Canon

painful incidents are coupled with irrational decisions and forcefully imprinted during moments of pain and diminished consciousness, we may later be prompted to be *reenact,* automatically and unconsciously, the original irrational and counter-productive meanings, feelings, and behavior contained in those incidents, however ancient and forgotten their origins.

In fact, *any* decision, however convincingly "right" it seems, that is *imprinted on the subconscious mind,* is likely to cause problems later, if only because *no* decision is right or useful *all* of the time.[40] It may seem reasonable and even practical to *"Say nothing to a (real) attacker,"* if he has a knife at one's throat. It is however, entirely impractical to "say nothing" to a *sub*consciously cued and indiscriminatingly superimposed *mental-picture* of a forgotten *past* attacker; confused, *in the present,* with a completely different *past* person and event, whether in a business, marriage, or *any* social situation.

Negative Conditioning: A "Revised" Perspective

Historically, the chain of events described above has been generally referred to as "negative or operant conditioning." Countless experiments have been done with animals[41] to document its occurrence. For example: one study of particular interest found in our own review of the literature was conducted

---

[40] As the saying goes…Even a broken clock is "right" twice a day…

[41] There are anecdotal accounts of how the "father" of operant conditioning, the physiologist Pavlov, was inspired by watching Russian circus performers "train" their famous "Dancing Bears." They would heat coins, place them on the ground and lead the bears over them, while playing a musical instrument. The animals soon "performed" without the inspiration of the coins, as did Pavlov's laboratory dogs who salivated on a bell-ring "cue," in a later scientific application of the principle.

> "Each fact is *more* than its form. The definitiveness of fact is due to its *form* but the individual fact is a *creation*, and creativity is the ultimate *behind* all forms, inexplicable *by* forms."
> -- A. N. Whitehead, philosopher
>
> "Pictures…look at *us!*"
> -- Paul Klee, artist

Chapter V - Consciousness: A Triadic Mysterium

by Dr. E. L. Hunt and reported in the Journal of Comparative and Physiological Psychology as early as 1949:

> *In Hunt's experiment, a spasmodic reflex was induced in chicken embryos by subjecting them to the sound of a bell, along with a series of electric shocks, while they were still in the shell. After they were hatched, the same chicks responded spasmodically to the bell alone, while a control group which had not been given shocks ignored the sound.*

Obviously, there are crucial and dramatic differences between negatively (i.e. traumatically) influenced human beings and similarly *conditioned* baby chicks! Chief among them is the fact that as Holons, we have the higher causal and *cognitive* capacity of a reasoning *consciousness* to potentially *"extinguish"* (erase) any installed compulsive behavior patterns.

Once we become *aware*[42] of the hidden, imprinted images and "out of date" meanings compelling our actions and discomfort; once we view them directly and realize their irrationality, all tension-based command power for mindless re-enactment *erases*. They shift immediately into consciously recallable (and controllable) experience, and like the *awareness*-cancelled post-hypnotic suggestions discussed can no longer compel our thoughts and feelings.

Historically, the early "traumatic-incident-reduction" approach to explaining human aberration was also *reductionist* in its assessment of *no* degree of human *volition*. This view has, of course, been greatly modified and extended by cognitive researches, (both

---

[42] As in the post-hypnotic suggestion example, as well as being a guiding principle of behavioral reflex or "referent extinction" in other "therapeutic" approaches that seek to mechanically "remove" trauma without reference to the full spiritually contextual *Kosmic* theory and background contained in Holosophy…

> "Experience is not what happens to a man, but what a man *does* with what happens to him."
> -- Aldous Huxley, author
>
> "A good and reasonable philosophy can be written containing nothing but *jokes* (without being facetious)."
> -- L. Wittgenstein, philosopher

Chapter V - Consciousness: A Triadic Mysterium

technically and philosophically) to include the spiritual nature and true causative capabilities of the Holon;[43] as an ultimately free and responsible *agent;* its core commitment is to creatively maintain (not obey) a wider *Kosmic* dialectic "blueprint" or *guiding* template for game participation and action.

In earlier chapters, for example, we have suggested that *every* moment of our existence is recorded and somehow "stored" in the form of potentially *recreatable* mental-pictures and computations. We have also, based on wide and careful research, suggested that our *memorial* existence as Holons may span *many* distinct lifetimes and genealogies. If this is the case, memory storage is *not* brain[44] or genetic based, but is a matter of an *innate cognitive* familiarity-capacity of the Holon to *know again* and to creatively *re*-vision and *erase* through *Transformation Dialogue,* any unwanted residual or *unconsciously copied* effects of its Kosmic adventuring. (Shades of Plato!)

At this point, however, we might again pose and consider a key question underlying the issue of all aberrant behavior: Why, in the *deepest* sense, do people respond differently to the "stored" imprinted material in the *sub*conscious? Why are some deeply and permanently affected by a post-traumatic *re*-activation of a painful experience and others only mildly if at all? Why do some soldiers, for instance, recover quickly from

---

[43] Many of the salient distinctions between the materialistic, reductionist approach to the mind and the higher cognitive and spiritual focus of cognitive optimization are outlined in Appendix II.

[44] Some physicists have theorized that the observational capacity of the Holon (consciousness) may be *selectively* correlated with use of "brain states" to directly influence and *selectively* "collapse" the quantum wave function.

> "We possess *art*...lest we should perish of the truth...art, in which precisely the *lie* is sanctified."
> -- F. Nietzsche, philosopher
>
> "The atheist finds creation so perfect that he can dispense with a Creator."
> -- Marcel Proust, author

Chapter V - Consciousness: A Triadic Mysterium

wartime traumas, while others continue to feel victimized and devastated by "post-traumatic syndromes" for years afterwards?

In fact, we observe a distinct correlation between each person's unique degree of ability to *confront*, i.e. remain optimally aware of, and to *restore and acknowledge causal ownership* of the created mental response to a traumatic event, and the rate of recovery from, any profoundly traumatic experience.[45] What, then is the true archetypal source and nature of victimhood, and its final *erasure* or deconstruction[46] in the Cognitive Optimization Dialogue?

A deeper, more exacting, and probative, answer to this from Holosophy's extensive researches, can perhaps be summarized in two words: *success-reluctance*...A discussion of this complex and seminally important phenomenon and its profound kosmic-theoretical implications follows in the final chapter. *(Please see Appendix XIV, Consciousness as a Scale of Knowing.)*

---

[45]For example, observations made during WWII of survivors of merchant ship sinking's confirmed that men who succumbed to hypothermia in open life boats were *not* the old timers, "out of shape" and middle aged, but the 18 to 25 years olds, in the prime of life and otherwise healthy and strong! The difference seemed to lie in the ability to *confront*, of the older people, longer *hardened* by experience of war, training and the stress and vicissitudes of the natural social environment and work place. *Victimization* is essentially the disabling sub-rational feedback of blame, mal-emotion and total denial of personal responsibility, following the receipt of the unwanted or injurious effects, whether real or imagined. Such residual "post-traumatic" effect, *when* fully confronted in a compassionate, *not* "sympathetic" dialogue setting, is obviously a target of erasure in counseling.

[46]We must remember that the Transformative Dialogue *is creative de*construction, and as used in Dialogue, must *feature* the pragmatic goal of *erasure,* and not *mere endless semantic re-formulation*. There must first be the accurate description or episodic *denotation* of the event and then the gradually revealed and inferred *connotations* of image, idea, and value-redundancy, and finally the cessation of all false signification and iteration ...The *signifier* must emerge "whole" from the signified, as is always the priority, with any objective epistemic paradigm. Post-Modern De-Construction is acutely situational, and relativistic, tending to ignore this anti-relativist admonition against infinitely regressive parsing in any mode of communication.

Chapter VI - Success Reluctance

Chapter VI
Success Reluctance: How the Kosmic Code sets the Stage for Subrationlity

> "There is no evil committed, even for its 'own sake,' or for *no* reason, that is not selected, therefore preferred, therefore *valued,* and that therefore *must* be referencing a *scale of value* containing and implying a range and extension of some *higher* acknowledged Good…"
> -- Holosophy Canon
>
> "Success and failure are equally disastrous."
> -- Tennessee Williams, playwright

Chapter VI - Success Reluctance

VI - Success Reluctance
How the actual Kosmic pattern sets the stage for *SUBRATIONALITY*

It has been the abiding and seminal theme of this book that, to have a game or an interactive *consensus thralldom*, Holons must collectively and continuously create, reify, and make "substantial," from a *mutually enthralled* source[1], the essential *projected* aspects, or *domains:* the Kosmic game"s reified arena of play.

Since we are playing within a physical universe, for example, a continuum of matter, space, energy and time must be initially constructed[2] and *jointly* perceived as real and *persisting*. In that we are playing, using bodies, which are dependent on other life-forms, those bodies and their symbiotes must also be made to persist. Since, also, to accommodate the essential *exchange-* related nature of *gaming,* we gather and form *inter*acting alliances; societies, nations, companies and groups. These too, must be made to endure as part of the over-arching Kosmic fabric of agreement.

In perpetuity, or for as long as we agree to *create*, have, and use them, do they actively constitute the artifacts,

---

[1] The 8th domain is an infinite potentiality…but a *potential*, infinite or otherwise, is not yet a *game*; the Kosmos actualizes that potential through a co-existing consensus of *Innate Ideas* made manifest…A primal and immanent fabric of Dualities, that, reified in creatively projected *alternation*, bring about the primary plus and minus boundary delineations of all emergent existence…(See the Kosmic 'equation', appendix III).

[2] Recall that in quantum physics, *conscious* observer-participancy is required to collapse the wave form, i.e. *extract*, through an act of perception and 'measurement'…a specific *emergent* event from a cosmic background of merely *possible* eventualities…

> "Archetypes are the innate thematic determinants of existence."
> -- Amit Goswami, physicist
>
> "Thralldom is the forgetful but self-determined and benevolent pretense of *not* knowing in order to *stage* ordinary experience with full conviction and believability."
> -- Holosophy Canon

Chapter VI - Success Reluctance

accouterments, or shared realities of the Kosmos. Actors need their particular costumes, props and stages only for as long as it takes to enact a scene, or the play itself; however long that may be. It might require billions of years for the planet nurturing blaze of a sun, or eighty plus years for the current average human span, or a scant few days for a family reunion. There must be a shared and on-going *co*-creation[3] of all such game enabling realities which contribute to and support a vital and tacitly *complicit Kosmic* continuity and co-survivorship!

We might reasonably deduce, that there must be a shared or agreed-upon core-archetypal schematic "blue-print" of the universe--in other words, the consensually encoded *deep*-structured and templated *meaning-potentials* for all domains; or category realms and *knowings* forming Kosmic actualization.

The *Kosmic* Life-Game must remain relatively constant, reliable, referenceable, and pragmatically *true for all*. It must be continuously intended and *endowed,* but "*un*consciously"[4] i.e. with an enthralled but *selective un*awareness; a *primal,* bounded, and creatively filtered frame-work for recreational[5] pretense and dis*play,* for all Holons, and for the duration of the Kosmos.

Modern physics suggests that, indeed, the instrumentality of

---

[3] Creation in this ultimate sense is selective subtraction from the infinite possibilities of Being by coordinated acts of *specified* knowing, ordered and *formed* through *intended* paradoxically framed and projected exception, to the innate non-duality.

[4] In the sense that *any* supporting foundation can exist stably and unseen, but subject in this case to the review, adjustment, and *repair* of Cognitive Optimization.

[5] It is this most fundamental and powerful intentional capacity of each Holon, the mockery and displacement of which, endows and converts 'it' into a *pictured* case-contour replication of the basic metaphysical urge for Kosmic continuity and community.

> "Our belief and attention (to something) are the same fact."
> -- Wm. James, philosopher
>
> "To logically assert the 'untruth' of objective truth, is, at once, to *confirm* it."
> -- Holosophy Canon

Chapter VI - Success Reluctance

consciousness itself, transforms, by what must be, inherently *generative* acts of "observational participancy"… the inchoate "*un*conscious" *potentia* of the physical quantum-microcosm "*into*" the orderly *actualities* of ordinary experience. This is apparently done in a deeply coordinated harmony by *all* sentient beings, in what Holosophy holds to be a *designed* dis*play*, manifesting as an orderly and innately templated *Holo*archy, the eight domain "Lila:" the *Kosmic* Life-Game.

Obviously, in the "macrocosm" of daily existence, we *intend* to have our bodies breathe, we *intend* to maintain balance while moving and we intend to digest our food; yet we do so in fact, with little or no *awareness* of any underlying *micro*-events or any supposedly *correlated* electro-chemical brain mechanisms of such subliminal intending.

If indeed we *had* such broad and complex micro-sentience there would still seem to be no window *framing* mechanisms i.e., *selective* private landscapes, or "limiting fields of perception,"[6] necessary for bringing about and *managing* the grosser activities that require *particular and generic* circumstantial discernment. One cannot steer clear of the pothole in the road ahead if one is focusing all of their attention on micro-managing the exact and minute quantum-physical "reductions" involved in depressing the car's gas or brake pedals.

---

[6] We can refer here to the 'basis' problem in quantum physics. How does consciousness experience qualia, or 'selective perceptual slices' of the universe, instead of a 'smear' of unfiltered *micro*-cosmic quanta, of which our 'organs of perception' are *themselves* supposedly composed? In other words, *how* are the quantum dots "connected" within a particular perspective and *what* connects them *purposively* to *form* the qualia or gestalts of ordinary experience?

> "No more good must be attempted than the public can bear."
> -- Thomas Jefferson
>
> "Fortune and adversity *both,* challenge the sub-rational mind to disable 'itself.'"
> -- Holosophy Canon

Chapter VI - Success Reluctance

The multi-dimensional survival-contexts of life, then, i.e. the *stable data* of the universe and the attendant conditions of the Kosmic "consensus-community" *game,* are preserved without our being *directly* aware, in the moment, that *we are* preserving them. Just as the actor cannot act effectively if he is, at the same time, also *thinking* about acting; neither can we directly experience the "enchanted loom," the complicit and complex fabrication of the "*un*truths of convenience" the artfully managed *selective unawareness* that characterizes the tacitly enthralling "grid" of the Life-Game.

If however, we know *fully*, in the immediate and active sense, that *we* are actually the enchanters and grid-makers, the spell is broken. *The light from the sun is useful and enabling, as long as we don"t look at the source directly.*[7] This is the *essence* of the Vedic Lila's; "divine play," or as Holosophy interprets it, the Kosmic Code of playfully realized *consensual thralldom.*

The apparent objectivity of life, the sense that it exists "apart" from *us*, is a constructive illusion; a *useful* untruth, which *unifies* primordial conceptual duality, *selectively,* into an apparently independent-*thing*ness; which we ourselves foster and create "*un*consciously." How do we do this? How do we create without knowing *we* are creating?

Is it by our known capacity to make *mental-images* more and

---

[7] Reminiscent of the Neo-Platonist "Deus *Absurditus*" the *hidden* deity, 'perfect' but not fully manifest. From Holosophy perspective, there must rather be distinctive conceptual realms of *actualizing* polarities forming the reified dialectic and emergent category-domains of a Kosmos, *necessarily* 'unseen' concepts made 'flesh.'

> "It is the *theory* that decides what we can observe. Imagination is everything, it is the preview of life's coming attraction."
> -- A. Einstein
>
> "That which is at variance with itself, *agrees* with itself."
> -- Heraclitus

Chapter VI - Success Reluctance

more *vivid*, extended by some latent, but *unlimited*, power and degree to an ultimate and actual *created solidity?* By a kind of rationally synchronized, on-going *co*-creativeness; and from a fixed archetypal core of thematic regularity and meaning, do we imaginally externalize and call into substance our *souls conceptual-code as* the Kosmos?

This seems accomplished by being, doing, and having, with a rational *suspension* of full awareness; an automated selectivity or *grooved* observer-participancy. An intrinsic "grid of the psyche" which filters, extracts, endows, *projects,* and gives "surface" and materiality, to the innate *meanings* of the Kosmic matrix, or 7th domain, producing an effortless and unfolding verisimilitude.[8]

Considered more narrowly, there are, however, *degrees* of automaticity or habituation. Involuntary bodily functions for example, such as heartbeat, respiration and digestion are reflexive; the strongest and most permanently bio-programmed or ingrained, because the survival of the body (the basic, requisite "piece" for playing the game) depends utterly upon their uninterrupted and efficient bio-functionality.

The impulses to sneeze or scratch an itch are, by degree, less reflexive. They are necessary functions much of the time, but not always, and can be, and often are, controllable. The ingrained routine of brushing one's teeth in the morning is

---

[8] Perhaps in this context, the Leibnitzian paradigm of a universal 'pre-established harmony' seems a useful analogy. To this we add the idea that the quantum 'collapse of the wave form' into macro-cosmic events and solidities, is an aspect of the potential imaginal capacity for the consciousness of the Holon to *bring into being*, any idea, form or *degree* of substance or solidity i.e.; to construct *any* universe by intentional incrementality.

"Attribution is both the imaginal permission and *command* to *be*."
-- Holosophy Canon
"Effective leaders put words to the formless longings and deeply felt needs of others."
-- Warren Bennis, executive

Chapter VI - Success Reluctance

merely helpful, not immediately indispensable, and therefore constitutes a usefully "weak" level of automaticity or self-directed habituation. Those impulses or automaticities constitute the limiting boundary conditions agreed upon to be the level of conscious "filtration" that is *fundamental* to continued game perception and participation.

These are the thematic rules and constraints which *must* go on "backstage" as *deep-structured co-creation,* regardless of what we are aware of "onstage." This *core belief-encoded* and limiting, "self"-containment is the Holon's most deeply valued, and automatic *kosmic capacity*; and *is* what makes the whole enthralled experience of game-play both *valuably plausible*[9], and selectively *noticed.*

However necessary for the sustainment of the Kosmic Life-Game, automaticity or habit, *is a fact* nonetheless, like anything not totally controlled, it is subject to a gradually increasing *cosmic* randomization; to a tendency toward chaos, increasing entropy, or *disorder*, with a commensurately increased *imprecision* of action and intention with often injurious consequence. Some more obvious examples:[10]

> *Things can go wrong when one's attention is not consciously and precisely directed. The phone rings; the homeowner's attention goes to the caller, not to the bathtub she is filling; the water rises, spills over, and damaging leaks occur. A baseball player runs with narrowed focus to catch a fly ball; he collides with an unseen fellow player; both men sustain injuries. The driver of an automobile, drowsy from long hours at work, falls asleep at the wheel and drives his car into a ditch. All selected instances of*

---

[9] Here the earlier used word 'verisimilitude' or 'believable and authentic *appearing*', might again be apt.
[10] As evidenced in the cosmic (as distinct from Kosmic) cyclical tendency for Order to descend through increasing entropy and randomization, into a chaotic finality.

> "In order to make a mistake, a man must *already* judge in conformity with *mankind.*"
> -- L. Wittgenstein, philosopher
>
> "Bernstein uses music as an accompaniment to his conducting."
> -- Oscar Levant, pianist/humorist
>
> "We cannot speak of a reality which endures, without inserting consciousness into it."
> -- Henri Bergson, philosopher

Chapter VI - Success Reluctance

broader, unintended, but consequential harming based on game limiting (and enabling) lack of discernment.

Cosmic randomization can also work to one's benefit, of course, as well as to one's detriment. Against astronomical odds, a man can win the lottery, *or* be struck by a lethal bolt of lightning. Statistical randomness can be seen, in fact, to be as much a necessary and essential proviso of the Life-Game as the warmth of the sun; its apparent purpose being to lend interest, by way of an adventurous unpredictability, to the quality of play. What fun would a game be if one knew in advance the *total* magnitude or extent of its challenges; or what moves would be made, or exactly what its ultimate experiential outcomes would be?

The point, however, is that when we make *any* aspect of the Life-Game automatic by design, even if only in the necessary and routine habituation of daily living, we are then no longer fully in *control* of it, and thus subject, eventually, to unintended *random* effects *(ludens accendens.)*[11] We make mistakes. We fail to maintain perception with the degrees of *precision,* accuracy, and discernment required for the cognitive optimization of choice and control of our actions, and, ultimately, their outcomes.

And in making on-going *mistakes*, miscalculations and "bad" choices, we eventually and inevitably violate the current "rules" of

---

[11] The 'breaks of the game.' In this context and with a global macro-statistical inevitability that is 'built-in' to the original game enabling pattern, it is *possible* for 'bad things to happen to good people,' still maintaining the ultimate responsibility for each volitional and *knowing* game entry, as *Kosmic* responsibility context for all subsequent eventuality, contingency, and Holon *response.*

> "The essence of ethics is the most broadly informed *Kosmic* exercise of *rational* choice."
> -- Holosophy Canon
>
> "Reason is the true self of every man, since it is the supreme and better part."
> -- Aristotle

Chapter VI - Success Reluctance

the game in ways that do damage to ourselves and to others. We overfill the bathtub, break limbs and drive cars off the road. But living to *play the game* is our deepest commitment, and because our participation in it depends on playing ethically and rationally, we also tend to make reasonable future-determining efforts to correct and *limit* those *errors* stemming from a naturally diminishing capacity, that is gradually perceived to be a *harmful* condition.

In such cases, we repair the damages, accept the consequences, and take more care in the future by gradually imposing rational *error limits* to awareness, *ability* and behavior; which also incidentally provides the *natural* extension and enhancement of the game through the introduction of complexity-generating "solutions" to error. These natural "error-limiting" boundary constraints act to further provide, and maintain, through a game sustaining and progressive alteration of conditions… a *devolving* and descending continuity, a sustained dialectical *continuum* or "play-fabric" of the total Kosmic game-cycle.[12]

But in other cases, as has been emphasized, we sub-rationally take an *additive* and *sub-rational* tack: INSTEAD OF MODERATING

---

[12] Games like all events on the physical (cosmic) plane of existence are cyclical, i.e. begin, continue, and conclude. The Kosmic *source* of the game may be 'timeless' and therefore unending, but its manifest game *activity* ceaselessly begins, continues, ends. Then begins anew, without descending fully into *cosmic* chaos. Acting *intentionally and knowingly* not for the *actual* greater good is an 'evil' departure from the game in progress. An *injected* false purpose, *via* the *sub*-rational 'case-contour' which imposes redundant and *mis*habitual restraint to 'prevent' evil and restore 'goodness,' results in an accelerated down-spiral of self-sabotaging constraint. The resistance insures the continuity of the sub-optimum activity which is resisted. It might be interesting here to consider *ethical* uses of destruction as a point of contrast. For example, the oriental Samurai Code of Bushido (martial service), as do martial arts generally, practices an ethos of rational restraint *and* destruction including the *capacity* to 'kill with *love*' in the service of a higher value or 'good:' a deeply personal, gesturally expression of spiritual integrity.

> "It matters not how straight the gate, how charged with punishments the scroll. I am the master of my fate, I am the captain of my soul."
> -- W. E. Henley, poet
>
> "The devil made me buy that dress."
> -- Flip Wilson, comedian

Chapter VI - Success Reluctance

OUR USE OF ABILITY THROUGH THE PROGRESSIVE FORMATION OF A RATIONALLY LIMITING PERSONAL CHARACTER IN A GIVEN AREA TO REDUCE THE MAKING OF *ERRORS*, WE MAY ACTUALLY *INCREASE* HARMFUL ERROR-MAKING THROUGH *MIS*-HABITUATION…I.E., THE COMPULSIVE AND IRRATIONAL *TRAUMA*-INDUCED , LIMITING OF ABILITY BY THE IMPRINTED *CASE-CONTOUR* IN ORDER TO GRATUITOUSLY "COPY-PROTECT" THE GAME FROM WHAT IS THEN *FALSELY* ASSUMED TO BE DESTRUCTION BY FORCE OF THE ACTUAL KOSMIC PATTERN AND SUB-RATIONALLY REQUIRING A POST TRAUMATIC REPLACEMENT *COPY*, TO *ENSURE GAME-CONTINUITY*.

Error-Limits to a Fault:
Redundantly Imprinted Self-limitation

By virtue of manifesting as a *rationally* reduced and filtered first domain consciousness, it is the authentic Holon *character*-foundation which ensures both playing the game *and* game-sustaining player *mistakes*. However, because of the resulting selective *sub*-awareness and game-enabling *in*ability to be, do, have, or know, *all* things all of the time--individual Holon-players, may come, *with* imprinted traumatic case-contour feed-back, to *fixedly* regard the exercise of certain native abilities as harmful and therefore seemingly "evil."[13]

A hunter who accidently shoots a friend in the foot during a hunting party may come to condemn *all* hunting, or deny and totally negate his own marksmanship. An investment advisor who loses a substantial amount of client money on the stock market may conclude that *any* financial risk-taking is unacceptable. A trucker who overturns a semi on a busy

---

[13] 'Evil' like a poor work of art, fails to fully depict and capture its inspiring *subject*…which is always the Good. But evil, as localized *denial* of that primary Kosmic value consensus is *locally real*, as such, but ultimately untrue.

> "They who forgive are cured…"
> -- Holosophy Canon
> "Love is metaphysical gravity."
> -- R. Buckminster Fuller, designer/inventor

Chapter VI - Success Reluctance

highway may decide that *all* or any, big rig driving is too hazardous…

By *responding sub*-rationally to the episodic traumas or engrams of life, an individual forms gradually, through cumulative stimulus-response, a *parasitic* "armoring" of his basic character, i.e., the much described case-contour, a traumatically installed egoic "self"-*image* or *pseudo*-templated vehicle to impose sub-rational compulsion, limitation, *dis*ability, *false* belief and identity.

These virtual false identities divert and feed off the Holon's *natural* self-actualizing endowment of energy and intention[14] and, when confused with the actual self…sub-rationally *displace* it, substituting past traumatic experience and thought for rational action and choice. The *total* elimination of this false engramically imprinted "blue print" for sub-volitional *re*-action and *dis*ability has been stressed as the deeper focus and goal of the Holosophic Transformative Dialogue.

As we have discussed in previous references to Ethics, nothing *existential* is inherently "good or bad," or "right or wrong," since existence is *manifest,* not innate, as is the realm of *value.*[15] However, this description does reference implicitly that objective realm as a *spectrum* of game-serving qualitative value-options for choice, the reasonableness, of which, stems entirely

---

[14] As has been suggested, nothing is more powerful and unrelenting than the Holon's primal intentional self-endowment as participant-player in the Life-Game…or when the power of that commitment is deceptively transferred to the case-contour or 'shadow self' to impose sub-rational 'ethical' restraint and limitations.

[15] Value judgments do however, have *objective* reference to the primary *agreed upon* hierarchical value-spectrum of 'Greater Good,' the enduring non-material and conceptual standard for discernment and rational choice that underlies, guides, and perpetuates Kosmic play. Evil is the *personal* sub–rational displacement of that objective value primacy.

> "There is no '*key*' to the Kosmos, but fortunately it was left unlocked,
> accessible only to an honest witness."
> -- Holosophy Canon
>
> "There can *be* no rules for creatively *violating* rules."
> -- Max Black, philosopher

Chapter VI - Success Reluctance

from the primal agreed-upon Kosmic obligation to perceive fully each situational *context* of *innate* value application, and *choosing* the action (or *in*action) that *best* achieves Life-Game *optimization*. Ideally this "*Calculus* of Greater Good" rationally is applied across the *full* Kosmic domain spectrum of choices.

Of course, being human, one's full capacity for data extraction and evaluation from the *totality* of domains, is, in any given circumstance, naturally limited in degree. One therefore *reasonably* settles for "good" *enough*; optimizing becomes choice, *guided* practically *and* rationally in common experience, by the *higher* qualitative standard of the *most attainable* betterment, minus sub-rational influence.

It is obviously and grossly inappropriate to impulsively murder an annoying neighbor, or succumb to "road rage," for instance, but entirely appropriate to take *any* action necessary to restrain an armed and marauding burglar who enters one's home threatening to injure or kill family members.

However, when, based on, and driven by a *sub*-rationally predisposed *core-belief* matrix or frame,[16] an individual, reacting to the *challenge of an event requiring increased ability to handle,* "knows" *sub*-rationally, that newly required ability to be the "same" as the one earlier applied harmfully, or in error, and therefore is *inherently* "bad," "evil" and *out-of-bounds*.

While engaged in the normative ethical play of the Life-Game, he

---

[16] "Matrix...that which, or within which, and from which, something originates, takes form, or develops." -- Webster Unabridged Dictionary ...i.e., Holosophically, where conceptual templates or contexts confirm or establish meaning, belief, or usage, and form the basis of choice, for evaluating action and optimized eventuation...

> "In our 'understanding' of human nature we have gained determinism, but lost *determination*."
> -- A. Wheelis, psychiatrist
>
> "He who ignores small things, perishes little by little."
> -- R. W. Emerson, essayist
>
> "Real capacity is never compulsive."
> -- Holosophy Canon

Chapter VI - Success Reluctance

may then, *subrationally* attempt, by activating and *"wearing"* the limiting shell of the case-contour, to incapacitate, by degree, *or even completely purge*, that "evil," previously misused, ability.

It is *subrationality* consigned there-by to a selectively *safe* category of *disabled in-action*.[17] The person then begins *restrained automated* use and occupation of that range of "protective" incapacity; now appearing as a plausibly disabled "victim," (usually of the very suppressed "ability" one used, *priorly*, to *cause* victims!) now effectively "forgetting" having *any* causal role in currently suffering the "unwanted" *victimized* condition!

Such a solution is, of course, irrational; an *aberrated* trauma-based *sub*conscious use of the *naturally* error-correcting limitation template originally established to maintain, a suitably *enthralled*, Kosmic game progression.[18] One remains, also, as above, artfully and selectively *un*aware, to prevent a "too" revelatory *knowing*…i.e., one does *not* admit to oneself that; under stress one has, in fact, *decided* that:

> *"To ensure that I'm not an evil person, I'm going to (without awareness) reduce my "dangerous" ability to shoot people in the foot by feeling a sudden and intense antipathy toward guns that I will then believe is caused solely by the harming event," or better, by something now unknown and forgotten (all occurring in a "flash" of coordinated and then occluded postulation, i.e., "uncaused" restructive believing).*

But irrational, *sub*conscious, and forgotten, as such a complex mental construct may be…it *can* profoundly, and negatively influence, distort, and *impair*, the ways in which the Holon

---

[17] A variant would be a *compulsion* to act, which is still the *dis*ability to *withhold* action.
[18] Rational 'error-limits' accommodate authentic character *formation* through the planned, orderly, involution and subsequent ascendance of the universal Kosmic game-*cycle* itself.

Chapter VI - Success Reluctance

> "Things bad begun make strong themselves by ill."
> -- William Shakespeare, Macbeth
>
> "Pain is necessary to give seriousness to life."
> -- F. Nietzsche, philosopher
>
> "For all we know, this world is very faulty and imperfect and was only the first crude essay of some infant deity, who later abandoned it."
> --- David Hume, philosopher

participates in the Life-Game, from then on.

Normal every-day challenges that could stimulate personal growth, can gradually become a restrictive pattern of *unknowing cues to sub-rationally enact and display disability,* via the case-contour.[19] Why? Because the related ability-increase would seemingly "unleash" the individual Holon to *repeat* the forgotten and unconfronted harming of others, by *compulsively* exercising *again* that *same* (or similar) harming ability, perhaps rooted and originating, in some darker and *more* ancient "evil" antecedent which *must* remain *forever* inaccessible and forgotten!

Gradually, retreating from the normal challenges of life requiring *any* expanding exercise of ability, the former Holon-*player* assumes the diminished mantle of a "success-*reluctant*" *pawn. The* fully formed, energized, and "sub-rationally self-displacing" case-contour now has a trauma-based, self-generated and *belief-sourced* unwillingness to restore *any* original, "harming" degree of ability for fear of abusing it *again.*

Fortunately, through focused dialogue, we discover and can confirm, that *re*-enabling an individual's *full* power of choice to expand optimally, any awareness or creative response to life's challenges, *frees* them from the sub-rational grip of the past[20];

---

[19] The case-contour could also be viewed as a complex of past sub-rationally assumed *belief perspectives* (with attendant traumatic imagery) which 'solves' confusion and stress by *re*-enacting *loss* and *dis*ability, and is triggered by any challenge that requires enhanced but *sub-volitionally* 'proscribed' being, doing, having or *knowing (*falsely deemed 'harmful') because, ultimately and at *core* it is considered unethical *game-revelation!*

[20] Factually, the restored ability to confront and fully 'own' the past commission of *any* act, re-enables the capacity to refrain from *any* compulsion to *repeat* that act. Recall Holosophy's precept that a restored capacity does *not* dictate or automatically compel its re-use. The restored *ability* to "*ethically* harm" is the only 'guarantee' of the re-*enabled* power of choice to "ethically *refrain* from harming."

> "Restoring the full ownership of an ability, however mis-used or 'evil' in the past; .reasserts the rational metaphysical pimacy which subordinates its choiceful exercise, in the *present,* to the higher consensus valuation of the *Good.*"
> -- Holosophy Canon
>
> "Politics is the grim jockeying for position, the ceaseless trading, the deliberate use of words to screen intention. A splendidly exciting game for those who play at it."
> -- Gore Vidal, author

and that…a restored ability or capacity is *never* a restored *compulsion* to harm. *Real capacity is never compulsive, because it always serves the calculus of rational choice!*

The Retributive Reflex: Kosmic "Karma" Re-Visioned

The obvious problem with the irrational *sub-volitional* reduction and *mis*-automation of an ability, is that it handicaps one's effectiveness in the Life-Game, thereby making the playing of it much less productive and much less *fun.* Consider the timid individual who never takes a risk, *never* tries anything new, for fear of hurting herself or another. Not only is her experience of life limited and dull; she is also of little use to anyone else, and indeed, is actually *harming* others in small increments, by consistent *in*action and by *abdicating* the normal inter-active and *personal* contributory playerhood, which benefits *all* domains.

But there is another contra-survival aspect of such *irrational* automaticity, one which has even farther-reaching effects: It leads, by endowing, and chronically *re-enacting*, the case-contour to replacing one's natural limits and *exercise of judgment* with a grafted-on "pseudo-*conscience,*"[21] which, in turn, *re*-enacts an insidious sub-rational dramatization-cycle of victimization and villainy; the individual being first the victimizer, and then the

---

[21] The case-contour could be considered as a 'pictured' replacement-*conscience* 'used by' the Holon to perpetually 'guarantee' its 'innate goodness' i.e. by the sub-rational auto-suppression of *any* 'evil' (intentionally harmful) act, *forever*; which can become a *very* 'convincing' and necessary enslavement to *disability*. The Holon, in an effort to be 'good' *uses* the case-contour as a 'success-limiter' to curtail its power to do 'harm to others 'and prevent restoring levels of 'evil' ability abused in an earlier, darker and anciently imprinted past.

> "All beings are owners of their Karma. Whatever volitional actions they do, good or evil; of those they shall become the heir."
> -- Gautama Sidhartha the Buddha
>
> "It was when the Great Way declined, that human kindness and morality arose."
> -- Lao Tzu

Chapter VI - Success Reluctance

victim; called, in Holosophy, the "Retributive Reflex-cycle."

At some point, given the fullness of Kosmic time, an *irrationally* self-limited individual (one with an *imprinted* trauma-"solving" series of belief-*identities, i.e.,* case-contour) will inevitably experience a situation in which "he" or "she" is challenged by someone or something requiring the *same,* but previously shunned and discarded level of *supposedly* "unethical" (evil) ability to handle effectively.

Unable to rationally and *currently own,* that increment of restored ability, i.e. unwilling to *mentally* confront, and *re*create it, now (and thereby *re*assume the capacity to use it) for fear of obsessively harming, *again*--the Holon may instead *sub*consciously assume a false "suffering" identity to be "victimized" by the ability's presumed harmful effects. The Holon thereby, at once, expiates (through sub-rationally *staged* compensatory suffering) the "guilt" for the commission of the regretted act *and* also demonstrates to all, as a now disabled "victim," its *incapacity* to have ever committed the act as a "villain"…An interesting cinematic parallel:

> *The 2003 movie "Shine," based on a true story, shows a suggestive example of a Success Reluctant conflict between David Helfgott's "conscious" mind wanting success and his "sub"-conscious mind concerned with the "threat" of being internationally recognized as a concert pianist. As he labors through a particularly challenging performance, he forces "himself" to stay in charge i.e. exercise the requisite ability, while his "sub"-conscious mind fights to take disabling control of his skills and body. Minus cognitive optimization as an option, Helfgott "wins" over the reactively imposed restraint to perform, by an exhausting effort of sheer will; but it proves a hollow triumph, since he emerges from the conflict insane.*

> "To 'counter' is to provide rational and *facile* opposition to something *sub*-optimum. To forcefully *resist* something unwanted, is to blame it for *being,* which *empowers* it."
> -- Holosophy Canon
>
> "The conditions that determine the logical possibility of *error*, must themselves be absolute truth."
> -- Josiah Royce, philosopher

Chapter VI - Success Reluctance

An individual similarly conflicted, and looking thru the sub-rational case-contours *lens*, might even see *any* possessor of "his" disabled ability as "wrong," and may attribute motives of evil intent to them, while seeing "himself" as right or good for *not* possessing or using such "evil" ability…This is evidenced, also, of course, by the covertly contrived "fact" that he as a *victim*, is now suffering (or *might* suffer) from its prior "bad" effects! Most importantly, he will insistently fail to see how he may have had *any* degree of responsibility whatsoever for his *current* unwanted condition[22] and continuing "victimized" plight.

Let's look a bit deeper at the *actual* cause and effects involved. This is where traumatic imprints, as previously discussed, have quasi-"karmic" application. Imprint "implanting"-- the purposeful imposition and embedding of fixed or counter-productive decisions, conclusions or beliefs on the *subconscious* mind during *traumatic moments* of pain and reduced consciousness--actually *only has subsequent compelling, and unrealized effect* when present circumstances are triggering "reminders" of earlier times when *we* abused, even in the most general sense, the very ability, and harmful effects, that we are now being *reluctantly victimized* by.

If we, now "wearing" the limiting belief-formations of the past conclude, for instance, that public speaking is "dangerous" (as in

---

[22] Victimization is the 'suffering' through *selective unawareness*, of the *false* necessity, inevitability, and unchangeability; of a covertly self-imposed and *persisting* but unwanted condition. It is *not* the mere 'un-caused' passive receiving of an unwanted or harming *effect* as commonly understood, but also requires the action or *perpetration* of continuing to *blame* that effect for being 'unwanted cause'.

> "A clearly enlightened person falls in the well. How is this so?"
> -- Zen Koan
>
> "*Extended* individuality requires gradual and confident mastery of all *eight* domains, not just 'number one'."
> -- Holosophy Canon

Chapter VI - Success Reluctance

the earlier case-example of the college student, become troubled executive), and thereby do it poorly or avoid it altogether, we effectively (if misguidedly) sidestep causing harm *again*, by selectively self-imposing an incapacity to speak, *now*, and, with post-traumatic generalization, to *any* public!

What sort of harm? It could be any kind of *earlier* injurious action, depending upon how one's *case-contour* or sub-rational templated "identity" and traumatic event-history, are *configured*: e.g., "pied-piper" demagoguery, inciting a riot, grossly misleading the public, or grievously injuring a political rival, to name just a few antecedent "evil" possibilities and purposes.[23]

After blaming another, then, for "causing" *his* unwanted condition or *victim*hood, an individual whose pattern of *contrived* suffering has become "Karmically" unbalanced and excessive, may sub-rationally require a *reversal* or "balancing" of flow, and retaliate with "new" *retributive* acts, or a reversed "villainous" behavior of his own,[24] an "unknowing" actor in a hidden, scripted, dialectic drama of progressive violence.

Now, *he* is in the role of villain. However, compulsively attacking, regardless of the circumstances, is fundamentally unethical, because such acts are never in the service of the greater and *actual* Kosmic good. But, *en*tranced and driven by trauma-based imprinting, the now "villain" does not "see it" as

---

[23] Of course this is all 'theory' until confirmed and demonstrated by the graduated access to and erasure of the relevant *core* imprintings, the certainty of mnemonic reference to *reality* is apparently proportional to the surface 'charge' erased and removed.

[24] A classic example is the victimized 'worm' *turning* and becoming a mindless robot of destruction, a perpetrator of *serial* 'evil' or compulsively compensatory or *obsessive* harming.

> "To be *able* to act 'as if', anticipates the innate capacity so to *be*."
> -- Holosophy Canon
>
> "Knowing*ness* is not itself an object, only *specified* knowing is also a possible projected *be*able."
> -- Holosophy Canon
>
> "Minds are not in space, nor are their operations subject to mechanical laws."
> -- Gilbert Ryle, philosopher

Chapter VI - Success Reluctance

anything but the *right*ful redress of an *earlier* "wrong" suffered by *him*.

Increasingly trapped in such alternating sequences of *subrational* identity "role-plays," created to maintain and rationalize the unwitting dramatization of the *case-contour's* "evil-preventing," sub-patterned ability-*aversion,* he then feels justified in having inflicted harm upon his "persecutors," or even against *anyone* else who might even *seem* to *represent* such an "enemy". But those receiving his "retaliations" will most likely feel victimized in turn, and respond with *their* counter-attacks.

Inevitably, there will ensue a prolonged, fixed, and increasingly destructive cycle of violence. All such action and *re*-action fueled, ultimately, by a failure to *rationally* enact the Holon's enthralled, selectively unaware, but *optimal limitation* of ability. By the *sub*-conscious *harnessing* of that native ability, by the *entranced*[25] surrogate "self" in the form of traumatically "*bundled identities,"* the case-contour, is robotically executing a restrictive, and disabling pattern of *action-prohibition*, but in broader fact, a sub-rational *success reluctant* assurance of goodness.

Character vs. Case-Contour: The Primal Error

---

[25] En*trance*ment is reactively *pictured* (copied) thralldom. Goodness or Kosmically enhanced (choice is rationally) *enacted* thralldom. Evil is that natural benevolence enforced by trance into a sub-rational compensatory 'iteration'…compelling decisions and perceptions made and recorded under extreme duress, and later "applied" strategically to "solve" that *false* stress-born confusion. Both neurotic and psychosomatic symptoms are apparently *condensed* and disabling replays of traumatic experience, *used* sub-rationally to *solve* a challenging life-situation. Illness and disability are ultimate "*problem solvers"* mistakenly and redundantly self-imposed by the Holon to restore and/or ensure ethical and "harmless" Kosmic participancy.

> "There is scarcely any man sufficiently clever to appreciate all the evil he does."
> -- Duc deLa Rochefoucauld
>
> "To blame, is to *empower* the 'unwanted'."
> -- Holosophy Canon

Chapter VI - Success Reluctance

Success-reluctance, and the destructive and unethical cycle of alternating "victimization and villainy" it produces, is begun and sustained, as research indicates, through trauma-occasioned[26], but ultimately *self*-induced, *responsive mis*-habituation.

Habituation, like a morning walk, can be enjoyed and helpful, *when knowingly* created and controlled. But when *sub*consciously or traumatically imposed, it is induced and maintained *compulsively*. By *re*-acting from this false and distorted perspective, "we," as sub-volitional a belief-identity "memory-cluster," or *case-contour*, resist "unleashing" any past, allegedly *un*ethical and "evil" ability that we are "challenged" to restore, or exercise *rationally*, in the *present* - a case of *authentic,* ethically evolving, *kosmic play*-activity gone awry.

In fact, this very act of irrational resistance brings *about* the generalized endowing or empowering of *the things resisted*, as the very evils and conditions "prevented" by the imposed disability. As in the "tar-baby" fable, we are forced, thru our own resistive impulse, and with diminished faculty and awareness, into *becoming*, i.e. being "stuck on," and *with,* the mental-images we subliminally (and paradoxically) keep with us *in order* to resist their *sub-rationally framed* "bad," reoccurance![27]

The individual tends to sub-rationally memorialize *all* the pain-associated sights, sounds, smells, tastes, tactile sensations,

---

[26] As we have stressed, it is the Holon's self-determined and memorialized postulate-*response* to traumatic experience, that is the final but *remediable* causal determinant of its personal sub-rational condition.
[27] To borrow Shakespeare's famous metaphor, we are 'hoist by our own petard'. We subliminally empower and *direct* our 'fates'.

> "No meditation on any kind of *object* is helpful. Meditating on an object whether concrete or abstract, is *creating* duality.
> …Meditate on what *'you'* are."
> -- Ramana Maharshi
>
> "The attunement of the world is of opposing tensions, as is that of the harp and the bow."
> -- Heraclitus

Chapter VI - Success Reluctance

and dramatis personae, present in original traumatic incidents -- along with all irrational *decisions and conclusions* arrived at, including the retributive, action-sequence that we *un* knowingly are re-enacting and "obeying" in the present; all to *sub*-rationally and illogically *ensure* our inherent sense of goodness, justice, and commitment as Holon life-game participants.

The philosophical irony is that we, like an actor performing from an extra (but subliminal script) must, at some level, *already* know and be mentally *re-creating* exactly what it is we *refuse* to admit knowing in order to simultaneously *avoid* knowing it.[28] That which is "solved" through denial, blame or the energizing force of *resistance*, is thereby, actually empowered and continued!

Why then, do we so often, vehemently *resist* any accountability for, or remedial insight into, the supposed "evil"[29] ability that attacks, dominates, or destroys, in a traumatic *victimization* cycle? We have already touched on an apparent cause and effect, between the imprinting of false limitation and the resulting *success-sabotaging* behavior that seems to ensure "goodness" and more basically…the *survival* of, and ultimate fealty to, *Kosmic* reality.

Evidently, from a deeper perspective, it is a matter of a deceptively mis*placed* primal allegiance to the actual and continuing

---

[28] *Selective* unawareness requires an infinite contextual 'basis' of potential *knowing* to make *particular* choices possible and Kosmically relevant, even when reactively 'filtered' by and through the case-contour.

[29] 'Evil', can be observed to be derivative. In this sense, a distorted, exaggerated, or misdirected *Good,* and is therefore fundamentally *parasitic* in nature, since Goodness i.e. the original , postulated, *ethos* or value-essence of the co-created Kosmos is both ultimate, primary, and precedent to any 'Evil' that 'feeds' on it. However, that derivative 'evil' *is* real in the sense that any actual *failure* is real, even when derived from or motivated by an ideal or rational aspiration. All experience of *value* even though it fails to represent fully, the ideal, has existential integrity *as a meaningful referent.* Such imperfect knowing can be 'real', even when not *ultimately substantive.*

> "If a man tries to fail and *succeeds,* which did he accomplish?"
> -- Holosophy Canon
>
> "Sometimes it proves to be the highest understanding *not* to understand."
> -- Gracian, philosopher

Chapter VI - Success Reluctance

value-integrity of the Kosmos...with a *traumatically injected* and *falsely* equivalent and "borrowed" valuation, which demands making *any associated replacement* "game," however inappropriately redundant, and sub-rational, *persist*!

As has been emphasized, Holons are essentially ethical and rational beings initially committed to the intrinsic "rules" of engagement, necessary for playing the *Kosmic* Life-Game. Evil, essentially seen as *unethical harming,* violates those rules. By sub-rationally assuming, identities and beliefs contained in the compulsive shell of the *case-contour,* the Holon seeks an *ultimate good,* even by the *sub-rational sub-mergence* and handicapping of its own character! It attempts to prevent *by such resistance*, the recreating of what "appears" to be its *own re-*occurring "evil" ability,[30] now to be safely "contained" by self-imposing a sub-rational "conscience" of restraining disability.

This stress-responsive assumption of a false and *disabled* victim identity, seems to demonstrate and *prove* that *we* are *in*capable of such evil, and therefore falsely reassures us *by proxy*, that *we* are natively *not* evil. The *resistance* to being bad, then, is an ill-conceived method of remaining "good"; by imposing the disempowering, disabling, and enforced *in*capacity to *be* (or *do* or *have*[31]) *anything* irrationally considered "evil."

At the same time, the compulsive *sub* volitional duplication of

---

[30] Evil is also the *pictured impulse* to harm *or* to 'suffer' harm; while assuming the case-contour's surrogate identities, which substitute for the rational non-pictured and innate *Kosmic* value-consulting power of choice of the unencumbered, *actual* Holon-agent.

[31] Deprivation in any form, can be sub-volitionally 'planned'. Any creativity if not exercised within the Holon's innate ethical constraints, is subject to the 'self-sabotaging' mechanism of the *subrational* mind

> "A man that studieth revenge, keeps his own wounds green, which otherwise would heal."
> -- Francis Bacon, philosopher
>
> "He who seeks God under *settled* form lays hold of the form, while missing the God contained in it."
> -- Meister Eckhart, contemplative

Chapter VI - Success Reluctance

all engramic content -- i.e., *everything* that is traumatically sensed and recorded *while* the "evil" is being *resisted* -- is imbued with equivalent "survival-value". That *everything* seems, to the cognitively diminished Holon, to require the "same" primal endowment for eternal continuity and playerhood, that the Holon's *true character* accomplishes by rationally enthralled and *volitional* occupation of all domains, of the Kosmos, in *perpetuity*.[32]

Succinctly re-stated, the *character* or "true-self" of the Holon, i.e. the *conceptual* form and power of the beings innate commitment, to the actual pattern of the *Kosmic* Life-Game, is *sub*consciously *copied* and *transferred* to an imprinted mental-image mockery of itself; a kind of "mind-*parasite.*" i.e. the case contour. This complex of past/painful mental images, contains the core-belief that to "survive," ethically, he must maintain that false, *pictured self* since he and "it" are *experienced post-traumatically, as the same persona* with the same commitment to Kosmic endowment and continuity.

Consider a case example: If, in an urban setting; two rival gangs have a confrontation in a public park, during the "rumble" a gang member is suddenly set upon by a rival, knocked unconscious and experiences the full traumatic effects of being beaten; containing the pain; the sensation of lying on grass; the shouted insults of attackers; the sounds of neighborhood traffic; etc; *including any sub-volitional "solving" decisions (charged*

---

[32] The Holon as an immortal spiritual being can do nothing *but* survive, not as a *particular* identity or persona, but as the first domain *source* of a vast lineage of consecutive player-personas, which is reduced as 'case-contour' to the narrow existential parameter of the cumulative identity-contents of each memorial life continuum.

> "The universe is God playing Hide and Seek…"
> -- Alan Watts, author
>
> "Surely *any* omnipotent Deity worthy of the name must have the relatively modest capacity for the benevolent and playfully forgetful self-limitation required to Kosmically enjoy Itselves."
> -- Holosophy Canon

Chapter VI - Success Reluctance

beliefs) made while unconscious.

During the confusion of the attack; the Holon, while "being" the *disabled* victim-identity, *sub*consciously records the *solving* of the confusion, and "tags" and files those mental-image pictures as cues for future *use*, (as the *case-contour*) to *post-traumatically simulate* the actual and *primally consensual* ethical postulation: **"Survival" = Eternal Kosmic-Game Commitment**, *as if* the *past* engramic *imprint* was still "his" actual *present* existence[33], but, like the Kosmos, endowed to "survive" and benevolently *displayed* forever!

Losing To Win: The Tactics of Sub-rational "Success"

That *post*-traumatic "use" may be triggered *every* time the, now conscious, individual encounters events reminiscent of the recorded traumatic "victimization". As if to warn him of impending danger (but actually triggering the success-reluctant disabling *re*-action), the traumatic mental-image pictures are automatically and immediately projected onto the *screen* of the Holon's mind, forming an ability reducing "perimeter."

The images have *command* value because *he* seems to be *being* "on the screen" with, and, *as* them; prompting him (as Holon) to react unconsciously and automatically to the present circumstances in much the same limiting way he (as the mentally *pictured* victim) did to the original threatening event:

---

[33] Opting, sub-rationally for continuing disability and 'ethical' limitation each time he is challenged to confront his actual causative role as Holon in the incident…'Survival' is then, in the higher Kosmic sense, maintaining and exercising one's ethical commitments as player-Holon, but is *reactively* reduced to the urge for a merely continued physical *existence, equated* with the 'valued' but literal word and perceptic command content of the 'survived' traumatic incident.

> "Modern physics impresses us particularly with the truth of the old doctrine, which teaches that there are realities existing apart from our sense perceptions, and that there are problems and conflicts where *these* realities are of greater value for us then the richest treasures of the world of experience."
> -- Max Planck, physicist
>
> "You cannot step into the *same* river twice."
> -- Heraclitus

Chapter VI - Success Reluctance

i.e., with passive and *disabled* behavior of some kind.[34]

To review: If by chance, our gang member at some later time finds himself in a place where traffic noises and the smell of dirt are present, his "re-minded" trauma-projected *past* "identity" may feel inexplicably "nervous and frightened," *or* hostile and aggressive and "ripe for a fight," depending on the original and personal *core case-contour* solution to being attacked, and the associated "harming" *ability* to be, or *not be*, violently causative.

Knee-jerk behavior is, of course, irrational and inappropriate, prompted and imposed, as it is by false cues from a narrowly perceived[35] and "survived" past, rather than by spontaneous choices based on *present* objective fact and reality.

Because the cued mnemonic images occur with such lightning speed, while containing the associated elements of force and pain; their re-enactment tends to be an automatic and *generalized* limiter of all present ability to perceive accurately.

The Holon, encased in these redundant mental-images, fails to notice their *true* source as a character-*leaching*, *re*-imposition of a false and disabling "assurance" of game-continuity; and *mis*-habitually succumbs to forgotten and *mindless* call to action, whose actual counterfeit nature is hypnotically *obeyed* but not actually seen or understood as pain-enforced re-enactment.

---

[34] A disabled passivity which rejects any possible incremental increase of awareness and *ability* which might 'successfully' *counter* or even defeat an overwhelming force.

[35] Perception through the distorting lens of *subrational* indicators is never accurate, since it is selectively imposed in a fixed, but no longer applicable belief-context, of *past* threat or menace to 'survival.'

> "JIVA • MUKTI": Jiva (soul) • mukti (enlightened); the ancient Vedantic reference to a fully realized being in living touch with its deepest Source of Being."
> -- Vedic Definition
>
> "Cogito ergo sum; Consciousness *hence* existence..."
> -- Descartes (An alternative translation)

Chapter VI - Success Reluctance

Further, intuitively *knowing* ourselves to be *good* or naturally ethical, we tend to rationalize our actions, falsely believing *we* are "surviving" (actually, as *past* "selves,") although the actions and viewpoints of these forgotten *surrogate* personas make no sense to our *true and present* selves! *"How can I be so unreasonable? "I'm a rational being!"*

Unfortunately, we also tend compulsively to seek out situations in which such aberrant and *dis*abled "survival behavior" can be *addictively* re-enacted again and again, because re-living such incidents seem to give opportunities to be vitally "right;" the *case-contour's* distorted application of the Holon's highest core purpose: *to ensure continued and optimized playerhood!*[36]

This repetitive compulsion to be compulsively "right" can result in a delusory fantasy-world supported by *failure*-prone beliefs and impulses that merely persist as *automata,* based and driven completely by an *imprinted* mockery of each Holon's self-determined participation in the actual Kosmos; to which that Holon maintains a fixed and eternal, but traumatically displaced and misguided, participating "loyalty."

To finalize our case example, our now *radicalized* gang-member may gravitate towards violence; "*un*able" to *counter* social challenges peacefully; or to be victimized again, now "*un*able" to oppose with rational force. The reaction depending

---

[36] An aberrated being would rather be 'right' than *rational,* a typical synonymic identification-distortion which sub-rationally links each Holon to its case-contour. This *most* fundamental rationality of Kosmic fealty and eternal commitment, *copied,* becomes the 'visceral' *felt and confirming rightness* of mere physical continuity as 'survival.'

> *"Cosmic causality, is consensus-attribution, a telic regularity that orders and enables all happenings."*
> -- Holosophy Canon
>
> *"All that exists... is rational..."*
> -- G. F. Hegel, Philosopher

Chapter VI - Success Reluctance

on which *deep*-volitional *compensatory* life-*dramatization* is being imposed to maintain the limiting "good," and avoiding the supposed unleashing of past "evil."

At the same time the Holon is compulsively avoiding the rational and *real* challenge to learn, and *increase ability,* contained in *all* adversity, experienced at effect; i.e. to restore, the awareness and circumstantial capacity necessary to confront, counter, or exploit, *any* of life's opportunities for an *active,* game-enhancing and *transformative acceptance.*[37]

The Holon's native *capacity is* to execute without irrational restraint, *any* "forbidden" or long suppressed ability to be fully, even if *dangerously, causative;* but, from a *novel* optimal, *freely-limited,* and truly ethical perspective.[38] Importantly, this on-going capacity for transformative discernment is essential to each Holon's *full* development and participation within the larger *non*-compulsive self-actualizing constraints of the Kosmic Game *cycle.*

The ability to *not* be irrationally or un-ethically destructive, must entail *power over* any imprinted trauma's full *intentional* content i.e. the restored willingness to perceive, confront and recreate *any* harmful identity or "evil" action from the past, *with full* understanding and *ownership.* It is the *full* realization of one's having limited one's *causal* intentionality that *enables its*

---

[37] True acceptance is not *resignation,* it allows novelty to creatively and actively to manifest.
[38] It is the sub-rational reinforcement of the primal Kosmic 'game-code' preserving, 'self-limitation' of the Holon's awareness and ability that, distorted, underlies *all* human aberration, and its 'personalized implementation'-copy was recognized as the *case contour.*

> "There is no such thing as absolute certainty. But there *is* assurance sufficient for human life."
> -- J. S. Mill, philosopher
>
> "Consciousness can operate beyond the brain, body, and the present as hundreds of experiments and millions of testimonials affirm. Consciousness cannot, therefore, be identified with the brain."
> -- Larry Dossey, MD, surgeon and author

Chapter VI - Success Reluctance

erasure! This restores the ability to ethically cause, or *not* cause, *any* such act or general *magnitude* of action.

Paradoxically, *only* a deep, clear, and *non*-dual understanding of an "evil" purpose as a sub-rational mockery of an intended, but *innately referenced goodness;* that re-enables and permits the *fully restored* ability to also destroy, *ethically!* This profound metaphysical insight frees the Holon from the disabling impulse to *unethically injure i.e., from* the "success-reluctant" *compulsion* to "ethically" restrain *any reasonable* (and ethical) destructive *capacity!*[39]

In the previous chapters, we have discussed from various perspectives, how past traumatic *imprint-related* mental viewpoints and images can impact upon our day-to-day lives, and how the systematic application of Holosophy enables their erasure.

If core mental-image pictures and their cumulative *"charged" "reminders"* make it difficult for us to perceive directly and accurately, the *present time behavior* which they prompt; the unpleasant feelings and attitudes which characterize that behavior, are usually obvious to all. We irrationally attack (from within a false but compulsive belief-frame) as *villains,* or alternatingly "retreat" as *victims*, from people or situations which have not actually threatened us. In so doing, we *display*, but also, *covertly execute,* with *selective disability, and with*

---

[39] It is only the full restoration of *any* ability, which includes its *control,* that enables and guarantees its free and rational use or *dis-use* .minus the oppressive 'conscience' personal disability dictates of the case-contour. All destruction (or *erasure*) is not bad. We must occasionally raze a tenement to *raise* a sky scraper!

> "To be the master of any branch of knowledge, you must master those which lie *next* to it. Thus to know *anything*, one must know *everything*."
> -- Oliver Wendell Holmes, Supreme Court Justice
>
> "It is as if we all live in our own private 'inside-out' black hole."
> -- Leonard Susskind, physicist and Black Hole Theorist

Chapter VI - Success Reluctance

fixed sub-rational conviction, a stress-formed belief (survival *"conviction"*) *from the past.*

As a result of this hidden and distorting *memorial* core-belief residue, we eventually and inevitably experience as convinced "victims", a multitude of unwanted conditions and effects, such as fear, apathy, frustration, depression, confusion, rage, disgust and many more[40] each signaling a *successful-failure*; a sub-rational sabotage of our true and ascending purpose to fulfill our uniquely creative Kosmic destinies.

Thus is cast, in urgent and expanded ethical perspective, the challenge to *also* increase our ability as Holons to identify, confront, and *erase,* those often accepted as normative fixed behavioral mal-conditions, or "sub-rational indicators" that artificially obstruct the success of our highest, *natural and* mutually beneficial aspirations as Kosmic players.

However discomforting and disabling they may be, such unwanted conditions actually have important *indicative* value in counseling, not only because they are the surest and most immediate indices, (or *standards of recognition,*) that real self-*defeating* viewpoints, attitudes, emotions,[41] and *beliefs exist;* but also because their elimination, and subsequent stable *absence,*

---

[40] See Appendix II for a more detailed description…However, consider being the unwanted effect of an overwhelming force…even if the passive sufferance is apparently enforced irresistibly, is it ultimately *choiceful* if we can *conceive* of any alternative increment of betterment, e.g. even opting *ultimately* for an increase in *past-traumatic* awareness or capability?

[41] Holosophy is not *critical* of *any* emotive expressiveness, per se, even the negative ones. It councils a heightened awareness of a Kosmic standard for "transformative acceptance" or 'true witnessing' as the vital and *volitional* prelude to *erasure* of all *mal*-emotion, and the optimal restoration of a free, vivid, and 'wild'…i.e., *natural,* un-forced, and *efficiently* adventurous *rational* emotional life.

Chapter VI - Success Reluctance

> "An organized being is then not a mere machine, for that has merely moving power, but it possesses in itself formative power of a self-propagating kind, which it communicates to its materials though they have it not of themselves; it organizes them, in fact, and this cannot be by the mere mechanical faculty of motion. For a rational but finite being, the only thing possible is an endless progress from the lower to higher degrees of ethical and actual perfection."
> -- Immanuel Kant, philosopher

provides objective and useful guidelines *for recognizing* them as dispensable and harmfully redundant additives distinct from one's authentic character.

Additionally, as each Holon becomes gradually more familiar with its own uniquely personal pattern of such "indicators", these can be more confidently identified, viewed, and erased as *not "self"* i.e., recognized, through the transformative re-examination dialogue as being *dispensable* and contra-survival *additives, distinct from the actual Self,* or one's authentic character as Holon-Player.

Technically viewed, they also provide a bonus of *useful diagnostic* flags for accessing the deeper *true-self*-displacing *case-contour*. They can then lead us, through systematic dialogue, to the actual source and *lineage* of those indicators, so that the *core* fabric of sub-rationality can be finally and permanently *dismantled*, resulting in restored control, confidence, and authentic *personal causation* as Holon.

The advanced cognitive project of *extending* optimization capacity across the full game-spectrum of all *eight* Kosmic domains, and the erasure of the deep structured and formative dialectic patterns that constitute subrationality, i.e., the *primal* engramic, deceptive replication and imposition of the innate archetypal thematic-code undergirding *all* false Kosmic limitation will be more fully explored in future volumes of this series, and in other Foundation publications.

> "The empiricist thinks he believes only in what he sees. But he is much better at believing than *seeing*."
> -- G. Santayana, philosopher
>
> "Scientists animated by the purpose of proving them*selves* purpose*less* constitutes an interesting subject for study."
> -- A. N. Whitehead, philosopher

Chapter VI - Success Reluctance

We conclude with a final and definitive observation, variously fore-shadowed in previous chapters. *A Holon Knows.* It knows, evidently, because, through its innate seventh (and eighth) domain awareness and exchange capacities, it has extended *potential cognitive access* to the totality of *abilities* necessary for *fully realized* (optimized) agent-participancy in the Kosmos at large.

Apparently, a Holon does *not* require mental-image pictures of the past to make *knowing*, consistently informed and rational, choices in the present, since it must *already* know[42] as its true and authentic self, and with an ultimately *selective* conceptual capacity, *what is contained* in *any* mental-construction in order to produce, recognize, *find* and rationally *use* it, or not!

So, arriving full course in our commentaries, it seems both essential and axiomatic, that to know who, and what, we really are, we must know, again, fully and with confident certainty, what we are *not,* or, as the great mystic, Meister Eckhart put it: *"the less there is of self, the more there is of Self."*

> *"We all know that there are regions of the human spirit untrammeled by the world of physics. In the mystic sense of the creation around us, in the expression of art, in a yearning towards God, the soul grows upward and finds the fulfillment of something implanted in nature. The sanction for this development is within us, a striving born with our consciousness or an Inner Light proceeding from a greater power than ours. Science can scarcely question this sanction, for the pursuit of science springs from a thriving which the mind is impelled to follow, a questioning that will not be repressed.*

---

[42] Therefore, rational thought ultimately depends on an innate *un*pictured knowing potentiality, i.e. an infinite framing context of *conceptual* familiarity and capacity to project *specified ability* and intent…mental images, alone, don't *know* anything!

> "The *sleep* of reason produces monsters."
> -- Francisco Goya, artist
>
> "If you don't like my principles, I've got others."
> -- Groucho Marx

Chapter VI - Success Reluctance

Whether in the intellectual pursuits of science or in the mystical pursuits of the spirit, the light beckons ahead and the purpose surging in our nature responds."
-- Sir Arthur Eddington, Physicist

A semifinal "advisory": The most profound challenge to personal realization in Holosophy is the Holon's misguided opposition through the mechanism of *resistance* or *denied inference*, to prevent, erasing through targeted and effective dialogue, the false, *pictured virtual* self or presumed *"core* of its character," which, for so many eons it has, with the deepest conviction, assumed "itself" to be. To make that quintessential cognitive distinction through Kosmic implication and dialogue, requires a piercing honesty, a dedicated resolve and finally, a loving and compassionate *Self* forgiving of "self"… something truly *empty and marvelous!*

…RHT

ABOUT THE AUTHOR

Robert Thomas has spent more than 40 years of active professional engagement in the frontier edges of Consciousness Research and Human-Potential Development.

After a university education in Art and Philosophy, he co-founded and managed international organizations and consulting firms that feature transformative learning theory and applications. Bob has also, over many years, re-visioned in Holosophy the general subject of dialogue technologies, with the goal of extending their already broad, varied, and pervasive influence on the study of consciousness over the last half-century. To that end he has become affiliated with the Holosophy Foundation,® formed as a public education and service vehicle for those who might want to access and study Holosophy's deeper Kosmic philosophical perspectives and helping technology.

After years of living aboard and ocean sailing (a peripatetic global residency), he currently lives in Florida, and remains active as consultant to a select group of individual and corporate clients. Bob continues to research and write* about the farther shores and capacities of consciousness.

References

Aquinas, Thomas, "The Summa Theological," in *Great Books of the Western World*, volume 19, ed. R. M. Hutchins. (Chicago:

Arzy, S., M. Idel, T. Landis, and O. Blanke. "Why Have Revelations occurred on Mountains? Linking Mystical Experiences and Cognitive Neuroscience." Medical Hypotheses 65 (2005): 81-45.

Aurobindo. 1996. *The Life Divine*, Pondicherry, India: Sri Aurobindo Ashram.

Ayer, Alfred Jules. *Language Truth and Logic* (Oxford: Oxford Univ. Press. 1963)

Barbour, Ian. Religion in an Age of Science (San Francisco: Harper & Row, 1990)

Barrow, J.D., and F. G. Tipler. 1986. *The Anthropic Cosmological Principle*. New York: Oxford Univ. Press.

Beauregard, M., J. Levesque, and P. Bourgouin. "Neural Correlates of Conscious Self-regulation of Emotion." *Journal of Neuroscience* 21 (2001): RC 165 (1-6).

Beauregard, M., and V. Paquette. "Neural Correlates of a Mystical Experience in Carmelite Nuns." *Neuroscience Letters* 405 (2006): 186-90.

Beauregard, Mario, an O'Leary Denise. 2007. *The Spiritual Brain*. New York: Harper One.

Behe, M.J. 1996. *Darwin's Black Box*. New York: Simon & Schuster.

Benson, Herbert, and Mark Stark. *Timeless Machine: The Power of Biology of Belief.* New York, Scribner, 1996

Bergson, H. 1949. *Introduction to Metaphysics*. New York: Harper

Berlinski, David 2008. *The Devils Delusion*. New York: Crown Forum.

Blood, C. 1993. On the relation of the mathematics of quantum mechanics to the perceived physical universe and free will. Rutgers University, preprint.

-----------2001. *Science, Sense, and Soul*. Los Angeles: Renaissance Books.

Bobrow, Robert S. "Paranormal Phenomena in the Medical Literature: Sufficient Smoke to Warrant a Search for Fire." *Medical Hypotheses* 60.6 (2003): 864-68.

Bohm, David. "Postmodern Science and a Postmodern World," *The Reenchantment of Science*, David Ray Griffin ed. (Albany: State University of New York Press. 1988).

Brown, G. s. 1977. *Laws of Form*. New York: Dutton.

Bucke, R. M. *Cosmic Consciousness: A Study in the Evolution of the Human Mind* New Hyde Park, NY: Univ. Books, 1961. Originally published in 1901.

Bryant, Barry 1990. *Cancer and Consciousness*: Boston, Sego Press

Byrd, R. C. "Positive Therapeutic Effects of Intercessory prayer in a Coronary Care Unit Population." Southern Medical Journal 81.7 (July 1988): 826-29.

Capra, F. 1982. The Turning Point. New York; Simon & Schuster.

-----------1996. *The Web of Life: A New Scientific Understanding of Living Systems*. New York: Doubleday.

-----------Uncommon Wisdom: Conversations with Remarkable People. Phantom Books, New York, 1988

-----------Capra, Fritjof, and David Steindl-Rast. *Belonging to the Universe* (San Francisco: Harper San Francisco, 1991).

Cheek, David, B., MD Hypnosis: *The Application of Ideomotor Techniques*, Ellen & Baken, Mass. 1995

Cicero. *The Nature of the Gods,* translated by H.C.P. McGregor (London: Penguin, 1972).

Cohen, D. "Placebo-Induced Changes in MRI in the Anticipation and Experience of Pain." Science 303, no. 5661 (February 20, 2004): 52-70

Davis, P. 1988. *The Cosmic Blueprint*: New Discoveries in Nature's Creative Ability to Order the Universe. New York: Simon & Schuster

-----------*Other Worlds* (New York: Simon & Schuster, 1980)

-----------*Superforce* (New York: Simon & Schuster, 1984).

-----------*The Accidental Universe* (New York: Cambridge Univ. Press 1982)

-----------*The Mind of God* (New York: Simon & Schuster 1992)

-----------1999. *The Fifth Miracle*: The Search for the Origin and Meaning of Life. New York: Simon & Schuster

Information and the Nature of Reality, Cambridge, 2010

Dawkins, Richard. *The Blind Watchmaker* (New York: W. W. Norton, 1987)

du Nouy, Lecomte. *Human Destiny* (New York: Logmans, Green and Co., 1947)

Decety, J. "Do Imagined and Executed Actions Share the Same Neural Sub-state?" *Brain Research: Cognitive Brain Research* 3 (1996): 87-93

Dembski, William A. *No Free Lunch: Why Specified Complexity Cannot Be*

References, cont.

Purchased Without Intelligence. Lanham, MD: Rowman & Littlefield, 2002.
Denton, Michael J. *Nature's Destiny: How the Laws of Biology Reveal Purpose in the Universe.* New York: Free Press 1998.
D'Espagnat, Bernard. *Reality and the Physicist: Knowledge, Duration ad the Quantum World.* Cambridge: Cambridge Univ. Press 1989.
Dossey, L. 1992. *Meaning and Medicine.* New York: Bantam.
Drury, Nevill. *Reincarnation,* Barns & Nobel, New York, NY 1998
Eccles, Sir John, and Daniel N. Robinson. *The Wonder of Being Human: Our Brain and Our Mind.* New York: Free Press, 1984
Eden, Murray. "Inadequacies of Neo-Darwinian Evolution as a Scientific Theory," *Mathematical Challenges of the New-Darwinian Interpretation of Evolution,* P. Moorhead and M. Kaplan, eds. (Philadelphia: Wistar Institute Press. 1967)
Foster, John. 1982. *The Case for Idealism (England*: T. J. Press, Ltd.)
Girber, Richard, MD, *Vibrational Medicine for the 21st Century*, Harper Collins, New York, 2000
Gish, Duane. *The Challenge of the Fossil Record* (San Diego: Creation-Life Publishers, 1985)
Gonzalez, Guillermo, and Jay W. Richards. Privileged Planet: *How our Place in the Cosmos is Designed for Discovery.* Washington, DC: Regnery, 2004 Goswami, A. 1989. The idealist interpretation of quantum mechanics. *Physics Essays* 2:385-400
Goswami, Amit, PhD. "The Visionary Window" 2000. Quest Books, Wheaton, IL
Grad, B. 1964. A telekinetic effect on plant growth. International Journal of Parapsychology 6:472-98
-----------1965. Some biological effects of "laying-on of hands": A review of experiments with animals and plants. *Journal of the American Society for Physical Research* 59:95-127
Grinberg-Zylberbaum, J., M. Delaflor, L. Attie, and A Goswami. 1994. Einstein Podolsky Rosen paradox in the human brain: The transferred potential. *Physics Essays* 7:422-8
Grof, Stanislaus, MD *Beyond the Brain*, State of New York Press, 1986
Grossman, N. *Who's Afraid of Life After Death? Journal of Near-Death Studies* 21.1 (Fall 2002)
Hardy, Alister. *The Spiritual Nature of Man.* Oxford: Clarendon, 1979.
Harman, W., and E. Sahtouris. 1984. *Higher Creativity.* Los Angeles: Tarcher.
Harris, William S., Manohar Gowda, Jerry W. Kolb, Christopher P. Strychaz,
Herbert, Nick, *Elemental Mind*, Dutton, New York, 1893
Hillman, James, *The Soul's Code*, Random House, New York, 1996
Hoyle, Fred, and Chandra Wickramasinghe. *Evolution from Space* (London: J.M. Dent and Co. 1981)
---------*Religion and the Scientists* (London: SCM, 1959)
---------"The Big Bang in Astronomy," New Scientist, V. 92,No. 1280, November 19, 1981.
---------"The Universe: Past and Present Reflections," *Engineering and Science* (November 1981).
Hooper, Judith, and Dick Teresi. The 3-Pound Universe. New York: Macmillan 1986
Hughes, Robert, *Selected Essays on Art and Artists*, Knoph, New York, 1990
Hrobjartsson, A., and P. Gotzsche. "Is the Placebo Powerless? An Analysis of clinical Trials comparing Placebo with No Treatment." *New England Journal of Medicine* 344, no. 21 (May 24, 2001)
Hume, David. *Dialogues Concerning Natural Religion* (London: Penguin, 1990)
Huxley, Aldous. *The Perennial Philosophy.* New York: Harper and Brothers 1945.
--------*The Doors of Perception.* New York: Harper & Row, 1945.
Jaki, Stanley L. *Cosmos and Creator* (Edinburgh: Scottish Academic Press, 1980)
------*The Paradox of Olbers' Paradox* (New York: Herder and Herder, 1969)
James L. Hacek, Philip G. Jones, Alan Forker, James H. O'Keefe, and Ben D. McCallister. "A Randomized, Controlled Trial of the Effects of Remote, Intercessory Prayer on Outcomes in Patients Admitted to the Coronary Care Unit." *Archives of Internal Medicine* 159 (1999):2272-78
James, William. *The Varieties of Religious Experience.* New York: Random House, 1902
Janov, Arthur. *The Primal Scream* (New York: G.P. Putnam's Sons, 1970)
Jeans, J. *The Mysterious Universe.* London" AMS Press, 1933.
Joad C. E. M., 1949. *Decadence.* New York: Philosophical Library
Critique of Logical Positivism, University of Chicago Press, Chicago, IL 1950

References, cont.

Johnson, Phillip. *E. Darwin on Trial* (Washington DC: Regnery Gateway, 1991)
Jung, C. G. 1971. *The Portable Jung*, ed. J. Campbell. New York: Viking.
Koestler, A. 1978. *The Case of the Midwife* Toad. N. P.: Hutchinson
Laszlo, Ervin. Evolution. *The Grand Synthesis* (Boston: Shambhala, 1987)
Leibniz, G.W. *Theodicy* (La Salle, IL: Open Court Publishing company, 1985 Kelley E&E et al Irreduble Mind, Rowman & Littlefield 2008)
Lerner, Eric J. *The Big Bang Never Happened: A Startling Refutation of the Dominant Theory* of Universal Origins (New York: Random House, 1991)
Leslie, John. "Anthropic Principle, World Ensemble, Design," in *American Philosophical Quarterly* 19, (1982)
Lewis, C.S. *Christian Reflections* (Grand Rapids: William B. Eerdmans Publishing Company, 1967)
---------"*Encounter with Light.*" Taken from An Anthology of C.S. Lewis: A Mind Awake, Clyde S. Kilby ed. (New York: Harvest/HBJ Books. 1968)
---------*Mere Christianity* (New York: Macmillan Publishing Co. Inc., 1952)
---------*The Problem of Pain* (New York: Macmillan Publishing Co. Inc., 1962)
Libet, B., E. Wright, B. Feinstein, and D. Pearl. 1979. Subjective referral of the timing of a cognitive sensory experience. *Brain* 102:193
Lipton, B. 2005. *The Biology of Belief*. Santa Rosa, CA: Mountain of Love/Elite Books
Lovelock, J. 1982. Gaia: *A New Look at Life on Earth*. Oxford: Oxford Univ. Press.
Malin, Shimon. *Nature Loves to Hide: Quantum Physics and the Nature of Reality, a Western Perspective*. Oxford: Oxford Univ. Press. 2001
Marcel, A. 1980. Conscious and preconscious recognition of polysemous words: Locating the selective effect of prior verbal contexts. In *Attention and Performance VIII*, ed. R. S. Nickerson, 435-57. Hillsdale, NJ: Lawrence Erlbaum.
Marinoff, Lou, *Plato Without Prozac*, 1999. New York, NY, MJF Books
Maslow, A. H. 1971. *The Farther Reaches of Human Nature*. New York: Viking.
  Religious Aspects of Peak-Experiences. New York: Harper & Row, 1970.
MacGregor, G. 1978. *Reincarnation in Christianity*. Wheaton, IL: Theosophical Publishing House, Guest Books.
Mahadevon, T. M. P. 2000. *Upanishads*. New Delhi: Motilal Banarsidass.
McCarthy, K., and A. Goswami. 1993. CPU or self-reference? Can we discern between cognitive science and quantum functionalist models of mentation? Journal of Mind and Behavior 14:13-26.
McGrath, Alister, *Dawkins's God: Genes, Memes, and the Meaning of Life*. Oxford: Blackwell, 2005
Mensour, J-M. Leroux, G. Beaudoin, P. Bourgouin, and M. Beauregard. Separate Neural Circuits for Primary Emotions ? Brain Activity During Self-Induced Sadness and Happiness in Professional Actors." *Neuroreport* 14.8 (June 11, 2003): 1111-16.
Midgeley, Mary. *The Myths We Live By*. London: Routledge, 2003.
  Evolution as a Religion (New York: Methuen & Co., 1985)
Miller, Ed L. *Questions that Matter*, 4th Ed, McGraw Hill, New York 1995
Moura, G. and N. Don. 1996. Spirit possession, Ayahuasca users and UFO experiences: Three different patterns of states of consciousness in Brazil. Abstract of talk presented at the 15th International Transpersonal Association Conference, May 16-21, 1996. Manaus, Brazil. Mill Valley, CA: International Transpersonal Association.
Murphy, Michael, '*Future of the Body: Explorations Into the Further Evolution of Human Nature*' *(Tarcher/Perigee Books, 1993)*
Newberg, Andrew, Eugene D'Aquili, and Vince Rause. *Why God Won't Go Away*: Brain Science and the Biology of Belief. New York: Ballantine, 2001.
O'Leary, Denyse, *By Design or by Chance? The Growing controversy on the Origins of Life in the Universe*. Minneapolis: Augsburg, 2004.
Paquette V., J. Levesque, B. Mensour, J-M Leroux, G. Beaudoin, P. Bourgouin, and M. Beauregard.
Parnia, S., and P. Fenwick. "Near-Death Experiences in Cardiac Arrest: Visions of Dying Brain or Visions of a New Science of Consciousness." Resuscitation 52 (2002): 5-11.
Pelletier M., A Bouthillier, J. Levesque, S. Carrier, C. Breault, V. Paquette, B. Penfield, W. 1976. *The Mystery of the Mind*. Princeton, NJ: Princeton Univ. Press.

References, cont.

Penfield, Wilder, "Memory Mechanisms," A.M.A. Archives of Neurology and Psychiatry, 67 (1952): 178-198
Penfield, Wilder. *Second Thoughts: Science, the Arts, and the Spirit*, Toronto: McClelland and Stewart, 1970.
Penrose, R. 1989. *The Emperor's New Mind*. Oxford: Oxford Univ. Press.
Plantinga, Alvin. *God, Freedom, and Evil* (Grand Rapids: William B. Eerdmans Publishing Company, 1974)
Polkinghorne, John. *Science and Creation* (Boston: New Science Library, 1988)
Pols, Edward, 1967. *Whitehead's Metaphysics*. Illinois: Southern Illinois University Press.
Prigogine, I. 1989. *From Being to Becoming*. San Francisco: Freeman.
Radin, Dean. *The Conscious Universe*: The Scientific Truth of Psychic Phenomena. San Francisco: Harper San Francisco, 2007
Ramsdale, David & Ellen: Sexual Energy Ecstasy Phantom Age, New York, 1993
Ratzsch, Del. The Battle of Beginnings: Why Neither Side Is Winning the Creation-Evolution Debate. Downers Grove, IL: InterVarsity Press, 1996.
Reich, Wilhelm: the Cancer Biopathy, Dover, NY 1957
Ring, K. and M. Lawrence. "Further Evidence for Veridical Perception During Near-Death Experiences." *Journal of Near-Death Studies* 11.4 (1993): 223-29.
Ring, K. and Sharon Cooper. *Near Death and Our of Body Experiences in the Blind.* Palo Alto, CA: William James Center, 1999.
Ring, K. and S. Cooper. 1995. Can the blind ever see? A study of apparent vision during near-death and out-of-body experiences. University of Connecticut, preprint.
Ross, Hugh. *Genesis One: A Scientific Perspective* (Sierra Madre, CA: Wisemen Productions, 1983)
Russell, Bertrand, Religion and Science (New York: Oxford University Press, 1968)
Sabel, A., C. Clarke, and P. Fenwick. 2001. Intersubject EEG correlations at a distance – The transferred potential. In *The 44th Convention of the Parapsychological Association: Proceedings of Presented Papers*, ed. C.S. Alvarado, 419-22. Raleigh, NC: Parapsychological Association.
Sabom, Michael. *Light and Death: One Doctor's Fascinating Account of Near- Death Experiences.* Grand Rapids, MI: Zondervan, 1998.
Recollections of Death: A Medical Investigation. New York: Harper & Row. 1981.
Schwartz, J. M., H. Stapp, and M. Beauregard. "Quantum Theory in Neuroscience and Psychology: A Neurophysical Model of Mind/Brain Interaction." *Philosophical Transactions of the Royal* Society B: Biological Sciences 360 (2005): 1309-27.
Schwartz, Jeffrey M., and Sharon Begley. *The Mind and the Brain: Neuroplasticity and the Power of Mental Force.* New York: HarperCollins, Regan Books, 2003.
Schmidt, H. 1993. Observation of a psychokinetic effect under highly controlled conditions. *Journal of Parapsychology* 57:351-72.
Schrödinger, E. 1994. *What is Life*? Cambridge: Cambridge Univ. Press.
Searle, J. R. 1987. Minds and brains without programs. In *Mindwaves: Thoughts on Intelligence, Identity and Consciousness,* ed. C. Blakemore and S. Greenfield. Oxford: Basil Blackwell.
-----------1994. The Rediscovery of the Mind. Cambridge, MA: MIT Press.
Mind A Brief Introduction. Oxford: Oxford Univ. Press, 2004.
Sheldrake, R. 1981. *A New Science of Life*. Los Angeles: Tarcher
-----------1999. *Dogs That Know When Their Owners are Coming Home*. New York: Summit Books.
Siegel, Bernie, MD, 1988. "Love, Medicine and Miracles." New York, Harper and Row
Simmons, Geoffrey, M.D. 2007. *Billions of Missing Links*. Eugene Oregon: Harvest House.Chalmers, D. 1995. *Toward a Theory of Consciousness*. Cambridge, MA: MIT Press
Smart, Ninian. "Omnipotence, Evil, and Supermen," Philosophy, Vol. XXXVI, No. 137 (1961)
Smetham, Graham, *Quantum Buddhist Wonders of the Universe*. Shunyata Press, Sussex, England 2012
Smith, A., and C. Tart. "Cosmic Consciousness Experience and Psychedelic Experiences: A First-Person Comparison." *Journal of Consciousness Studies* 5, no. 1 (1998): 97-107.
Smythies, J. R. 1984. *The Walls of Plato's Cave: The Science and Philosophy of Brain, Consciousness and Perception*. Aldershot, UK: Avebury.
Spangler, Mark: Editor, Cliche´s of Politics, (FEE Inc. New York) 1996

Spitzer, Robert, New Proofs for the Existence of God, Eerdmans, 2010

References, cont.

Stace, W. T. *The Teachings of the Mystics*. New York: Macmillian, 1960.
Stapp, H. P. 1993. *Mind, matter, and Quantum Mechanics*. New York: Springer
"*A Mindful Universe*", New York: Springer (2009)
    "The Effect of Mind Upon Brain", Monograph, See http:stapp/stappfiles.html
Stevenson, I. 1974. *Twenty Cases Suggestive of Reincarnation*. Charlottesville: Univ. Press of Virginia.
Stove, David. *Darwinian Fairytales*. Aldershot, UK: Avebury, 1995.
Susskind, Leonard, *The Cosmic Landscape*, Little Brown, New York, 2005
Swimme, Brian. "The Cosmic Creation Story," David Ray Griffin, ed., *The Re-enchantment of Science*
    (Albany: SUNY Press, 1988)
Takahashi, T., T. Murata, T. Hamada, M. Omori, H. Kosaka, M. Kikuchi, H. Teilhard de Chardin, P. 1961.
    The Phenomenon of Man. New York: Harper & Row.
Tempel, R. "Implications of Effects in Placebo Groups." *Journal of the National Cancer Institute* 95, nos.
    1, 2-3 (January 1, 2003).
Tennant, F. R. "Cosmic Teleology," *Philosophical Theology*, Vol. II, chapter IV
    (New York: Cambridge University Press. 1930)
Trefil, James. *Reading the Mind of God: In Search of the Principle of Universality*
    (New York: Charles Scribner's Sons, 1989)
--------*The Dark Side of the Universe* (New York: Doubleday, 1988)
Van Lommel, P. "About the Continuity of Our Consciousness." In *Brain Death and Disorders of Consciousness*.
    Edited by Calixto Machado and D. Alan Shewmon. New York: Kluwer Academic / Plenum, 2004.
Van Lommel P., R. Van Wees, V. Meyers, and I. Elfferich. "Near-Death Experience in Survivors of Cardiac Arrest:
    A Prospective Study in the Netherlands." Lancet 358 (2001): 2039-45.
Von Neumann, J. 1955. *The conceptual Foundations of quantum Mechanics*. Princeton: Princeton Univ. Press.
Watts, Alan, 1957. "The Way of Zen", New York, Pantheon
Weil, A. 1995. *Spontaneous Healing*. New York: Knopf.
Wheeler, J. 1975. The Universe as Home for Man. In *The Nature of Scientific Discovery: A Symposium
    Commemorating the 500th Anniversary of the Birth of Nicolaus Copernicus*, ed. O. Gingerich, 262-95.
    Washington, DC: Smithsonian Press.
-----------1977. Genesis and observership. In *Foundational Problems in the Special Sciences,* ed. R. E. Butts and
    J. Hintikka, 3-34. Dordrecht: D. Riedel.
Whitehead, Alfred North, "*Adventures of Ideas*," Mentor, New York, (1959)
Wilber, K. 1981. *Up from Eden*. Garden City, NY: Anchor/Doubleday.
-----------1996. *A Brief History of Everything*. Boston: Shambhala.
Wyller, A. 1999. *The Creating Consciousness*. Denver, CO: Divina.
----------2003. Beyond Darwin's paradigm: Consciousness driving evolution. Unpublished manuscript.
Yoshida, and Y. Wada. "Changes in EEG and Autonomic Nervous Activity During Meditation and Their
    Association with Personality Traits." *International Journal of Psychophysiology* 55.2 (February 2005):
    199-207.

Appendicies

I. The Kosmic Domain Matrix
II. Truth Functions
III. Kosmic Equation
IV. Cognitive Optimization: A Comparative Analysis
V. Sub Rational Indicators
VI. Reality (density) Discrimination Guide
VII. Is The Brain Really Necessary?
VIII. Excerpt from "Recalling Nana's Face: Does Your Brain Store Memories?"
IX. The Paradox: Intimations of Non-duality
X. The *Powers* of Communication
XI. The Transformative Dialogue: (Sub-rational Resistance Markers)
XII. Kosmic Archetypal Agendas
XIII. Excerpt from "You Have to be Conscious to Deny Consciousness, and Other Conundrums" (Evolution News, 2015)
XIV. Consciousness as a Scale of Knowing: An Epistemic Hierarchy
XV. Seminal Holosophy Canon

Appendix I

Appendix I

The Kosmic Domain Matrix

Appendix I

The Kosmic Domain Matrix

The Holosophic diagram opposite symbolizes the basic structure, order, and thematic dynamics of the *Kosmic code;* an inately patterned grid or matrix that represents the functional and inter-active aspects of the eight life-game domains that *guide* Kosmic actualization.

First, the larger golden outer circle represents the 8th domain, the infinite potentiality which encompasses and grounds all other domains. The center (7th domain) contains the traditional Yin-Yang and the Greek letter 'psi' which is the mathematical unit of meaning for the quantum wave-form and its Consciousness related collapse into perceptibles… plus the addition of the letter 'phi' symbolic of its 'golden mean' or telic-cosmic proportionality. Holosophy adds to the traditional 'phi' interpretation to include *personification* as a non-material source of all volitional optimization. Therefore, each domain contains a proportional ratio of *personal* awareness of cognitive value parameters, which, when evaluated and *executed as rational choices* determine the scale of the greater good or degree of Kosmic betterment when superimposed over the ancient Yin-Yang symbol represents the primal capacity of the 7th domain which radiates out to actualize and reify domains 1-6. The arrows are variable in size and color to represent both the comparative degree of endowed order, and the implicit presence of *all* domains within each domain to enable the cognitive projected, manifest, and *optimized* exchange between them as Kosmic *Play!*

The overlapping hierarchy of domains show both a vertical and horizontal dimension ... implying relative size and comparative organization and order. The central Yin-Yang symbol combined with both the Golden Mean symbol and that of the quantum wave-function, represent a primary and functional synthesis of the epistemic and ontic aspects of reality[1]. The wave-function is placed more properly on the 7th domain since it symbolizes *potentia* of possibility and is not *actual* until made manifest as 6th domain…i.e., the collapse of the wave-form from *potentiality* into *actual* particulate 'substance' through *conscious specification* or observation. Thus 'phi' (proportion) and 'psi' (possibility) plus the dynamic logic of all projected eventuation (Be, Do, Have) added to the *plus-minus duality* of Yin-Yang, combine as a transcendent *Consciousness directed* potential for all existential formativeness. This primal directing consciousness is represented by the 7th domain, but is ultimately generated and divinely encompassed, as is *All,* by the Infinite Potentiality and personhood of the 8th.[2]

---

[1] Some quantum physicists hold that quantum states by their nature are a combination of epistemology (knowledge) and ontology (existence) thus the two words simultaneously reference the *material* and *non*-material. There is a union of these two perspectives, i.e., they then are *epiontic,* a neologism used to describe this metaphysical amalgam.

[2] See Chapter II, et al, for a more complete exposition of the full *Kosmic* rather than Cosmic aspects and implications of the domains. Consider also Aristotle's original concept of *hylomorphism*, i.e., that existence as merely an interactive combination of form and matter, or *substance*. This assumption seems to neglect the fact that that these two "fundamentals" are themselves, *in essence* innate knowables which Holosophy posits as a missing and essential cognitive *triadic* ground, i.e., *idea,* form and matter, *essential* for a complete Kosmic metaphysic.

Appendix II

> "Knowledge is justified true belief."
> -- Plato
>
> "*Value* refers to *worth* metaphysically... in a usefull, achieving, or revelatory sense, as a necessary *ascension adjunct* to the truth."
> -- Holosophic Canon

Hierarchy of Truth* Functions

∞ **DEFINITION:**

Transcendent Truth...
Infinite but *un*specified potentiality for all manifest or as yet *un*manifest knowability

Cognitive Truth...
Selective knowability of *innate* hierarchic degrees and levels of implicit meaning, order and *value*

Coherent Truth...
Knowing projected as *logically consistent* propositions or *any represented conceptuality*, e.g. ('unicorns have horns') or ('all crows are black')

Consensual Truth...
Knowing *objectified* as concerted, mutually combined, and shareable conceptuality

Corrospondent Truth...
Symbolically descriptive propositions that attempt to convey and share discrete co-realized empirical particulars, e.g. a ('that car is blue')

Pragmatic Truth...
Higher order truths usefully employed as means to achieve practical solutions or incremental betterment day to day

Perceptual Truth...
Truth as a primary *creative act* of accurate and immediate sensory duplication of an 'external' reality

0

∞ **COGNITIVE DESCRIPTION:**

Infinite *knowability-potential for all* universal modalities and reifications

Specifically known but as yet unmanifest, or projected as actual, real, or consensual

Manifestly known but *self-generated* (actual) projection of combined conceptuality as *arbitrarily representable* knowing

Mutually comprehensible (realized) agreements between multiple viewspoints consensually made manifest

Ideal one to one corrospondence of a symbolic reference to a mutually observable and usefully sharable recreational Kosmos

Degrees of truth value determined by workability or effectiveness of data-use in problem solving or further value-access

The immediate consensual re-creation of a *co*-experienced external reality using healthy organs of perception

0

∞ **UTILITY SCALE:**

Thoughts as a potential cognitive spectrum of all actualizable meaning, order and value

Thought as yet unprojected or managed knowables, provides potentially *useful* logical order and value gradients

Thought selectively realized as essentially *self*-endowed and projected logical order as symbolic knowables e.g.(poetry)

Thought used as the projected agreements and boundaries necessary for Kosmic game-playing and gradient value Revelation

Thought benevolently displayed to enable communication, interactive value perception, and game/domain exchange and participation

Thought as objective skill capacity in using the calculus of betterment to discern and enhance Kosmic play

Thought as the primary perceptual apparatus that *limits perception* to actionable, game enabling and sustaining barriers

0

---

*Truth, like all fundamental ideas, has many definitions, like those contained in the quotations referenced above. Holosophy describes 'Truth' basically as a cognitive hierarchy of symbolic and transformative *usefulness*, in both *representing* and *accessing* the full descriptive scale of the *total capacity to Know*. Ranging from the immediacy of raw perception, up through symbolic representation and its formal logical order, to ultimate *reminding* access to the primal non-material Forms or Source-as the ultimate *patterned potentiality* for Existence, e.g. both as *cognitive* Universals ('Beauty') *and*/or specified particulars (Mozart's 'Requiem').

Truth as *value* is the higher cognitive framing or motivating ideal for *optimal use* of perception and ideation. Not as mere pragmatism, which is a much *narrower* focus of purpose on an immediate planned result. It is in this higher sense that a great work of art has truth *value*. The perceived aesthetic object or symbol serves as a reminding reflection of a higher cognitive order,** a realm of transcendence to which all *value* of symbol, object or act, gives revelatory access.

Truth, then, considered as more than mere logic or particular description, reflects an implicit scale of exemplary *values*, providing a playfully instructive and accessing doorway and staircase to the sublime, qualitative essence, or patterned universality, of the Kosmos.

**Cognitive order refers to 'thought' as *represented knowability* including the full range of truth functions as optimally applicable judgements or 'true' 'propositions' or premises. The classic order adopted by Holosophy and applied as a graduated cognitive 'vehicle' to provide access to ultimate truth-*value*, is as follows:

    I...Epistemological Order: Conceptuality as cognitive potentiality for *all* meaningful order, value, and actualization
    II...Ontological Order: Capacity to specify meaning as *realized being* inherent in and derived from acts of knowing
    III. Teleological Order: Innate reconciled duality, devolving to the *manifest* duality of consensually realized purposiveness
        The above summarizes a practical Holosophy definition of thought as *projected knowing* with graduated degrees of reification

Appendix III

Appendix III

A supposedly ancient "woodcut" by C. Flammarrion (1842 – 1925), showing a medieval searcher breaking through the natural boundaries of the Cosmos to reveal what Holoshophy freely interprets as an *innate* answer to the mystery of life; that it is what the ancients term a "lila" or divine game enjoyed consensually by all Holons as an ultimately benevolent and playful cosmic *display*"

Appendix III

Kosmic Equation

$$\chi\rho = H^{\cdots n} \ll \overbrace{\left[\pm (b)(d)(h)\right]}^{\infty}{}^{\aleph} \gg 5 \cdot D^{\cdots n}$$

The Kosmic "equation," or "optimizing algorhythm," above is intended as a symbolic representation of the complete and actual Kosmic pattern of existence. Where $\chi\rho$ is considered the divinely proportionate (and personified) matrix of all eight Kosmic domains which then equals infinite potentiality ∞ (eighth domain) bracketed below from which are derived its emergent aspects. First in rank, is the conceptual potentiality for manifesting the innate archetypal category themes of the primal game template: Being, Doing, Having (7th domain). This then selectively brings about the necessary emergent ordering of the other domains beginning with the Holon ($H^{\cdots n}$), the individuality or player consciousness which provides the active agency and window of participancy (1st domain) necessary to experience the remaining five domains ($5 \cdot D$). These comprise the interactive fields of life and existence that Consciousness-at-large (7th and 8th D) imposes on the physical universe (6th D) as the Kosmic Life Game.

Legend

$\aleph$ = a specifiable and derived infinity of potentials... also implying the "collapse" of an infinite possibility into a *selected* actuality

Φ = divine proportion; contains interacting hierarchic symmetries and order of the Kosmic domain template, including *personification*

[= contains the category matrix of of the primal domain elements

(= contains distinct conceptual potential for each of the catergory meaning domain sources

$\ll$ = source of, and of greater magnitude than

$\cdots n$ = volitionally imposed limit to actualize each infinite possibility

Archetype = a priori (conceptual) *source* of symbolization, sometimes refers to (and is confused with) the primary *source* of representation, combined conceptuality itself.
- It is the redundant or "shadow *copy*" of the authentic, *primal* Kosmic template, that, unknowingly endowed and confused with that actual pattern provides the origin and command value of the sub-rational mind with its false game limitations and irrational fixed belief system
- Kosmic: An ancient Greek term used by Pythagoras and borrowed by Holosophy to refer to the entire universe in all its multi-dimentionality, i.e. Spiritual, mental, emotional and physical... and contrasted with "Cosmos" in its modern usage which refers only to the physical realm.
- Domain: each of the 8 primary interactive meaning-spheres of Kosmic existence... in the form of which the Life Game Themes playfully emerge and inter-acts... self, family, community, humanity, all life forms, the physical universe, Conceptuality and Infinite Potential.

Appendix IV

Cognitive Optimization: A Comparitive Analysis

"*Holosophy* is concerned with removing through *spiritually* directed communication technology (Transformative Dialogue) all aberrant effects caused by the person's continuing mental-image reaction and underlying *volutional response* to traumatic events in the past; and their selective and aberrative, reiteration and re-imposition as 'solutions' to present challenges and confusion."

PSYCH-(OLOGY/IATRY) Vs. TRANSFORMATIVE DIALOGUE

	PSYCH-(OLOGY/IATRY)	TRANSFORMATIVE DIALOGUE
1.	Reductionist "nothing but" – ism. Usually materialistic.	Non-Reductionist. Open to higher spiritual truths, non-materialistic.
2.	Free association. Non-directive, undisciplined communication.	Directive, disciplined, focused communication system.
3.	Techniques: Non-systematic, variable, usually "personalized."	Techniques: Systematic, replicatable, rigorous, consistent.
4.	No use/awareness of repetitive communication cycle to erase.	Use of repetitive communication cycle to reveal and erase.
5.	No generally agreed upon technology or standards for practitioners.	Agreed upon technology and standards for all qualified practitioners.
6.	No awareness of GSR[1] application in detecting tension and confirming its erasure. (Usually not considered possible.)	Research & optionally use GSR applications to detect tension and confirm its reduction.
7.	Evaluative, speculative.	Non-evaluative. Observational.
8.	Often uses hypnosis.	Non-hypnotic, no 'power of suggestion' used
9.	Goal: neurotic raised to normal.	Goal: 'normal' raised to a 'meta'-normal optimum (fully realized potential for optimization)
10.	Mind *is* brain. No Holon (soul).	Mind distinct from Brain. Holon as spiritual entity, and is distinct from both.

---

[1] Galvanic Skin Response – a physiological change in the electrical resistance in the human skin which has been found to correlate with mental and myological tension and reaction. (One of the elements used in a lie detector.)

Appendix IV

PSYCH-(OLOGY/IATRY)   Vs.   TRANSFORMATIVE DIALOGUE

11. Limited or no responsibility; client as "victim" of genetics or environment. No real personal responsibility for condition.

    Total responsibility context of application, non-victim orientation for client. Ultimate responsibility for personal condition.

12. Doesn't seek to improve general abilities. Limited scope.

    Seeks to improve all ability. Unlimited scope.

13. Optimum personal state unknown or denied.

    States of Optimum defined and achievable.

14. No concept of Optimization or states beyond normal as existent or attainable.

    States above Optimum identified and achievable through graduated erasure by domain.

15. No standardized training for practitioner or evaluation of client progress.

    Standardized training for practitioner as well as evaluation of client progress.

16. No objective monitoring or indication of result or objective therapeutic closure.

    Objective indication of process closure within counseling technique (Defined and targeted responses indicate erasure of mentally charged material).

17. Subconscious mind with variable definitions and explanations of content.

    Sub-*rational* mind with precise definition and erasure of content as goal

18. Imprecise distinction between various conscious and subconscious 'minds'.

    Clear distinction of Volitional and Reactive minds with emphasis on the restored rational mind as ultimate source of betterment.

19. Mechanistic concept of trauma removal; electric shock; use of "aversion techniques" to modify behavior.

    Precise erasure of traumic content with volitional and self-determined client changes of behavior; no duress or violently invasive approaches used.

20. Additive, suggestive, and evaluative attitude toward client.

    Subtractive; non-invasive; removes barriers to emerging *self*-reliance.

21. Reconditioning, re-programming, often use and reliance on drugs.

    De-conditioning, de-programming, no use of drugs.

22. Ideal: "adjust" to reality; conformist social or situational norms.

    Ideal: *creates* own reality; non-conformist; seeks to attain higher universal norms.

PSYCH-(OLOGY/IATRY) Vs. TRANSFORMATIVE DIALOGUE

23. Secular beliefs often imposed or required to effect change.

    No beliefs imposed or necessary for dialogue process workability.

24. Theoretical: assumptions unscientific, unproven.

    Axiomatic: assumptions self-evident and verifiable.

25. Deterministic. Past conditioning is sole source of persons present actions and difficulties.

    Self-deterministic; past is ultimately irrelevant to the being freely operating in the present.

26. Narrow in focus. No effective applications to other fields, e.g. learning, management, society.

    Has wide practical application to other fields, e.g. study and general life skills.

27. Assumes a limited deterministic decision making capacity with regard to life. Character determined by genetic background and conditioning. Limited or no ethical template.

    Assumes a basically free and unlimited decision making capability. Character self-determined. Rational, ethical, optimization template for decision making.

28. Creativity considered stemming from subconscious, recombined memory, non-volitional.

    Creativity is volitional, *not* ultimately subconscious in origin, and not strictly memory-based.

29. Non-Metaphysical; no recognition of ancient spiritual traditions or wisdom.

    Based on and utilizes the highest metaphysical traditions of East and West.

30. Creativity is nothing but a 'sublimation' of unconscious instinctual forces and drives.

    Creativity resides potentially in the innate state of the Being (Holon) emerging freely from this Spiritual nature when *un*blocked.

31. Assumes that man is driven wholly by animal instinct (Id) or is a conditioned result of genetic inheritance and therefore needs to be contained or restrained in order to *construct* an adjusted social being.

    Man is basically *good*. Needs to be *un*restrained to enable him to be the naturally and spontaneously social being he inherently is.

PSYCH-(OLOGY/IATRY) Vs. TRANSFORMATIVE DIALOGUE

32. Narrow by secular scope of source and application of belief systems. Limited to current life; earth bound.

    Operates at much greater scope and depth in terms of the considered non-material boundaries of experience. Allows unlimited perspective for core beliefs: e.g. reincarnation; life and *life origins* culture beyond earth.

33. Ethics are arbitrary social standards imposed to rationalize mere self-interest or justify conditioned behavior. *Ex*clusive of free-will or authentic altruism.

    Ethics are the co-postulated and agreed upon value-norms of Reason used as a guide in the *free* and optimizing choices in life. e.g. *authentic* self interest balanced by an *in*clusive non-material concern for the greater good.

Appendix V

Sub-Rational Indicators:
A General List of Unwanted (Sub-Optimal) Conditions

The Sub-Rational Indicators

The sub-rational indicators are a compendium of the character, emotional and attitudinal traits symptomatic of *re*activity which we have observed over the years to *fall away*[1] in the course of the Holosophic Counseling Programs, and which have been arranged and codified in the categories, and with the specific characteristics provided below. While not necessarily exhaustive, they are a good cross section of the observable range of reactive experience, and will be more than sufficient to assess, plan and customize the identification, examination and erasure of specified unwanted and sub-volitional behavior. The client should, however, feel free to expand the list based on his own personal experience. Increasing familiarity with the list will better enable him to do so…

The sub-rational indicators below comprise over 150 *typically* redundant and *sub*-optimum (i.e., destructive, contra-survival) mental and emotional states and conditions which though comprehensive are *not* complete…These have been defined, codified, and arranged alphabetically into eight general sub-rational categories: Mal-Emotion; Criticalness; Continuity; Dis-Interest; Confusion; Dis-Ability; Generality; and Mis-Perception.

I. MAL-EMOTION

Definition: an irrational, ineffective and *un*pleasant emotional reaction; ingrained uncontrolled negative emotion, usually irrelevant to the actual experience of the moment and continuing long past the circumstance or event assumed to be its cause, and experienced with an often compulsive urgency and seeming lack of volition.

Alienation: withdrawing or distancing oneself from things, persons, or former attachments; self-exile or "lonerism," often tinged with self-pity, "woundedness," "numbness," or steely resolve to be invulnerable to the "pain" of *any* disappointment or betrayal.

Anger: physically aggressive feeling of displeasure, antagonism or hostility toward another person or thing with characteristic and stressful disfunction.

---

[1] These categories convey (based on long term observation) types of specific unwanted conditions that are extinguished or "un-created" when fully inspected during dialogue. We suggest that the sub-optimum psychological conditions which improve or *erase* during their address in counseling are also sub-*rational* to begin with. Their erasure restores the optimum and rationally natural state. Remember that the list has helpful but *limited*, 'solo' application. Some indicators require deeper viewing and access, more proper to an assisted Cognitive-Optimization program.

Appendix V

Anxiety: a painful or apprehensive uneasiness of mind, usually over an irrationally anticipated or impending ill; fearful concern or interest; self-doubt about one's capacity to cope with a fancied adversity.

Apathy: dispirited lack of any appropriate feeling, emotion, caring or concern.

Boredom: an unpleasant state of being irresponsibly devoid of interest or purpose.

Carefulness: marked by excessive concern or solicitude, by extreme caution, wariness, or prudence, or by an overly painstaking effort to avoid errors or omissions.

Covert Hostility: secret enmity or hidden unfriendliness, injuriousness or ill-will; antagonism, opposition or resistance in thought and/or action accompanied by pretended liking.

Degradation: a shameful or humiliating sense of diminished or lost status, rank or worth.

Envy: a painful or resentful awareness of an advantage or possession seemingly or actually enjoyed by another often joined with a compulsive desire to exclusively possess the same advantage or possession.

Fear: a strong sense of dread, alarm or panic generally accompanying an anticipation or fixed awareness of danger whether real or imagined.

Grief: a sense of deep, enduring and poignant distress often accompanying, extending and recurring beyond an apparent or actual loss, e.g., of a loved one or a valued object or condition.

Guilt: an oppressive sense that one has solely caused, and is "to blame" for, the suffering or condition of another; obsessive, regretful "self"-condemnation…

Handle It Myself: a conviction, decision or resolve, tinged with covert anger or resentment that one *must* handle something oneself if it is to be "done right" or done at all.

Hate: extreme aversion, dislike, or enduring and active enmity or hostility toward something.

Hopelessness: a state of having no expectation of ultimate good or success; of not being susceptible to remedy or cure; of being incapable of solution, management or accomplishment.

Impatience: restlessness; extreme limited sufferance; shortness of temper, especially under stress, delay, opposition, or challenge.

Jealousy: excessive or victimized intolerance of rivalry or unfaithfulness; apprehensiveness of the loss of another's exclusive devotion; hostility toward a rival or another believed to enjoy a valued advantage regarding a situation, object or person, "rightfully" one's own.

Appendix V

Loss: a continuing sense of emotional harm, deprivation or desolation accompanying and persisting beyond a removal, absence or separation from something or someone of value.

Malaise: a vague sense of unease often associated with the onset of an illness, or impending loss or dissatisfaction.

Manic: excessively or unreasonably enthusiastic; irrelevantly hyperactive or loquacious; gleefulness'.

Misery: a continuous unhappy or emotionally distressing state of suffering and want, usually accompanied by an apparent deprivation or persisting affliction of some kind.

Nervousness: negative excitation; jumpiness, fidgetiness or oversensitivity accompanied by tense concern over a possible challenge, unwanted result, or possibility.

Outrage: being 'poised' for a victimized sense of injustice and aggressive susceptibility to being 'offended'; aggrieved, or disappointed.

Persisting Upset: a state of being mentally or emotionally troubled which continues or endures long after the act or event, which seemed to have caused it has passed.

Revulsion: a strong, often violent or "sickening" sense of being repelled, usually by something automatically deemed repugnant, offensive or evil.

Righteous Indignation: a "lofty" sense of moral up-rightness accompanied by a 'justifiable' outrage against the supposed offending party or circumstance.

Sadness: a persisting, emotionally painful, poignant or "bittersweet" feeling often associated with a sense of irretrievable loss of some kind, or an event or circumstance automatically thought to be "a tragedy" or a "a shame," such as an untimely death.

Sense of Failure: defeatedness; a deflating sense that one is congenitally unable to be successful, achieve goals or perform effectively the routine responses to challenge or functions of living.

Shame: a sense of self-abnegating guilt, shortcoming or social impropriety, or of humiliating disgrace or embarrassing disrepute or admonition.

Stubborn: intractable; unmanageable; obsessive unwillingness to deviate from a fixed pattern; heedless of suggestion.

Suspicion: the act of critically suspecting that something is wrong or amiss without proof, or on insufficient evidence.

Sympathy: commiserating with and therefore validating another's victimization; an automatic, often deemed virtuous or even morally obligatory, habitual co-experiencing or *sharing* of another's

Appendix V

suffering, sadness or grief; co-suffering, as contrasted with empathy or compassion, based on the assumption that *self*-reduction is required to help or communicate to a suffering or disadvantaged person…'feeling their pain'.

'Tolerance': exhibiting strained forbearance, endurance or "putting up with" often under hidden protest.

Unhappy: typically not cheerful or glad; habitually causing or "subject to" misfortune; without a sense of purpose, participation, productivity or fulfillment in life.

Worry: mental distress or agitation resulting from exaggerated concern, usually for something impending or anticipated; obsessively visualized threat, menace or negative consequence.

II. CRITICALNESS

Definition: an obsessive, unreasoned and hostile devaluation of persons or things; the habitual, often rationalized minimizing, attacking or negative distortion of any actual value or worth, which masks the deeper, sub-rational intention to destroy or remove by force, anything that 'shouldn't be' in the moment when it actually *is*...

Abandonment: critical departure from or isolation of a blamed person or situation usually to covertly punish.

Argumentative: obsessive election of opponency; unproductive conflict; habitual protest or "againstness" based on hidden destructive need.

Asserted Rightness: compulsively and insistently positing the "validity" or superiority of one's viewpoint, position or actions; needing to assert one's "rightness" with the implied wrongness of another; a fixed "knowing best."

Belittling: making less, little or nothing of others; compulsively including deprecating or critical comments in one's demeaning appraisal of another.

Blaming: denial of any personal responsibility while mal-emotionally attributing injurious, censorious or "bad" cause or agency to others; holding others solely and punitively responsible for one's (or any) unwanted condition.

Contemptuousness: diminishing criticalness or hostility toward those (including self) seemingly incapable of, or inherently deficient in exercising a desired degree of intelligence, skill, judgment, expertise, etc.

Defensive: self-justifying; protectively explaining or rationalizing one's behavior or actions in an effort to diminish an apparent threat and prove self right (or not wrong) and others wrong (or not right.)

Appendix V

Disapproval: judging to be unworthy, immoral, unacceptable or wrong.

"Don't Need Help": a conviction, usually tinged with defiance, stubbornness, or denial that some real and possible assistance is unneeded; or that one can do alone that which might actually requires cooperation or assistance.

Gossip: the often gleeful or titillating spreading of rumors or reports of an intimate, salacious, sensational, malicious or privileged nature which, by virtue of its harmfulness or demeaningness, actually represents an indirect criticalness toward, or attack on another or others.

Grudging: giving or allowing unwillingly or reluctantly; ambivalent or resentful compliance or acknowledgment.

Hidden Standard: all or nothing thinking; which doesn't allow gradient, requiring of oneself or others a higher level of understanding, achievement, expertise or accomplishment without allowing for intermediate steps or gains; habitually minimizing progress by negating any step toward the goal because it is not the "final" attainment; "everything or nothing!", a persisting sub-rational and *losing* comparison.

Hostile Individuation: excessive, often arrogant sense of separateness from rational participation in a group often following harmful acts against that group and usually based on a hidden need to protect the group from one's continuing harmful intention; compulsive abandonment of allegiance accompanied by a false devaluation of the group or individual abandoned to obviate the harm caused.

Ignobleness: characterized by baseness or meanness of spirit.

Invalidating: weakening, making little or less of; destroying the truth, legitimacy or worth of something, often to explain earlier offenses against that thing.

Making Wrong: a compulsive proving or showing of another's convictions or actions to be wrong, unjust or unreasonable, often by a contrived victimization of self by the other.

Martyrdom: a sense of suffering "willingly but undeservedly" for some cause or person, allegedly for the sake of one's principles; covertly self-interested suffering.

Misemotional Evaluation: a decision, conclusion, judgment or assessment tinged with or stemming from negative emotion such as anger, resentment or jealousy.

No Trust: a belief or attitude that the character, ability, strength or truth of other people or things can "never" be relied upon.

No Remedy: the irrationally self-serving conviction, often militantly and aggressively asserted, that help or any degree of betterment is impossible, non-existent or harmfully intended.

Appendix V

Protesting: ineffective and contentious complaining, objecting, actively resisting or displaying unwillingness, usually to an idea or course of action.

Reductionism: the tendency to reduce complex data or phenomena perceived as hostile to one's fixed ideas to simplistic, less significant or 'nothing but' causal terms; devaluation by habitual, usually materialistic, interpretation which omits vital data, context, consciousness, or other aspects of total existence from consideration as to cause or source.

Regret: persisting grief or pain, tinged with mal-emotions such as disappointment, longing or remorse, over some past event, action or occurrence; the irrational, often debilitating longing for the reversal or cancellation of past events or misfortune.

Revenge: self-justified retaliation against the source of a real or imagined insult or injury.

Self-Critical: disparaging of self; considering self to be intrinsically flawed or unacceptable; self-compulsive effacement.

Suspicious: premature, and often undeserved assignment of wrongness, potential enmity or harmful purpose.

Tense Denial: a negating or protesting of something, usually the assertion or accusation of another, accompanied by nervousness or stress, or the feeling of being undeservedly attacked.

Too Intense: overly serious; morose; preoccupied to the point of tense and persisting urgency or distraction.

Unforgiving: unable to give up a persisting bitterness or resentment of, or claim to requital for, a past "victimization" by a person or event.

Victimization: unadmittedly failing to assume responsibility for one's own condition; resentfully attributing one's failure, injury or unwanted condition wholly to others; dishonest "suffering," or confusion.

III. CONTINUITY

Definition: the apparency of sameness or unchangingness; of seamlessness or on-going, effect contrasted with the actual discontinuous and novel seriality of each differentiated and unique "moment-to-moment" interval of experience.

Excessive 'Need' To: an overly pronounced sense of obligation, requirement or pressure to be, do or have something.

Fanatic: marked by excessive and irrational zeal and often intense, belligerent and uncritical devotion to (or opposition to) a belief or opinion.

Appendix V

Fixed Attention: inability to shift one's attention from one thing to another at will; a compulsive focusing on or returning to something; obsessive introversion or extroversion; mental 'stuckness'.

Habit or Addictive Behavior: automatically repetitive or compulsive indulgence in or abstinence from something, such as alcoholic drinking, promiscuity, compulsive gambling, overeating, smoking or any obsessive activity.

Looking That Doesn't Change a Mental State: inspection of a sub-rational indicator which does not result in alleviating or dissolving it because of an interjected but unnoticed "slant", hidden perspective or standard preventing direct observation and therefore *honest* communication and erasure. "I see it...but it dosn't change."

Misplaced Concreteness: attributing solidity or dense unchangeability to that which is persisting but purely conceptual or symbolic, such as 'hopelessness' or "no money."

Perceives 'Factoid' in Place of Fact: perceives or accepts as objective fact an observation which is actually overlaid and distorted by subjective opinion, supposition or conjecture.

Persisting Unwanted Condition or "Stuck Picturing:" an undesired state of mind, set of mental images, conditions, or preoccupation, which seems to continue despite one's desire to be rid of it.

Procrastination: unreasonable neglect, or postponing attending to something, usually accompanied by a rationalized negative attitude, dread or aversion projected onto the omitted obligation, whether noticed or unnoticed.

Self Consciousness: undue preoccupation with the impression one is making upon others; over-concern with obtaining approval or reassurance; morbid and sustained introspection.

Subjective Problem: internal mental conflict or picturing, projected outward and seen as an unwanted and seemingly "unresolvable" or unchangeable external condition which also *demands* solution; an attitudinal "can't" or specious personal disempowerment

Uncaused/Uncreated: 'menacing otherness': feeling as if one is a "victim" of an overwhelming and uncaused existence or presence; a sense of being at the personally uncaused menacing effect of someone or something over which one has no ownership, authorship or control.

'Worn Outness': feeling emotionally or psychologically thwarted or beaten by life, either in general or by a convincing set of too "real" circumstances, events or onuses that have 'obstructed' one's aspirations.

IV. DIS-INTEREST

Definition: Covertly suppressed or misplaced interest in an area of life, where such interest and its resulting contact, confronting and interaction would reveal and eventually *erase* a sub-rational "protective" commitment to valuable fixed or habitual ideas, attitudes or disabled behavior about that part of life.

Arrogance: actively diminishing the value of others while asserting and exaggerating one's own.

Can't or Must Create Interest: an inability to find value in something actually worthwhile, or a sense that one *should* find value in or interact with someone or something, arising from fixed notions about the absence or presence of value or worth.

Can't Remember: apparently unable (or convinced that it is impossible) to recall something; feeling blocked, fogged in or continuously blank about some past thing; sub-volitionally selective unawareness of the past.

Complacency: lackadaisical or incurious self-satisfaction usually accompanied by habitual unawareness of any actual dangers, deficiencies or need for betterment.

Contactlessness: obsessive disconnectedness; a sense of not touching or being a part of anything; alienation; enforced remoteness or dissociation.

Distracted by Lesser Priorities: an automatic drifting of attention or consciousness away from important or priority matters onto less important or trifling matters.

Elsewhereness: not being present in the moment; automatically or unconsciously dwelling on the past, or daydreaming ineffectively about the future; thinking of other things distractedly, rather than with the attentiveness the present moment demands.

Emotionless: deadness, numbness; feeling "no feelings"; passive insensitivity.

Facetious: jocularity or levity in an often clumsy or inappropriate manner to mask hidden mis-emotion or intent.

'Got it made': a sense of exaggerated confidence or fixed self-assurance, usually tinged with arrogance or complacency, which ignores the big picture or larger issue of sustaining and increasing betterment, and instead clinging to a rationalized and unchanging "positive" self-image.

Humorlessness: 'deadpanish'; literalness: seeing no humor or lightness in anything; focused solely on the "serious" side of life; inability to get distance from, or "lighten" an experience.

Ignoring 'Small' Awarenesses of Causation: not noticing or "listening" to one's subtle intimations; discounting discernment, promptings or intuitions of possible incremental betterment and change; 'always knew' any realization resulting from a dialogue…

Laxity: undutiful neglectence, or omission of discipline, resolve or intent necessary to accomplish a rational task or result.

Appendix V

'No Sympathy': a harsh, cold or defensively indifferent attitude toward another's suffering, as opposed to a position of being neither sympathetic nor unsympathetic but compassionate (a distanced but rationally caring and active benevolence.)

Non-Participation: fixed avoidance of joining in; typically abstaining from group efforts or alliances; acting the "loner."

Not Confronting known and actual importances: ignoring the obvious; "backing off" or resisting facing and handling difficult but important issues, people or events, present or past.

Not Enough Time: an enervating sense that sufficient 'time' does not exist to accomplish something, as opposed to knowingly prioritizing and apportioning time as a *controllable* resource for accomplishment

Remote: cut off from, distant; unattached to; obsessively disconnected.

Same Realization Over and Over: a repetitive "knowing," awareness or insight which is not applied, or does not result in change of condition or deepen or expand in time; habitual adherence to an unchanging philosophical core belief or ineffective "common sense" conviction or "fixed idea."

Stuck in an Accomplishment or Win: resting on one's laurels or living in the past; dwelling on or continuously returning to a past achievement, without adding to one's store of progressively evolving accomplishments and wisdom.

Uninteresting Object or Person: considering a person or thing to be intrinsically "uninteresting" or without merit, as opposed to recognizing one's capacity to generate interest or choose to withhold interest or selectively *intend* interest to accommodate ethical goals or projects.

Unwilling to Apply Ethics: willfully ignoring what would be best for the greatest number effected and instead choosing to act with a narrow and perverse focus of interest, negating the wider rational balance of concerns which achieve the greater good for all domains.

V. CONFUSION

Definition: a persisting seemingly 'honest' failure to comprehend, a convincingly oppressive mental disorganization of thought process and attention, which actually overlays a sub-volitionally selected and fixed balance of opposing convictions regarding a resisted or desired subject, situation or person.

Blankness: persisting dullheadedness; mentally "frozen" or stubbornly numb; seemingly unable to think:, imagine, or recall.

Appendix V

Can't Assign Correct Importances: calculated inability to prioritize or evaluate the worth or importance of some things in relation to others in order to prevent realization decision or planned achievement.

Conflicting "Truths:" inability to establish shades of difference between opposing ides or issues, which appear to be equally real, true or factual resulting in a self-serving impairment of action or judgment.

Convinced after Impact or Duress: "brainwashed"; having the "truth" stressfully; enforced, delusional believing or adamant conviction after suffering stress, pain or punishment to "correct" or "reform" a previous state of non-believing; "post-traumatic;" or post-hypnotic suggestion.

Dogged Assertion of Conviction: a compulsive or stubborn adherence to a false belief despite established contrary evidence, observation, or reasonable argument and discourse.

Dopey: semi-comatose; an enduring state of mental sluggishness, 'thick'ness, dullness, stupidity.

Insolubility: the apparency that a particular problem or condition cannot be resolved or changed no matter what effort is applied to it; a hopeless and menacing dilemma which yet demands a solution and fixes attention.

No or Slow Cognitions: failure to have normal insights or realizations when new, and particularly profound material, is presented to one; selective incomprehension in the service of a fixed pattern of avoidance or sub-rational preservation.

Persisting Complexity or Mystery: failure to grasp the meaning of something despite repeated and varied exposition; *selective* unawareness of the larger, rational context which, when understood, erases the narrower, fixed context of an apparent insolubility formed in the past and misplaced in the present.

Robotic: automatic, machine-like; going through motions; falling into habit, repetition or echoing rather than bringing fresh awareness and intent to something; irresponsibly following orders or assigning external cause for one's actions; mindless reenactment.

Slow or Unstable Learning: sluggish or resistive grasp of new information, often characterized by lapses, setbacks or forgetting; "stupidity;" sub-volitionally patterned mental resistance.

Sudden Tiredness: "feelings" of fatigue brought on "mysteriously," or by enervating negative "feelings" or "thoughts" rather than by physical exertion or strenuous effort.

Trouble with Concepts, Words, and Study: a persistent resistance to the learning of theoretical or conceptual material; a defensive "blockheadedness" or a covertly purposeful blankness with respect to such learning.

Appendix V

"Wondering or Wandering": "analysis paralysis;" fruitless or purposeless speculation, questioning or attempting to "figure out;" irrational demand to solve what one is covertly convinced is insoluble. Unwillingness to use 'working solutions' to get on with it.

Wrong Target: assigning blame, discredit or cause of action inappropriately as a tactic of avoidance.

VI. DIS-ABILITY

Definition: apparently unwanted but covertly intended impairment or reduction of a previously existing ability or faculty to support a hidden reactive agenda for failure, or self-restraint as a player, as opposed to the authentic limitation of ability (inability) requisite to attain an as yet unattained or unrealized state of capacity; disabled as opposed to unabled.

Back Off: the irrational but knowing avoidance of or retreat from observing or handling a situation that is recognizably sub-optimum; a reactive unwillingness to accept a challenge requiring incremental growth or expansion of ability to handle or correct a sub-optimum condition.

Can't Be/Do/Have: a false and covertly self-serving conviction that one is inherently unable to be, do or have something, despite the fact that such capacity is routinely demonstrated in life by others or by self at other times.

Can't Change a Condition: the sense that one is "innately powerless" over or cannot alter for the better an unwanted circumstance, condition, or behavior.

Can't Focus: apparent inability to direct and maintain one's attention or awareness toward something; rambling or distractedness in the service of sub-intentional non-arrival.

Can't or Must Control Something: a sense that one is dangerously powerless over something, or that one must exert power over it with exaggerated urgency.

Can't Refrain from Causing: a seeming inability to cease a compulsive and repetitive doing of something, such as mental chattering, "volitional" but unwanted smoking or drinking, repeatedly using a catchphrase, complaining, and so on.

Can't Waste: a sense that one must not lose, misuse, discard, or fail to use something, usually accompanied by an anticipation of dire penalty or other unspecified negative consequence if one does.

Disorganized: "scatterbrained," unprepared, unfocused; "unable" to control one's time, possessions or thinking in a covert pattern to prevent achievement.

Appendix V

Don't Notice: obliviousness; unheeding failure to perceive one's surroundings or to note obvious importances or significant things as an insulation from the betterment derived from systematic noticing and remedial action.

Greedy: unethical desire for possession, sensation or status in excess of what is rationally necessary, appropriate or fair.

Illness/Injury Prone: tendency to frequently experience and suffer from proneness to physical ailments and accidents.

Inattentive: unwilling to concentrate or pay attention; revelation avoidance.

Incompleteness: a troubling sense that one is fundamentally flawed, or not whole or sufficient, or that something vital is missing from a product or experience.

Indecisive: wavering; unable to make decisions or choose; perpetually at "loggerheads;" submerged in a covertly self-imposed dilemma.

Intemperate: given to excessive and unthinking indulgences, particularly of appetite or passion, as in intemperate drinking or drug use.

Knowingly Dishonest: consciously and willfully misrepresenting the truth of a situation, often to justify unethical behavior.

Know it's Wrong: compulsive action desire or decision with a partial knowledge of inappropriateness that is insufficient to enable rationale restraint or control; rationalized obsessive need, greed, or infatuation.

Lacking Intention: aimlessness, purposelessness; taking no responsibility for causing harm, or failing to help, by volitional reservation of the sustained intent necessary.

Loses Gains: forgets, "unlearns," consistently reverts to previous state of lesser knowledge or ability to sabotage an ultimate or progressive revelation or rehabilitation.

Need to Please: obsessive, often obsequious unwillingness to be thought ill of or be disliked; prone to servility or propitiativeness to gain imagined favor, approval, or affection.

No Goal: having no dreams, no desires, no ambitions, no game, no purpose, no obstacles to overcome; an unwillingness to participate in and be a full player in the game of life.

Perversity: capriciousness as contrasted with spontaneity; willful rejection, corruption or abuse of a known good; intentional irrationality; arbitrary harming action despite prior agreement with norms or codes of behavior.

Procrastination: habitually avoiding the willed or volitional compliance with or completion of a task, duty or other commitment.

No Confidence: "wimpishness," low self-esteem; representing oneself to be unable or ineffectual.

Self-Sabotage: the obsessive re-enactment of a hidden scenario from the past to bring about an apparently "uncaused" failure or self-limitation in the present.

Uncommunicativeness: an irrational conviction that communication, or direct, honest confrontation, will not help, resolve or improve an unwanted condition, or achieve a wanted one.

Unfocused: "Fuzzy," indirect wavering of intention or resolve which impedes accomplishment; hesitant or scattered.

Unhandled Physical Condition: calculated neglect of or failing to attend to or remedy an illness, injury or physical deficiency, which then becomes a continuing and chronic distraction.

Unproductive: lazy; working without result; contributing little or nothing; avoiding accomplishment or real exchange.

Unwilling to Take Action: factual but irrational passivity; deleterious neglect.

Vacillating: oscillating between two positions; harmful failure to make a decision or choice; shifting compulsively between viewpoints or peaks and valleys of sub-rational emotion or intent to achieve inaction.

VII GENERALITY

Definition: a non-legitimate symbolic totality or "allness" not subject to confirming observation; non-specific; usually attributed without full *contextual* awareness and incorporated in a fixed, sub-rational belief system to avoid precise and direct viewing or handling of a real situation or problem, or to legitimize a reactive agenda.

All Inclusiveness: lumping a class of things together inappropriately; failing to make distinctions between separate things, even if similar..."everybody knows."

'Always': seeing things as being invariably one way or another, failing to allow for exceptions.

Blurred Distinction: failing to make a distinction between approximately similar things; non-specificity.

Confused Levels of Meaning or Abstraction: failing to perceive the distinctions in definition or concept with multiordinal (i.e., a full range of) meaning; confusing "map" with territory; undifferentiated nuances, no 'gray-scale'.

Appendix V

Category Error: sub-rational confusion or blurring of distinction between conceptual realms or domains of meaning or existence, e.g. picture/concept, holon/mind, self/image, etc.

Enforced Equivalence: tendency to insistently equate one thing with another rather than allow for the possibility of many different relationships and distinctions between them.

Everyone Knows: irresponsible, generic attribution of a particular point of knowledge to 'everyone', or a general grouping; not allowing for the possibility that some do not know or for specific origin. Use of 'they': referring to an unspecified grouping of others to assert, allege, prove or disguise a point.

Fixed Context: habitual viewpoint; unwillingness to consider or imagine alternative or expanded perspectives, which might positively reframe a particular experience; no awareness of broader or deeper context for a negative experience.

Fixed Definition: perceiving only one definition or meaning for a word or symbol versus recognizing and utilizing its full spectrum of applied meaning.

Illogical: falsely assuming, or denying, a relationship between concepts or things; faulty reasoning which inhibits rational choice and judgment.

Literalness: focusing on accuracy or inaccuracy of a detail as opposed to the big picture; adhering to the "letter of the law" rather than the intent of the law; context insensitivity as in lacking a sense of humor.

'Never': dismissing of all possibilities, allowing for no possibility.

Non-Multiordinality: considering a word to have a singled or fixed meaning rather than a full spectrum of meanings depending on a changing context; fixedly non-interpretive.

Unwarranted Generalizations: global assumptions or assertions which are not demonstrable or have no basis in logic or fact and which mask direct viewing or support a conviction irrationally.

VIII. MIS-PERCEPTION

Definition: the sub-aware superimposition of mental images from the past over the reality of present experience to bring about an unknowing and distorted perceptual conformity of the present to the dictates of a hidden traumatic past; a post-traumatic re-enactment; delusional returning to the "safety" of the past; replacing fact with "factoid," including the reimpositions of the original perceptions contained in the trauma; psychosomatic sensation.

Appendix V

Compulsive Mis-valuing: habitually viewing certain sensations or substances as being so scarce, important or desirable as to crave or irrationally "need" them; or seeing them as so menacingly overwhelming as to compulsively avoid them or find them repulsive.

Association of Words or Concept with Thing: failing to distinguish between symbol and conceptuality, such as perceiving patriotism and the flag as one and the same.

Attributing Past to Present: compulsively perceiving something in the immediate environment in a past (and often painful) experience-dictated context; overlaying percepts in the present with significances of the past (factoids).

Confusion of Picture and Fact: failing to distinguish a distorting mental representation or image from the fact it represents or substitutes for.

Delusory Menace: False attribution of "present" menace or threat to a person or thing because of physical sensations which actually stem from a past, but similar trauma; (people think: because they "feel nervous" there "must be" something unnerving around them.)

Disassociation: Compulsive mental disconnection from or avoidance of ordinary experience which has been unknowingly associated with past traumatic events.

Distorting Self-Reference: describing oneself in terms which one deems to be factual or true, but which actually characterize only a habit, a fixed aspect or fragmental perspective of personality, or a current unchanging condition. Example: "I'm the kind of person who leaps before he looks," or "I can't stand opera."

Enervation: Exhaustion not connected to physical duress; chronic tension-based "mental" fatigue.

Fanaticism: the fixed and uncritical distortion of perception and action characteristic of the "true believer" or zealot.

Gullibility: Susceptibility to flattery, influence, manipulation or any other form of disingenuousness which distorts common sense perception; susceptibility to hypnosis or to brainwashing, or ready inculcation by stress of false perceptions and assumptions.

Indistinct Pronoun Usage: referring to or connecting I, you, he, she, it, we, you (plural) or they with sub-rational qualities or attributes which are not authentically the person's own, but which originate from past sub-rational perspectives (trauma formed identities).

Intransigent Unforgiveness: implacable, unwavering enmity or vengefulness, which clouds perception; a tenacious, sub-volitional and false attribution of enmity to another; reenactment of ancient and unresolved conflict.

Misdefinition: assigning wrong meaning to a word out of a fixed and post traumatic context.

Appendix V

Negative (or Positive) Coloration: the superimposition of a mental image from a past moment of pain, stress or unconsciousness which creates a delusional reframing of the actual experience of the present in terms of the earlier trauma. Something quite harmless can seem menacing: dog = bite = all dogs bite = all dogs dangerous (by irrational association.) Non-differentiation of Word and Thing: failing to distinguish between the symbolic nature of a word and the thing it represents.

"Not Invented Here" Syndrome: an unfriendliness toward things not created or approved by self or one's group.

"Too Many," "Too Much:" attributing negative or disabling cause over one to an apparently excessive quantity or degree of something experienced, rather than to the present context from which a thing is controlled or used or enacted; inhibition of the capacity for self-renewal of purpose, interest, or perception; not in the (new) moment.

"Positioning:" Unethical emphasis or exaggeration of the supposed "desirable" (or undesirable) qualities of a person, place, thing, event or circumstance to persuade or influence another's viewpoint or perception to accept or reject it.

Preference for "Packaged" Perceptions: Unnoticed or obsessive reliance on authority or on "pre-digested" or externally managed perception; attribution of inordinate value to rumors herd mentality, gossip, third-party perceptions, media "facts," docudramas, "sound bites," sensationalism or group biases.

Psychosomatic Sensations: superimposition on the body of past physical perceptions contained in traumatic experiences; unwanted non-relieved physical and/or emotional sensations not connected to actual physical pathology, impact or injury; tension-based sensations (such as "nervous stomach") often resulting from the stress of conflicting purposes contained in past mental pictures; "post traumatic syndrome."

Time Distortion: the oppressive sense that time is passing more quickly or slowly than it actually is, often related to a duress which activates the reactive indicator.

Selective Unawareness: unknowing but volitional unwillingness to experience; contrived obliviousness in the service of sub-volitional agendas. This may be observed in the disavowing of a previously confirmed and demonstrated certainty that a specific reactive indicator is reactive and can be erased. The indicator may occur in a new context in which it doesn't "seem" reactive, until erasure of this variant reactive indicator reveals again the pattern of covert selectivity.

Spatial Distortion: the oppressive sense of insufficient, tight or "collapsed" space (or claustrophobia), or of overabundant or unpleasantly boundless space or time; "endlessness."

Trivialization: Devaluation of important significances, values, experiences or things perceived, to eliminate them from consideration as data in a context of realization.

Appendix V

"Ugly/Big Nose" Syndrome: automatically *mis*perceiving a factual irregularity as a factoid deformity; feeling a knee-jerk revulsion toward something, the action of which is supported or "justified" by commonly-held bias against or preference for that thing; a self-serving and false authentication of reactive criticalness, justified by a critical, pictured, superimposition over the actual presence of a suboptimum object or fact.

Garrulousity: empty talking; unknowing but strategic avoidance of real communication; substituting a mannerist mode of communication for authentic being and connection; hiding behind seemingly rational verbiage, or "occupying the buzzword bushes."

Malaise (see also under mal-emotion): a vague sense of dis-ease...often associated with the onset of an illness, and is often psychosomatic.

Appendix VI

Reality (density) Discrimination Guide

Holosophy holds that:

Truth is a logical coherence *balanced* by descriptive correspondence: derived from a higher apriori, and ultimate idealized Truth that provides rational meaning and value context for both. (See appendix 1.)

Fact = agreed upon reality co-perceived volitionally in the context of an actual or potential Ideal scene.

Factoid = sub-rational and redundant mis-perception of fact to sustain and accommodate the duration of a pre-existing compulsive agenda (case-contour-imposed compelled or *reactive indicators*).

	Fact (Holon As 'True Witness' No reactive lens of perception)	Vs.	Factoid (The Lens of Perception *through* Sub-Rational indicators)
1.	Analytical (not sub-volitional influences)		Reactive
2.	Perceived volitionally (as authentic Self) *own* viewpoint		Perceived sub-volitionally (as false pictured 'self') Other viewpoint, mis-owned
3.	Thick, Dense, Palpable Solidity		Thin, Diaphanous, lacks solidity
4.	Public, Observable by others		Private, Non Observable by others
5.	Life Game relevant (objective problem)		Redundant to Life Game (Subjective problem and non-relevant)
6.	No Reactive Indicators, present or associated		Reactive Indicators present or associated
7.	Novel, changing "unscripted"		Imitative, unchanging, "scripted" sub-rationally
8.	Agreed to apparency in present time		No agreement on deceptive 'past as present'
9.	Refreshes, but does not *erase* when confronted		Erases when confronted and fully *owned*
10.	Not easily re-located without physical contact & force		Relocates automatically as vp (perceiver) moves or relocates
11.	Enduring ownership or co-ownership possible objectively "perceived" and acknowledged.		Perceived *because* mis-owned, vanishes *when* owned
12.	Volitionally co-perceived by multiple rational consensus		Sub-volitionally perceived, no rational consensus
13.	Imaginal illusion in *present* (no present mental mass) as past or present		Pictured deception from *past* (mental mass, confused with present)
14.	Thralldom – volitional source implicit		Trance – *non*-volitional source believed, enacted

Appendix VI

Fact (Holon As 'True Witness' No sub-rational lens of perception)	Vs.	**Factoid** (Case-Contour Perception *through* sub-rational indicators)
15. Co-perceived objective eventuation & non-eventuation		Forced delusional eventuation & non-eventuation
16. Consensual, benevolent pretense		Arbitrary, suboptimum alteration as 'lie'
17. Predictable variation & stability of appearance		Unpredictable, 'invariant instability' of appearance
18. Degree of flexible certainty of observation …(rational)		Inflexible tendency of absolute "conviction" concerning…(rightness)
19. Continuum of events, changing		Continuity of "event", fixed reoccurrence
20. Exact stable repetitive locatability possible		Exists *because* of mis-location…endowed sub-rational and automatic persistence
21. Participatory, (interacts constructively with other players in Life Game		Non participatory (no other players *real*)
22. Not *connected* to past trauma conscious selectivity possible		Past trauma reenacted, limited and compulsive selectivity
23. Available as data for rational ethical choices		Fixed, unknown data past, use produces unethical choices
24. Multiordinal* contextual, holon conscious of abstracting		Non-multiordinal fixed frame, and context no awareness of abstracting
25. Freely remembered, familiarity possible		Obsessively enacted, no familiarity or self-determined knowingness present

* Susceptible to conscious reframing

Appendix VII

Is the Brain Really Necessary?

This was the question asked by British neurologist John Lorber when he addressed a conference of pediatricians in 1980. Such a frivolous sounding question was sparked by case studies Lorber had been involved in since the mid-60s. The case studies involve victims of an ailment known as hydrocephalus, more commonly known as water on the brain. The condition results from an abnormal build up of cerebrospinal fluid and can cause severe retardation and death if not treated.

Two young children with hydrocephalus referred to Lorber showed normal mental development for their age. In both children, there was no evidence of a cerebral cortex. One of the children died at age 3 months, the second at 12 months. He was still following a normal development profile with the exception of the apparent lack of cerebral tissue shown by repeated medical testing. An account of the children was published in Developmental Medicine and Child Neurology.

Later, a colleague at Sheffield University became aware of a young man with a larger than normal head. He was referred to Lorber even though it had not caused him any difficulty. Although the boy had an IQ of 126 and had a first class honors degree in mathematics, he had "virtually no brain". A noninvasive measurement of radio density known as CAT scan showed the boy's skull was lined with a thin layer of brain cells to a millimeter in thickness. The rest of his skull was filled with cerebrospinal fluid. The young man continues a normal life with the exception of his knowledge that he has no brain.

Although anecdotal accounts may be found in medical literature, Lorber is the first to provide a systematic study of such cases. He has documented over 600 scans of people with hydrocephalus and has broken them into four groups:

- those with nearly normal brains
- those with 50-70% of the cranium filled with cerebrospinal fluid
- these with 70-90% of the cranium filled with cerebrospinal fluid
- and the most severe group with 95% of the cranial cavity filled with cerebrospinal fluid

Of the last group, which comprised less than 10% of the study, half were profoundly retarded. The remaining half had IQs greater than 100. Skeptics have claimed that it was an error of interpretation of the scans themselves. Lorber himself admits that reading a CAT scan can be tricky. He also has said that he would not make such a claim without evidence. In answer to attacks that he has not precisely quantified the amount of brain tissue missing, he added, "I can't say whether the mathematics student has a brain weighing 50 grams or 150 grams, but it is clear that it is nowhere near the normal 1.5 kilograms."

Many neurologists feel that this is a tribute to the brain's redundancy and its ability to reassign functions. Others, however, are not so sure. Patrick Wall, professor of anatomy at University

Appendix VII

College, London states "To talk of redundancy is a cop-out to get around something you don't understand."

Norman Geschwind, a neurologist at Boston's Beth Israel Hospital agrees: "Certainly the brain has a remarkable capacity for reassigning functions following trauma, but you can usually pick up some kind of deficit with the right tests, even after apparently full recovery."

This case is by no means as rare as it seems. In 1970, a New Yorker died at the age of 35. He had left school with no academic achievements, but had worked at manual jobs such as building janitor, and was a popular figure in his neighborhood.

Tenants of the building where he worked described him as passing the days performing his routine chores, such as tending the boiler, and reading the tabloid newspapers. When an autopsy was performed to determine the cause of his premature death he, too, was found to have practically no brain at all.

Professor Lorber has identified several hundred people who have very small cerebral hemispheres but who appear to be normal intelligent individuals. Some of them he describes as having 'no detectable brain,' yet they have scored up to 120 on IQ tests.

No-one knows how people with 'no detectable brain' are able to function at all, let alone to graduate in mathematics, but there are a couple theories. One idea is that there is such a high level of redundancy of function in the normal brain that what little remains is able to learn to deputize for the missing hemispheres. Another, similar, suggestion is the old idea that we only use a small percentage of our brains anyway – perhaps as little as 10 per cent.

The trouble with these ideas is that more recent research seems to contradict them. The functions of the brain have been mapped comprehensively and although there is also a high degree of specialization – the motor area and the visual cortex being highly specific for instance. Similarly, the idea that we 'only use 10 percent of our brain' is a misunderstanding dating from research in the 1930's in which the functions of large areas of the cortex could not be determined and were dubbed 'silent', when in fact they are linked with important functions like speech and abstract thinking.

The other interesting thing about Lorber's findings is that they remind us of the mystery of memory. At first it was thought that memory would have some physical substrate in the brain, like the memory chips in a PC. But extensive investigation of the brain has turned up the surprising fact that memory is not located in any one area or in a specific substrate. As one eminent neurologist put it, 'memory is everywhere in the brain and nowhere.'

But if the brain is not a mechanism for classifying and storing experiences and analyzing them to enable us to live our lives then what on earth is the brain for? And where is the seat of human intelligence? Where is the mind?

Appendix VII

The only biologist to propose a radically novel approach to these questions is Dr. Rupert Sheldrake. In his book '*A New Science of Life,*' Sheldrake rejected the idea that the brain is a warehouse for memories and suggested it is more like a radio receiver for tuning into the past. Memory is not a recording process in which a medium is altered to store records, but a journey that the mind makes into the past via the process of morphic resonance.

But, of course, such a crazy idea couldn't possibly be true, could it?

Anthony Smith "*The Mind*" New York Viking Press, 1984, p.230
Roger Lewin "*Is Your Brain Really Necessary?*" Science, 210 December 1980, p. 1232
Richard Milton Category Science, December 1, 2003

Appendix VIII

Excerpt from *Recalling Nana's Face: Does Your Brain Store Memories?*

A singular consequence of the materialist-mechanical metaphysics that permeates our culture and our sciences is that we commonly hold basic beliefs that are abject nonsense. One such belief is the almost ubiquitous one -- among ordinary folks as well as neuroscientists and surprisingly many philosophers -- that the brain "stores" memories. The fact is that the brain doesn't store memories, and *can't* store memories.

It has been known for the better part of a century that certain structures in the brain are associated with memory. The amygdala and the hippocampus in the temporal lobe, and some adjacent cortical regions, have been shown to be associated with the act of remembering in animals and humans. The research is fascinating and important, and in my own work as a neurosurgeon I have to be aware of these regions (especially the hippocampus and the fornix and mammillary bodies, to which the hippocampus projects). During surgery, injury to these critical structures (if bilateral) can leave a patient incapable of forming new memories, which is a crippling disability.

But these physiological facts do *not* imply that the brain stores memories in the hippocampus or amygdala or elsewhere. How so?

It's helpful to begin by considering what memory is -- memory is retained knowledge. Knowledge is the set of true propositions. Note that neither memory nor knowledge nor propositions are inherently physical. They are psychological entities, not physical things. Certainly memories aren't little packets of protein or lipid stuffed into a handy gyrus, ready for retrieval when needed for the math quiz.

The brain is a physical thing. A memory is a psychological thing. A psychological thing obviously can't be "stored" in the same way a physical thing can. It's not clear how the term "store" could even apply to a psychological thing.

Now you may believe -- as most neuroscientists and too many philosophers (who should know better) mistakenly believe -- that although of course memories aren't "stored" in brain tissue per se, *engrams* of memories are stored in the brain, and are retrieved when we remember the knowledge encoded in the engram. Indeed neuroscientists believe that they have found things in the brain very much like engrams of some sort that encode a memory like a code encodes a message.

But that too is nonsense. To see why, consider a hypothetical "engram" of your grandmother's lovely face that "codes" for your memory of her appearance. Imagine that the memory engram is safely tucked into a corner of your superior temporal gyrus, and you desire to remember Nana's face. As noted above, your memory itself obviously is not in the gyrus or in the engram. It doesn't even make any sense to say a memory is stored in a lump of brain. But, you say, that's just a silly

Appendix VIII

little misunderstanding. What you really mean to say is that the memory is *encoded* there, and it must be accessed and retrieved, and it is in that sense that the memory is stored. It is the engram, you say, not the memory itself that is stored.

But there is a real problem with that view. As you try to remember Nana's face, you must then locate the engram of the memory, which of course requires that you (unconsciously) must remember where in your brain Nana's face engram is stored -- was it the superior temporal gyrus or the middle temporal gyrus? Was it the left temporal lobe or the right temporal lobe? So this retrieval of the Nana memory via the engram requires *another* memory (call it the "Nana engram location memory"), which must itself be encoded somewhere in your brain. To access the memory for the location of the engram of Nana, you must access a memory for the engram for the location for the engram of Nana. And obviously you must first remember the location of the Nana engram location memory, which presupposes another engram whose location must be remembered. Ad infinitum.

Now imagine that by some miracle (materialist metaphysics always demands miracles) you are able to surmount infinite regress and locate the engram for Nana's face in your superior temporal gyrus (like finding your keys by serendipity!). Whew! But don't deceive yourself -- this doesn't solve your problem in the least. Because now you have to decode the engram itself. The engram would undoubtedly take the form of brain tissue -- a particular array of proteins, or dendrites or axons, or an electrochemical gradient of some specific sort -- that would mean "memory of Nana's face." But how can an electrochemical gradient represent a face? Certainly an electrochemical gradient doesn't *look* like grandma -- and even if it did, you'd have to have a little tiny eye in your brain to see it to recognize that it looked like grandma. Whatever form the engram takes must be a code, and you must then have a key to the code, stored in your brain just like the Nana memory is stored. But then you must remember where the key to the code is stored, which is itself another memory which must be stored and remembered. And to remember the location of a location for the key for the code for the engram requires another engram to remember the location of the location code, which must be located and decoded, which requires another key engram which you now must locate...

And if you think that remembering your grandmother's face via an engram in your brain entails infinite regress, consider the conundrum of remembering a *concept*, rather than a face. How, pray tell, can the concept of your grandma's justice or her mercy or her cynicism be encoded in an engram? The quality of mercy is not strained, nor can it be encoded. How many dendrites and axons for mercy?

You see the nonsense.

By Michael Egnor, MD., Neurosurgeon

Appendix IX

The Paradox:
Intimations of Non-Duality

Contemplate and discuss each dichotomy. Then proceed further by reversing the words (and concepts) to gain playful access to the Infinite Landscape of Knowing that projects and frames all Paradox, the rhythmic ambiguity of the 'Gateless Gate,' or "Portal to Potentia."

1. A tiny hugeness
2. A blazing darkness
3. A future yesterday
4. A weightless heaviness
5. An approaching leaving
6. A dull radiance
7. A meaningful blankness
8. A past future
9. A hollow density
10. A spaceless solid
11. A glowing dullness
12. A missing presence
13. A full emptiness
14. A present absence
15. A boundless perimeter
16. A distant nearness
17. A solid space
18. An empty solid
19. A freezing fire
20. A dubious certainty
21. A different similarity
22. An identity in difference
23. A blind viewing
24. A helping harm
25. A forgotten remembrance
26. A smooth roughness
27. A powerful impotence
28. A colorful grayness
29. An deafening quiet
30. Within an outside
31. A past now
32. A persisting termination
33. An open closure
34. An ordinary uniqueness
35. A novel imitation
36. A pointless emphasis
37. A fixed flexibility
38. A precise inaccuracy
39. A guilty innocence
40. A serious game
41. A solid without particles
42. A personal otherness
43. A forgotten remembering
44. A distant nearness
45. An actual potential
46. A powerful weakness
47. A sourceless origin
48. A painful numbness
49. A beautiful ugliness
50. An unconnected linkage
51. A energetic lassitude
52. A purposeless goal
53. A soft hardness
54. An unconscious awareness
55. A meaningless significance
56. An appearing vanishment
57. A cheerful sadness

Appendix IX

58. A passive dynamism
59. An active stasis
60. An ancient future
61. A painful pleasure
62. A clear ambiguity
63. A thrifty wasting
64. A greedy giving
65. A causative effect
66. A unified diversity
67. An unmoving motion
68. A vacuous plenum
69. An anguished happiness
70. A differentiated similarity
71. A distinct blur
72. A successful failure
73. A random choice
74. An unthought concept
75. An existing nothing
76. A free enslavement
77. A divided non-duality
78. An interested boredom
79. A heated frigidity
80. An asymmetrical symmetry
81. A sacred profanity
82. An unaware consciousness
83. An unconscious awareness
84. A temporary forever
85. A virtuous vice
86. A commanded freedom
87. A blind seeing
88. An existing essence
89. A multiple singularity
90. An unprovable proof
91. An impossible likelihood
92. An abundant scarcity
93. A designed accident
94. An instant eternity
95. A final almost
96. A designed accident
97. A contemptuous Admiration
98. A frenzied calm
99. A fanatic moderation
100. An Absolute relativity
101. A pointless necessity
102. A measurable infinity

Appendix X

The Powers of Communication:

Communication has been called "a universal solvent." It has however, a great many more aspects and powers than solving or *dis*solving. It is the essence of Act and Intent that propels and instantiates all Kosmic Order and Existence. It is the manifest instrument of *all creative* Agency and Player Participation in the Game of Life. As such, it is the Proper Study and a priority *restorative* and creative Interest for all Holons.

Some of the Capacities of Communication to consider and discuss:

1. Creates spaces
2. Transmits concepts/convinces
3. Reifies objects
4. Separates locations
5. Enables exchanges
6. Limits/extends knowing
7. Separates viewpoints
8. Defines identity
9. Enables portrayal/enactment
10. Actualizes consideration
11. Defines power by emission-rate
12. Transmits quality
13. Locates and enables source-points
14. Locates receipt-points
15. Carrier of sensation
16. Sorts disorder/introduces order
17. Provides perception grids/frames
18. Directs attention
19. Establishes lines of connection
20. Moves symbols
21. States periodicity
22. Enables alteration
23. Enables duplication and persistence
24. Enables *im*persistence/curtails infinities
25. Is restorable
26. Is recreatable
27. Certifies rank
28. Can be graduated/gradient
29. Can convey emotion/inflame/inspires
30. Transmits understanding, projects vectors
31. Sets objectives
32. Can denote
33. Can connote/frame knowledge
34. Can conceal
35. Can be withheld
36. Can refer/intimate
37. Can be referred *to*
38. Can congeal and solidify
39. Can mis-represent
40. Can clarify
41. Can undulate
42. Can particulate
43. Is synchronous
44. Can create ambiguity
45. Restores knowing
46. Reveals distinctions
47. Harmonizes/reconciles opposites
48. Is a 'nothing'
49. Is a 'something'
50. Is a meaningful combination of both
51. Enables a cognitive *inference cascade* in dialogue

Appendix XI

The Transformative Dialogue:
(Sub-Rational Resistance Markers)

Clients experiencing difficulty or persisting reactive indicators should review full list below and discuss any confusions, or disagreements, or applicability of any item with facilitator,cognitions are permitted…even encouraged.:

1. Is an upset present that is denied, justified or 'explained'? ___

2. Something persistently concealed? Not discussable? Too embarrassing or 'off limits'? ___

3. Some resistive hidden standards (diminishing or odious comparisons):

    - If it doesn't erase immediately then any additional communication isn't validated as a gateway to erasure…i.e. must get rid of it *now*… ___

    - A 'small' or introductory awareness or communication gradients not considered 'enough' to *begin* a pathway to erasure…an interrupted inference? ___

    - Failure to notice 'close-in' *ideas* as an incremental gradient of erasure or betterment of conditions? Not enough progress being made? ___

    - Unnoticed 'valuable' mental-image connections to and framing of something seemingly unwanted…something better not said or revealed ___

    - Comparing each realization to a hidden fixed goal or standard…'Does this get rid of or 'solve' my (pain, problem, compulsions)?' ___

4. Selling/asserting something vs. witnessing and describing everything honestly in a dialogue? Facilitator doesn't understand? ___

5. Mental mass or condition seems like it's "everywhere?" ___

6. 'Factoid' not gradually revealed and recognized as a reactive *picture*? ___

7. Reactive indicator 'explained away' or justified as 'not really reactive' to perpetuate and accommodate a specific dramatization? ___

8. "Honest" confusion asserted as fact…Any hidden intention supporting it denied or un-noticed? Something insoluble? A persisting mystery? ___

9. Covertly resisting a 'dangerous' inference or implication to prevent an erasure or preserve a false but disabling belief? ___

10. Unwanted condition or picture 'moving around' but not erasing? ___

11. Poor or uncertain density discrimination…*picture* seems solid or 'real', no sense of looking *as* a pictured identity, or *through* the picture? ___

Appendix XI

12. Using *im*personal pronoun or *name,* in describing a situation; generalizing without a *specifying* awareness of distinction (it's, they, she, Joe, etc.)?

13. Poor sense of subjective location…unwanted "fact" seems physical, or seems physically placed and uncausedly "there." (Something *there* seems *here*.)?

14. Lost any sense of emergent degrees of erasure pathway (no inferential gradients e.g. first intimation not developing to full appearance and erasure of picture)?

15. Unnoticed 'resistive-qualification' of answers in dialogue-cycles…"I guess, maybe, perhaps, I think", etc. to avoid fully 'owning' and confronting of erasure path?

16. Verbal abstraction or generality used to 'describe', without being noticed as a resistance to *direct* perception (*inexact* time, place, form or event) preventing the description 'as it *is*' necessary for erasure?

17. Event *location* 'confusion': "There is 'here'…Here is 'there'…Past is 'now'?

18. Trying to get "rid of" or "solve" a persistent unwanted condition instead of '*dis*solving it' by inspection and dialogue?

19. Failing to improve recognition of a 'close-in' *thought* as a hidden connector to, or precursor of, a reactive picture or condition? A 'reasonable' suffering?

20. Failure to notice assemblages of pictures as generalized interpositions, or fixation on multiple or grouped 'picturings' without selecting *one* to view and handle?

21. Consistent failure to notice that seeing is *not* being (viewing *requires* distance)?

22. '*Mere Expressing*' without realization as a dramatization or obsessive experiencing …and *not* a reducing/erasing description of something; leading to an erasure pathway? Dialogue is becoming a 'disagreement', or argumentative?

23. Failure to notice a 'capacity is compulsion' computation?…'if I restore this ability, I'll be dangerous…again'…? Denied past of having or using an ability?

24. Selectively disabled willingness to *admire* or be admired, i.e. to perceive beauty, rarity or value…in an object, condition, or person…to 'prevent' becoming (or causing) the involuntary or seductive victim of the thing admired?

Corollary:
Anything to *be* erased must be 'appreciated' in a wider integral Kosmic context…admiration is volitional and does *not* equal or result in vulnerability.

25. Diving for 'deeper' meaning or 'awareness' to avoid confronting an *immediately* accessible picture, which would more easily access an available erasure pathway?

26. Resistance based on the false assumption that the memory or recreation of an evil act or purpose *fixes* one in that condition…The creative *source* of a condition is not ultimately fixed in it, or *defined* by it…

Appendix XI

27. A hidden, obstructing thought process which denies or avoids the certainty that *anything* unwanted has *some* gradient and accessible context for *viewing*, betterment and/or erasure? ___

28. Failure to look at, or be aware of the 'nearer' or closer in, thought *about* the thought, picture or condition that seems unwanted and persistent? No separation from a sad or unwanted 'fact'? ___

29. Neglected or selectively 'denied familiarity' of reactive categories or indicators that enables making the same mistakes over and over? ___

30. Selective (tactical) unfamiliarity with the full complement of reactive indicators especially, to not recognize one that's typically valuable, present, applicable and viewable? Something persisting doesn't 'seem' reactive ___

    Corollary:
    Any Reactive Indicator is always an apparently involuntary, but actually *tactical* departure from an ideal scene, and therefore *harmful* to some degree...and therefore carries a primary ethical obligation to erase or 'rise above' it... ___

31. Denied or delayed familiarity with the basic resistance markers, concepts, and the temporal *sequence* of handling? Some things better left forgotten? ___

32. Deciding to passively accept blankness, confusion, forgetting, boredom, disinterest as "reasonable" or "special" exceptions to erasable reactivity? ___

33. Persistently unaware of *selective* un-familiarity with a repeating mechanism or condition. "Confused again", "lost again", "same thing again?" ___

34. Expressing or describing again an unwanted condition while un-admittedly attaching reactive indicators to it so it doesn't erase? ___

35. Un-admitted or *knowingly* unacknowledged personal intentionality concerning some value or aspect of a 'picture' or persisting, unwanted condition? ___

36. Fixated on the need to handle *another's* condition or upset...'first'? ___

37. Concerned about loss of 'self' or possession when erasing because of hidden identification of the reactive mind with the Life Game, or one's character with the 'case-contour'? ___

38. Asserting responsibility *without* good indicators...concealing hidden blame... 'Toughing it out' as an escape mechanism...Being "courageous" (or 'stupid enough') to have been, or *remain* connected to, or victimized by, a present source of upset or menace?...rightfully critical? ___

39. Consistent failure to break down the complexity or generality of a condition or problem to its *erasable* components and hidden, conflicting intentions? ___

40. Is there a framing sentimentality? Sub-rational 'victim' validation, i.e. superficial mis-emotion that is 'protective' or reactively indulgent but *not* transformative? ___

Appendix XI

41. The apparency of an 'undeniable fact' that is hopelessly unchangeable? ___

42. Is what seems 'here and now' really 'there and then'? ___

43. Overwhelmed?…'too many'; 'too much', unhandled cycles piling up, often un-communicated therefore persisting beyond capacity to conclude or complete? ___

44. Disguised victim: No apparent reactive or 'mental' context available for an effect "being honestly or factually suffered?" Just being *human…unchangeably*? ___

45. Mislabeling or 'not noticing' incremental small or preliminary erasures as 'not enough'…suppressing, burying or holding off available and *new* material and perception to prevent full and realized access to an erasure pathway? ___

46. Un-acknowledged mini-overts accumulating to require the inevitable compensatory 'unwanted' effect…suffering that is blamable, periodic, and suitably retributive? ___

47. 'Convinced' by a feeling or mental effect which is not recognized as the falsely appearing deeper stage of an *erasable* blankness and confusion, e.g. the 'valid victim' dramatization? ___

48. Asserting that 'feelings' are more important than 'mere intellectualism', assuming concepts are junior to sensation, therefore, *postulates*, being falsely devalued, tend not to erase? ___

49. An imposed reactive pattern is a *pictured* continuity; a generalized *pattern* can't be instantly erased (the *whole* and actual pattern is never there)…'continuing' trauma 'complex' acts as a hidden standard to prevent the earlier-similar inference cascade *starting* with a particular accessible element leading to erasure? ___

50. Something *apparently* whole, but just grouped sensations or elements? ___

51. Is what's looking for "it" *being* in the same space as the "it?" ___

52. Has some *conviction* (pictured decision) displacing *familiarity* (non reactive cognitive *re*framing capacity)? Some undeniable *rightness* persisting? ___

53. Asserting (limiting) a realization as relative to only one domain or life context… tending to have little 'ripple-effect' or 'resonance' of realization with other domains. ___

54. Item or condition mentally placed on wrong domain…'self' as brain…picture as reality?...mind as 'neurons'…? ___

55. Not yet aware of "it" as a pronoun which can sub-rationally 'connect' an external *object* or condition to a 'self' *picture,* through a *personal* pronoun e.g. 'me'…? ___

56. Need pictures to maintain objective standards (reality)…failing to realize that one must first 'Know' what's in a picture *in* order to create a picture?...objective standards are *innate* Kosmic *priority* knowings… ___

57. Confusing hidden 'equally' conflicting intentions, or 'problem' with a *condition* (no perception of the personal countering *intention* contained in, and *making persist,* what *is* 'unwanted')? ___

Appendix XI

58. Selective unwillingness to *know* enough data-content and its *context* to spot actual departures from ideal scenes or objectives…(rational choices and familiarity *inform* ideal scenes enabling corrections of any departures)…tactical un-awareness of *inferences* thereby preventing any corrective learning steps or bettering path to accomplishment? ___

    Corollary:
    Realization is a *cognitive* enhancement, which rationally extends familiarity… (Dramatization is *sub*-rationally and selectively *denied* familiarity, inferentiality, or *contextuality*)? ___

59. Something still resolutely unforgivable?...persisting recrimination…still blaming? ___

60. Still savoring an old realization to prevent a *new* one, or 'waiting' for the *next* one? ___

61. 'Reframing' just to diminish an importance or 'value'? ___

62. More *knowing* than the facilitator, or Holosophy, or Facilitator not helping…? ___

63. Consider it's *all* 'just opinion'? Is one *opinion* just as 'true' as another…is there a relativism diminishing a rational importance? ___

64. *Forced* to continue playing a Game? Looking doesn't or 'can't' erase something? ___

65. Out of character…(being a false, pictured 'self' on *another* domain)? *Pictured* self put on 1st domain…pictured Mind/Brain on 6th? ___

66. What is truly *believed* about (the problem or thing unwanted)?...Do *you* believe that? ___

67. Does your identity, personality, or 'true self' exist prior to, or apart from, 'your' holon? Might *lose* a sacred 'part' of yourself? ___

68. Being 'right' or convinced of something despite the presence of a reactive indicator… rather be *right* than reasonable or accurate? (Perception is *never* accurate in presence of a 'lens' of reactive indicators.) ___

69. …If none of the above apply, check for a pulse!...or a forked tail and horns? RT ___

Appendix XII

Some Kosmic Archetypal Agendas

Be →	Do →	Have
Begin →	Continue →	Complete
Create →	Survive →	Destroy
Affinity →	Reality →	Communication
Truth →	Goodness →	Beauty
Start →	Change →	Stop
Plan →	Implement →	Result
Subject →	Verb →	Object
Possible →	Observation →	Real
Order →	Entropy →	Chaos
Cause →	Distance →	Effect
Space →	Energy →	Object
Differentiation →	Association →	Identification
Quality →	Relation →	Quantity
Plus →	Neutral →	Minus
Source →	Existence →	Condition
Concept →	Combination →	Appearance
Idea →	Intentions →	Action
Potentiality →	Possibility →	Actuality
Actuality →	Agreement →	Reality
Singularity →	Projection →	Entropy
Past →	Present →	Future
Birth →	Growth →	Death
Possible →	Observable →	Actual
Essence →	Choice →	Existence
Presence →	Transition →	Absence
Observe →	Evaluate →	Decide
Notice →	Duplicate →	Erase
Image →	Item →	Entity
Field →	Wave →	Particle
Energy →	Condensation →	Solidity
Semantics →	Syntax →	Semiotics
Self-determined →	Other-determined →	'Pan'-determined
Condensation →	Compaction →	Concretion
Thesis →	Anti-thesis →	Syn-thesis
Non-Duality →	Duality →	Paradox
Play →	Error →	Limit
Instantiation →	Alteration →	Continuity
Freedom →	Purpose →	Barriers

Appendix XIII

You Have to Be Conscious to Deny Consciousness, and Other Conundrums (Excerpt from *Evolution News*, July 6, 2015)

Would you have a rational discussion with a zombie? Materialists are forced into the position of discussing philosophy and science with the walking dead, since under their terms we are all that. Unless rationality is a mindful concept -- unless we are more than atoms in motion -- that's the logical result of denying mind and intelligence.

To deny that we are mindful creatures, the materialist also has to deny the existence of any realm of abstract concepts that a mind can access. Yet materialism itself is an abstract concept.

This seems intuitively obvious, but it's amazing how often materialists ignore the self-refuting nature of their assumptions. Nancy Pearcey wrote about this a few months ago, noting ways in which materialist claims commit the self-referential absurdity: "Applied to itself, the theory commits suicide."

A recent example is a new theory of consciousness from Ezequiel Morsella, a psychology professor at San Franciso State University. Morsella relegates consciousness to a minor, passive role as an interpreter of sensory data rather than a free agent of choice and deliberate thought.

"The interpreter presents the information but is **not the one making any arguments** or **acting upon the knowledge** that is shared," Morsella said. "Similarly, the **information** we perceive in our consciousness is **not created by conscious processes**, nor is it reacted to by conscious processes. Consciousness is the middle-man, and it doesn't do as much work as **you think**." [Emphasis added.]

So did Morsella think about this? Here's how you uncover a self-referential fallacy: you apply the claim to itself to see if it short circuits. He just made an argument, but said consciousness doesn't make arguments. He said consciousness can't create information, but he attempted to create information from his own theory. He said we don't really think, but told his readers "you think."

Consciousness, per Morsella's theory, is more reflexive and **less purposeful** than **conventional wisdom** would dictate. Because the human mind experiences its own consciousness as sifting through urges, thoughts, feelings and physical actions, **people understand their consciousness to be in control** of these myriad impulses. **But in reality**, Morsella **argues**, consciousness does the same simple task over and over, **giving the impression** that it is doing more than it actually is.

"We have **long thought consciousness** solved problems and had many moving parts, but it's much more basic and static," Morsella said. **"This theory is very counterintuitive. It goes against our everyday way of thinking."**

Some ideas are counterintuitive because they are wrong. Self-referential fallacies permeate these comments like white on rice. If "conventional wisdom" is not mindful, it is not wise -- nor is Morsella's alternative. If the human mind experiences its own consciousness but has no control, did Morsella have control when he chose to write this statement? If consciousness can't think, why does he keep referring to thinking? And what is "reality" if our minds are incapable of apprehending such a concept?

The **theory**, which took Morsella and his team more than 10 years **to develop,** can be difficult to **accept** at first, he said.

So did he think about his theory for all those years? Did he choose to "develop" it? Does he want our minds to "accept" it? We're watching a poor professor's theory implode. To take him seriously, we would have to treat him as a zombie going through motions and mouthing syllables. Nobody's home.

We see next that he builds his ideas on the theory of evolution.

The **study** of consciousness is complicated, Morsella added, because of the inherent difficulty of **applying** the **conscious mind to study itself**.

"For the vast majority of human history, we were **hunting and gathering** and had more pressing concerns that required rapidly executed voluntary actions," Morsella said. "**Consciousness seems to have evolved for these types of actions rather than to understand itself.**"

In other words, Morsella's theory is just a new way of hunting and gathering to pass on his genes. It has no more significance than that. It's not about making rational arguments in abstract realms of logic and understanding. Pearcey showed the suicidal inevitability of so-called "evolutionary epistemology."

By contrast, intelligent design is not self-refuting. If we truly are rational creatures with consciousness and free will, then we can talk about those concepts in a meaningful way. Our own awareness of our rationality and choice makes it reasonable to assume that our fellow humans experience consciousness like we do. When we bounce ideas off them, and analyze arguments, we can judge which are true or false by weighing their logical coherence or comparing their correspondence with reality.

Animals have ways of "making sense" of the world through their inputs and brains, as researchers at the University of Buffalo describe. But this does not mean that humans are just "more of the same" in terms of information processing. Four times the news item uses the word "understand" or "understanding" how animals do it. Understanding is superfluous to survival. For a bird, it is sufficient to know *that* a sound signifies a mate or a threat. Humans share that ability, but are exceptional in caring *how* or *why* sounds represent things.

Consider this on *Live Science* about the Euler Identity, named for Swiss mathematician Leonhard Euler and called "The most beautiful equation in mathematics." The simplicity of this

Appendix XIII

relationship, $e^{i?} + 1 = 0$, is indeed profound and beautiful. It brings together five mathematical entities in a purely abstract way, one of them being the "imaginary" number i. It is purely conceptual, the result of a long process of logical reasoning, using theorems of calculus. Yet its truth can be checked out against the real world by seeing how it works in applications as diverse as wave mechanics, half-lives, and compound interest.

One must also presuppose consciousness and free will to determine if a statement commits the self-referential fallacy. To prove this, we leave you with a choice to work the following logical exercise. You can quit now, or proceed. (Is that choice yours, or is your hunter-gatherer instinct controlling you?) If you choose to continue, look at any or all of the following statements and decide if they are self-refuting by posing a question referring back to the claim. We'll do the first three as examples. Have fun!

- Everything is relative. (Is that absolutely true?)
- Question everything. (Should we question the advice to question everything?)
- Only particles and forces exist. (Is that statement made of particles and forces?)
- All is illusion.
- Name-callers are idiots.
- People are really zombies.
- It's impossible to know anything.
- Only statements derived empirically are valid.
- Everything evolves.
- Morality is just an evolutionary strategy.
- Tolerate everyone.
- Co-exist.
- "They are in you and in me; they created us, body and mind; and their preservation is the ultimate rationale for our existence. They have come a long way, those replicators. Now they go by the name of genes, and we are their survival machines." (Richard Dawkins)
- "Naturalistic evolution has clear consequences that Charles Darwin understood perfectly... [including the idea that] human free will is nonexistent... Free will is a disastrous and mean social myth." (William Provine).
- Darwinism is like "a universal acid; it eats through just about every traditional concept and leaves in its wake a revolutionized world-view." (Daniel Dennett)
- "Nothing in biology makes sense except in the light of evolution." (Theodosius Dobzhansky)
- "But then with me the horrid doubt always arises whether the convictions of man's mind, which has been developed from the mind of the lower animals, are of any value or at all trustworthy. Would any one trust in the convictions of a monkey's mind, if there are any convictions in such a mind?" (Charles Darwin)
- We must take control of our own evolution.

By the way, Leonhard Euler was known to work out complex derivations in his head while blind. Of what possible use was this ability for survival?

Consciousness as a Scale of Knowing: An Epistemic Hierarchy*

∞
Potential = Infinite *un*specified *Potential* for all projected knowing*ness enabled* below as variably *displayed* meaning and its projectable *being* (elements of knowing *combined*)
↓

Know = Infinite capacity for *specified* knowables, i.e. *subtracted* primal agency conceptuality from the infinite totality of potential knowability
↓

Source = Innate conceptual and categorical templates for *specified* meaning as *potentially manifest* existential referents (combinable knowables)
↓

Create = Emergent Novelty: existential forms of being (as *combined* knowability) *projected* as *new* recreational actualities (manifest forms, events or possible occasions)
↓

Cause/Effect = Apparent spacio-temporal *ordering* of projected and manifest *being* as agree upon reality (*existential process* as volitionally coordinated knowings)
↓

Non-locality & Cosmic Remnant Entanglement = Cosmic background wave-potentia as the remnant quantum levels *underlying* all physical possibilities, contingency, or eventuality (selectively varied probability) reified statistically as the *re*vitalized co-perceived projection of extant Life-Game conditions and potentials.

*Holosophy considers the Kosmos to be an ultimately graduated scale of cognitive potential or knowing*ness* descending from the infinite potential for all knowing, through levels of cognitively specified, *then manifested* knowing down to the mere possibility of being known as an *observed* (selectively conscious) de-construction, i.e., the cosmic background wave form potential.

Apparently the reifying focus of conscious observation is necessary to extract the actualities of any *personal* experiencing from the un-distilled probabilities of the Kosmic background. This perceiving is both broadly consensual and coordinated, *enabling* the enthralled and consensual continuity necessary for Kosmic play and its naturally increasing cosmic entropy.

The scale presented above attempts to represent the scalar degrees of epistemic condensation of knowing which, integrated with the Truth Functions (appendix II) gives an useful philosophical spectrum of knowledge-essence and its existential application.

Appendix XV

Seminal Holosophy Canon:

A Reality is an agreement in progress...so is a game.
A Reality requires observer-participation...so does a game.
A Reality has variable options and barriers...so has a game.
A Reality can be won or lost...or transcended...so can a game.
A Reality contains arbitrary rules or "laws"...so does a game.
A Reality is not internally complete and consistent...neither is a game.
A Reality requires time, place, form and event...so does a game.
A Reality is not self-generated...neither is a game.
In a game the players can decide to resume play after an interruption...
...also in a Reality?

Any true metaphysic of consciousness must address three fundamental problems:

I. The "basis" Problem...
Why is it that we experience a mere "sentient slice" of the vast universe around us...why does awareness have a private perimeter if that defining perimeter is *itself*...part of an endlessly inter-connected and "smeared out" cosmic quantum background?

II. The "binding" problem...
How can the putative "neural correlates" of consciousness be *bound together* to provide both unity of awareness (personal agency) and unitized objects of perception which have *holistic* features seemingly different in kind from mere collections of discrete "synaptic firings" or other strictly *physiological* elements?

III. The "bestowing" problem…
Are Holons *"condemned"* to be free? How can a *personal* existence itself, including freedom of choice and responsibility be arbitrarily and individually *bestowed* by a benevolent diety without a prior *existential* capacity by each recipient to accept or reject such a demanding and deceptive bestowal of "Self"-creation?

> "Some of the greatest physicists believe that to seek *any* ultimate physical understanding is a dangerous and futile pursuit, and that such worrying is best left to philosophers, who have nothing better to do with their time."
> -- Jim Al Khalili, quantum physicist
>
> "The soul can be given a scientific meaning as one's immediate perception of one's coherent, uncollapsed wave-function."
> -- R. Rucker, mathematician

A brief summary statement of Holosophic cognitive and Philosophical researches to date…

Envoi

Finally, let's examine, in capsule, an overview of sub-rational belief and behavior… and attempt to provide a summary perspective as to its ultimate source and content:

Holosophy basically holds that all human aberration is traceable to a primal or core *sub*-rational Template which is a stress-formed post-traumatically imposed *mental-image copy, or memory trace*, substituting for the **actual archetypal[1] pattern of existence; itself a kind of innate "mandalic" paradigm** which, is central to *guiding, but not determining*, each Holon's *authentic persona,* intention, activity, and character formation, while living[2] fully, as a *Kosmic* participant.

---

[1] Archetype: To restate its holosophic meaning and usage… The a priori (conceptual) guiding *potential* for symbolization; sometimes refers to (and is confused with) the primary conceptual *representation*, or the symbol itself. Holosophy uses the term to refer to an *innate* specified signification, which when projected as a *combined meaningfulness* is the *source* of all substantive representations, symbols, or prototypes…

[2] When overwhelmed by the exigencies of living, a being tends to lose full sense of *Kosmic* player-hood, its natural connection to it, and responsibility for it - slipping into sub-rational *semi*-consciousness… a repository of stress-formed *memorial images* containing past sensations, impulses, *beliefs*, and surrogate identities … which deceptively replicate the Holon's natural persona, and is then re-activated by circumstances of similar stress to *compel repetition* of sub-volitional *past* "survival" behavior. Holosophy holds that this total accumulated traumatic past is intended to *mentally* preserve, *simulate* and activate the *actual* conceptual pattern forming of an overlaid mental-image *copy*, a core *reactive* or *sub*-volitional template of past behavior and belief, compulsively repeated…

> "How something is" or what its state is, is an illusion… It may be a *useful* illusion for some purposes, but if we want to think fundamentally we must not lose sight of the essential fact that it *is* an illusion…"
> -- Lee Smolin, quantum cosmologist

A brief summary statement of Holosophic cognitive and Philosophical researches to date…

To reveal, re-appropriate, and re-ensoul, the *actual* life-game template…one must expose the errant departures from it, and erase[3] the redundant *re*active mental-image additives encrusted on it ... which is essentially the goal of Holosophic Dialoguing...

When the Holon falsely copies its own character *under extreme duress*; it then tends to confuse - or "fuse" - *itself* with that substitute character-*image*! Subsequently, "it's" beliefs, activities and impulses tend to be directed by a duplicate, and *false* surrogate ego, formed under duress as a *"post-traumatic"* copy of its true actual persona, original *agency* capacity, and purposes.

In essence, the *sub*-rational mind is the traumatically *pictured* and multi-layered or encrustation of that *reactive* core belief template, which research has shown is each holon's redundant pain and stress-enforced *copy* of the *actual* archetypal pattern of Kosmic existence ... One that was originally and innately *co*-engineered to provide the natural limitations, intentions, and opponencies necessary to play a *Kosmic Game* of mutually enthralled and ultimately benevolent, *recreational display*-activity.

---

[3] Erasure is the capacity of the person to *volitionally cease to create* any sub-rational mental imagery, when perceived as redundant, unwanted, irrational, or *sub*-optimally destructive. This is based on the deeper holosophic insight that *all* persisting mental-images are created by the being itself and if created, can be optimally and *volitionally un*-created (erased).

> "Quantum theory provides a superb description of physical reality on a small scale yet it contains many mysteries. Without doubt, it is hard to come to terms with the workings of the theory, and it's particularly difficult to make sense of the kind of "physical reality" - or lack of it - that it seems to imply for our world…"
> -- Sir Roger Penrose, physicist

A brief summary statement of Holosophic cognitive and Philosophical researches to date…

That emergent *pattern* of co-existent intent essentially actualizes the primal "rules of the game," and with *tacit selectivity*, projects dialectically a universe of serial "plus/minus" eventualities unfolding variously through time as a living Kosmic Template… a celestial algorithm that describes how the Kosmos displays itself *as a game*. A vast *recreation* then enfolds, with its rules, purposes, goals, intentions, universal barriers and organized structure (the 8 domains), all based on a greed-upon, *game-determinate* archetypal categories and dichotomies, with their projected, *co*-perceived, and *enthralled* actualizations.

A *Kosmic* pattern is thus tacitly adopted by all Holons, to creatively *co*-actualize purpose through time … Goals and identities in cyclical opposition are projected to move freely in a serial cosmic path-way. However, the dynamic rules of the *Kosmos* have a designed order and proportionality of manifestation. As in chess, there are progressively tactical events, daily purposes and exchanges; and an overall strategic intent with end-game objectives … There is apparent local goal completion and finality … Then after each series of ended game-cycles, there is projected, a new game, *and* renewal of basic purpose, with a sustained Kosmic cascade of countering, or oppositional, *persona-progression*, providing *novel* future game-*sustaining* vectors, goals, and *identities*… ad infinitum.

> "The universe does not 'exist out there' independent of all acts of observation. Instead, it is in some strange sense a *participatory* universe."
> -- John A. Wheeler, physicist

A brief summary statement of Holosophic cognitive and Philosophical researches to date...

As each Holon-Player evolves, through a succession of solving and counter-solving game purposes and identities, there occurs, progressively, sub-optimal *error*[4], and a resultant *self-limitation* to correct its harmful effects. This *error-limit* factor ensures the cumulative and progressive variation and continuity of the Kosmic "Game at Large". Resulting, is a *pattern of existence* which has a fabric of serial goals that proceed through time one after the other, but are *connected logically*. The logical and thematic connection between the goals which descends through time, consists of projected and *reified* prime archetypal oppositions (be, do, have, *plus-minus*) which express the dialectic gaming-themes of existence, and emerge from its *innate conceptual source*... the 7th domain.

The corruption of the game, by an apparent *forcefully* deceptive intervention[5], at a primordial stage of play by those who opposed, or were trying to dominate from outside the "game in progress" ... tricked the Holon into creating and *substituting* under traumatic duress, *a pictured copy* of the actual game pattern, including its own original *conceptual* intentions and character. The Holon then *endows, and is sub-rationally entranced* and *led* by that injected game-*copy*, and substitute

---

[4] Review chapter six for discussion of how volitional, game-enabling, reduction of awareness and resulting *imprecision and harm* (error limit) are necessary features of Kosmic progressive *devolution*...

[5] This incident of unconfrontable "erasing" force contains revelatory input about the creative consensual limitation committed to, at the "inception of game" ... To avoid a seeming forced revelation which would spoil that, and *all*, *"game" enabling* thralldom, the Holon in a reduced state of awareness, unnecessarily and *pictorially recreates* its natural self-imposed state of "tacit" limitation in order to ensure the game is not erased by a "disenthralling" and unethical "revealing of pretense ..." (see other publications for more details).

> "The physicist John Wheeler once asked 'How can you describe quantum mechanics in five words or less?' The best answer he received was: 'Don't look waves, look particles!' "
> -- Sean Caroll, physicist

A brief summary statement of Holosophic cognitive and Philosophical researches to date…

"ego," instead of its own native character, forming the sub-rational mind (to "preserve the game" but now merely *an implanted replica*. The paradox is "how can an immortal, non-physical, being be so concerned about mere *survival*?" Of course, the *real* concern is the continuity, not of "self," *but of the Kosmic Game itself,* which is the vast co-created artifice of the Holon's ultimate and eternal consensual *participative* commitment, to maintaining the *shared* recreational *game-*display of the *total* Kosmos and its domains…

Every "stimulus-response" mental function that is not rational, spontaneous and in control, is by degree, derived from a *pain-installed* and redundant Kosmic-template- *copy* … We *sub*-rationally endow, i.e. "believe," that stress-born *fiction*, and make it "right" and meaningful because, in our "own" distorted belief-system, it convincingly "arises" in our consciousness, and "seems to *be*" real… deceptively *simulating our actual characters* and perceptions. This *subrationally displaces* the authentic windows of *agency* through which, is tacitly reified and projected, the *true* archetypal conceptuality, that, forms, or *instantiates,* the actual Kosmos…

Essentially, Holosophy holds that the 7th domain, which is *innately specified* conceptual potentiality, is selectively projected as all *manifest* existence … but the trick played upon the Holon is to convince it, *under duress*, that it needs to use the 6th domain (as a *material* copy) to protect and sustain all *non-*

> "The world is an illusion… but it is an illusion we must take seriously, because it is real… as far as it goes…"
> -- Aldous Huxley,
> essayist, novelist, and contemplative

A brief summary statement of Holosophic cognitive and Philosophical researches to date…

material postulates on the 7th … It believes that *it has to redundantly copy (picture) its primal conceptuality in order to continue to actualize it!* Once it *mis-habitually* "pictures" its capacity to *know*, such "thinking" is fixed and compulsive… as a *sub*-rational mockery of Kosmic Thralldom! The being agrees to pretend "not to see" the distinction between an *in*substatial but reifying conceptuality and its *material symbol*. This is deeply convincing because that same commitment to *rational* thralldom (usefully selective *un*awareness) is the Holon's most profound level of participative Kosmic game enablement, expressing the essential benevolent integrity of its *actual* character and mutually *playful* intent...

Player-hood requires such *willed* suspension of disbelief (or artfully adjusted *believ*ability) … a kind of contrived, and tacit, verisimilitude... "It's real and it's *out there!*"… The effort is to avoid the disturbing *un*reality of solipsism - which is the idea that only "you" are egoistically creating the whole universe (on all domains)! However, in serving the prime *rational* consensual tradition of avoiding any game-disruptive revelation, the holon, under extreme duress, *sub*rationally tries to prevent the forced and/or "un-timely" revelatory extinction of "the game"… i.e., the being comes, through a mentally pictured *response* to a *suggestive* trauma, *re*-actively and *irrationally* to pretend that the *substantial* implant-copy (mental image)[6] of its original

---

[6] Like the earlier discussion of "implanted" post hypnotic suggestion, severe trauma imagery can be used to forcibly inculcate (or remove) beliefs, ideas, attitudes, etc. This would be the case with an installed trauma with revelatory information which countered any intentional game preserving "unawareness" on the part of the subject.

> "The mind is a kind of theatre...where several perceptions successfully make their appearance."
> -- David Hume, philosopher

A brief summary statement of Holosophic cognitive and Philosophical researches to date...

conceptuality *IS* that primal *non*-material conceptuality! This makes the *knowing* illusion and benevolent *pretense* of thralldom, into the *unknowing* delusion and *lie* of a trance... by endowing that *pictured* conceptuality, through the same *window* (first domain) of meaningfulness and value that it endows the *actual* Kosmos!

The point of holosophic knowledge and practice is to enquire into and *discard* that whole distorting confluence ... to fully *de*construct it through dialogue, gradually but ultimately recognizing all of its aberrant shifts, shapes and complexities ... and finally to *cease to create all* sub-*rational "thinking" (as unnecessary memorial replication) that falsely simulates and "protects" the redundant "survival" of the ultimately inviolate and immaterial Source that generates and projects the Kosmos...*

This emerging insight "restores" the Holon's true Character as Player, i.e. as the manifest and *distinct* exchange agency between the 1st and 7th domains ... the *window* of personal *optimizing volition* through which all projection of *specified* conceptuality into *all* domains of the Life-Game occurs, and is made manifest ... The other domains *use* various organized forms of the 6th... Confusion of these domain-exchange capacities and distinctions as referenced above, further contributes to the formation of the *sub*-rational mind[7], which is

---

[7] See sub-rational synonyms list (Appendix V) and the discussion of how this mechanism acts to rationalize and perpetuate aberrant behavior and belief.

> "I will argue that in the literal sense the programmed computer understands what the car and the adding machine understand, namely, *exactly nothing*."
> -- John Searle, philosopher

A brief summary statement of Holosophic cognitive and Philosophical researches to date...

basically the 7th domain's *knowing* capacity redundantly projected and reified.

    Finally, and, *most* essentially: To rationally "stage," ethically source, and perpetually control an enduring *Kosmic Consensus*[8] requires an ultimate and tacitly creative *maintenance* by a supersensible yet *artfully*, "*Un*knowing"...Player!

Bon Voyage!
- RT

---

[8] See Appendix III for the Kosmic Equation: A primal post-traumatic identification or *in*distinction between the 6th and 7th domains both characterizes and enables all human aberration. The Holon submerged in and "dominated" by pain-enforced memorialization and belief is actually fulfilling a primal dedication to *preserving* the actual Kosmic pattern of existence. As an enduring and distracting paradox the sub-rational mind is a falsely valued mockery of that transcendental obligation.

Holosophy Foundation Press:
Holosophyfoundation.com

Holosophy Publications*

→ :: Holosophy: Restoring the Soul's Code Metaphysics of Consciousness
You are   Volume I (Revised)   Series Number I
Here!

:: Managing by Statistics   Introduction To Management
   Volume I   Series IV Number II

:: Problems and Paradox   Metaphysics of Consciousness
   (In Progress)   Series Number III

:: The Transformative Dialogue: Metaphysics of Consciousness
   Remedial Markers, Aphorisms, Prescriptions & Principles   Series Number IV

:: The Holosophy Dialogue Protocols (With appendices)   Metaphysics of Consciousness
                                             Series Number V

:: Success Reluctance: Metaphysics of Consciousness
   An Introduction to a Basic Element of Human Aberration   Series Number VI

:: Ethics and the State of Optimum: Metaphysics of Consciousness
   Gradients of Rational Behavior   Series Number VII

:: Sub-Rational Indicators: Metaphysics of Consciousness
   Emotion, Attitude, and Sensation   Series Number VIII

:: Alembications: a compendium of Holosophy Canon   Metaphysics of Consciousness
                                             Series Number IX

:: The Case For Consciousness and   Metaphysics of ConsciousnessIts
   its Survival of Bodily Death   Series Number X
   (A Research Supplement)

:: The Sub-Rational Synonym List   Metaphysics of Consciousness
   An Inventory of Mis-defined   Series Number XI
   Word-Triggers of Irrational Behavior

:: High Wisdom Quotations   Metaphysics of Consciousness
   (Holosophy Information Supplements)   Series Number XII

:: Kosmos vs. Cosmos: Metaphysics of Consciousness
   The Case for Intelligent Design and   Series Number XIII
   A Darwinian Revisioning
   (A Holosophy Information Supplement)

* As of Dec. 2016, selective editing and re-publication of all titles is in progress.